"Whatever you have planned for next we
read this book. Your heart and mind an
work of love for humanity from Ireland's
will take you from the paralysis of our visi
bole and limb begins to dance the univers
—Mary M(............. ~, ..~...~, 1997–2011

"Imagine a dream in which the makers and shakers of the modern world appeared, large as life, explaining what they were doing and what it meant: not just artists, musicians, poets, writers, and philosophers, but also scientists, economists, and politicians, all contributing, like the characters in Dante, to pull the world upwards or downwards. Now imagine the whole thing in flowing, vivid verse, arranged in five great sequences each with its own inner coherence and subtle blend of poetic form, climaxing with a gloriously unexpected heavenly conversation between modern saints. O'Siadhail has always invited us to taste the rich abundance of life. Now, in the best traditions of Irish hospitality, he spreads a lavish banquet for the ear, the intellect, and above all for the heart."

—N. T. Wright, *Professor of New Testament and Early Christianity, University of St Andrews*

"This is not an ordinary book of poems. It brings a vision of hope, an understanding about the evolution of our society in words of grace. Micheal leads us on to a road of peace."

—Jean Vanier, *Founder of L'Arche*

"With astonishing depth, breadth, and creative range, O'Siadhail interweaves paradox and contradiction across the centuries, conversing with history's greatest minds and evolutionary agents. This masterwork delivers a layered feast of wisdom and insight to inspire lovers of words, ideas, and action. Historians, politicians, artists, theologians, and economists alike will be delighted and nourished by this poetic tour de force."

—Jerry White, *Nobel Peace Prize Laureate and CEO, Global Impact Strategies, Inc.*

"As a scientist I am thrilled at the way *The Five Quintets* weaves the history and the individuals involved up to the present time into a rich poetic fabric which is remarkable in its depth of understanding, yet leaves the reader with a sense of awe and mystery. The reader is invited to immerse into this world and enjoy the pleasures therein."

—John Wood, Scientist, *International Research Infrastructure Policy Adviser, and Consultant to CERN*

"*The Five Quintets* unfolds slowly, the steady self-revealing of insights that catch the edge of thought and provoke an arrest of mind—the fruit of a life in languages and words and depth of perception in wisdom."

—Justin Welby, *Archbishop of Canterbury*

"As a composer of choral music, I try to allow the sung and the repeated word to point to new dimensions of awareness, contrition, joy, or grief. These astonishing words in their settings, combinations, repetitions, and choices resonate with my own efforts on a very special, spiritual and different medium, and I welcome and applaud them. They are of international significance."

—Paul Mealor, *Welsh Composer*

"I am in awe of the whole enterprise—the magnitude of it, the daring of it, and the easy competence of it."

—Brian Friel, *Playwright*

"*The Five Quintets* celebrates how the threads of our culture are woven together across the continents in a grand tradition extending back many centuries. As an astronomer, I resonate specially with a poet who acclaims science alongside humanistic culture. He celebrates the succession of great individuals who have probed the wonders and mysteries of our natural world—and what lies beyond. Nobody else could have created a work like this."

—Martin Rees, *Astronomer Royal, President of the Royal Society (2005–2010), Master of Trinity College Cambridge (2004–2012)*

"An unparalleled book of instruction for a troubled age, *The Five Quintets* retrieves and exhibits human gifts our own age may have lost, like the power to measure the merely probable or to shape verses whose pulse draws us to love. A book of poetry in the category of the epic, the encyclopedic, and the sacred."

—Peter Ochs, *Professor of Modern Judaic Studies, University of Virginia*

"Micheal O'Siadhail's *The Five Quintets* takes the premise of Dante's *Divine Comedy* and brings it into the current day. This epic poem is rich in language, complex in meter, but astoundingly modest in rhetoric. As Dante brought us to the circles of Hell, O'Siadhail brings us to the pinnacles of modernity. And as Dante brought out the humanity in characters of myth, O'Siadhail brings us to confront the humanity of the creators of today's dreams of perfection— scientists, economists, artists all get their due. Somehow he manages to explain how each one's work may approach perfection, even as he recognizes the humanity, incompleteness, and mortality of them all. It is a great work of humble humanism."

—Robert Pollack, *Professor of Biological Sciences, Columbia University, and author of* The Faith of Biology and the Biology of Faith

"Wading boldly into the murky waters of the past and its still swirling, dangerous depths, O'Siadhail offers us an angle of vision for the future that he invites us to create as he also gracefully enacts its unfolding. It is the perfect poetic intervention into the monstrous imperfections and possibilities of the present political moment."

—Serene Jones, *President, Union Theological Seminary*

The Five Quintets

The Five Quintets

Micheal O'Siadhail

CANTERBURY
PRESS
Norwich

First published in 2019 by the Canterbury Press Norwich
Editorial office
3rd Floor, Invicta House
108–114 Golden Lane
London EC1Y 0TG, UK
www.canterburypress.co.uk

Canterbury Press is an imprint of Hymns Ancient & Modern Ltd
(a registered charity)

Hymns Ancient & Modern® is a registered trademark of
Hymns Ancient & Modern Ltd
13A Hellesdon Park Road, Norwich,
Norfolk NR6 5DR, UK

Published in the United States in 2018 by Baylor University Press

Cover design by Aaron Cobbs
Cover image: *Violin and Guitar*, 1913 (oil on canvas), Gris, Juan
(1887–1927) / Private Collection / Photo © Christie's Images /
Bridgeman Images

British Library Cataloguing in Publication data

A catalogue record for this book is available
from the British Library

978 1-78622-195-7

Printed and bound in Great Britain by
CPI Group (UK) Ltd

For Christina

Contents

Acknowledgements

Some brief sections of this work appeared in *Prairie Schooner, Commonweal, Skylight 47, This Landscape's Fierce Embrace: The Poetry of Francis Harvey, The Clifton Anthology, Shine On: Irish Writers for Shine, Windows Commemoration Anthology, Spiritus,* and *Studies.* Thanks are due to the editors.

Acknowledgement

Introduction

How do we describe the contemporary world? There is greater fragmentation and crossover between "high" and popular art. We see growing divergence between the rich and poor in our world of globalisation and post-Fordian economics, and conflicts continue between those seeking justice with compassion and those opposed to any state control, who advocate a consumer society with a free market. Politics is riven with the contrary tendencies of globalisation and the politics of identity. In science, subatomic physics, relativity, complementarity and the uncertainty principle no longer allow us to imagine our world as graspable in the way we thought it was. Religion, which a certain post-Enlightenment mindset thought could be dismissed, has reasserted itself for both good and evil. Fundamentalists can wage war and wreak terrorist havoc. Theologies are no longer discrete and, some accepting no one has a monopoly on truth, are trying to draw on their resources to live with difference in peace.

In this twenty-first century we are facing the first global era in history. Given our world with instant electronic communication, immediate media reaction, and constant and rapid travel, all our cultures, economies, politics, sciences, and religions are more interwoven than ever before. How do we orient ourselves? Where have we come from? Have we a vision for the future?

No one agrees on what to call our current era. Some see a complete break with modernity, as we call the four hundred years or so stretching from the Renaissance to the late twentieth century, and speak of postmodernity. Others see our times as a new and different phase of modernity, naming it variously late modernity, chastened modernity, liquid modernity. In so far as we can have perspective on our own period, and bearing in mind that any such shifts happen slowly, it seems that there is agreement that some kind of change in our mood and attitude has occurred. Perhaps the hallmark is radical questioning of overarching certainties. The upside of this is a respect for what Jonathan Sacks calls the "the dignity of difference." The downside is the danger of excessive irony and meaninglessness.

But what was that journey across some four hundred years, and where is it now leading us? Historical periods are sweeping, wide-ranging, abstract descriptions of tendencies. Yet over time, for all their broadness, they have validity. But changes are brought about by people in community and institutions by the way they think and act. *The Five Quintets* is a meditation on these changes and on individuals whose lives contributed to them. These lives are complex and often full of contradictions. However, seen in the round and through the lens of history, many of the lives I engage with shifted the perspective of their times. Some, though deeply rooted in their context, seem in some way to transcend their time and place and point to a vision which we might share. While the choice of personalities to represent different phases may seem male-dominated, this is simply a reflection of the reality of history. The reader, however, will note the significance of the fact that the final canto of the fifth quintet reverses any notion of male dominance.

The title of each of the five quintets is a present participle: "Making," "Dealing," "Steering," "Finding" and "Meaning." Artistic creativity, economics, politics, science and the search for meaning in our lives are all works in progress. Each quintet has five cantos suggesting different phases on our journey through modernity to how we might envisage our future. The five phases in each quintet run very broadly parallel. First, there is a modulation to a modern outlook. Second, there is a shift towards either greater freedom or control. Third, there is either a phase of excessive individualistic freedom and interiority or extreme control by ideology and fixity. Fourth, there is a realisation of the need to attempt, however inadequately, to find a fresh approach. Last, in the company of those I admire most, I want to suggest some angle of vision for the future.

Each of the quintets is divided into five cantos which reflect these phases. To illustrate how this works, take, for example, the first of the five quintets, "Making," which deals with world of the arts. The cantos are "Transition," "Feeling Freed," "Labyrinths," "Breaking Out" and "Abundance."

Canto 1, "Transition," engages with Miguel Cervantes, John Donne, Peter Paul Rubens, John Milton and George Frideric Handel. Each, in his own way, represents the shift away from the medieval to the modern in terms of his perspective on medieval chivalry, his cosmology and his attitude towards the rising bourgeoisie and the Reformation and the move from the sacred to the secular. This is part of what Max Weber, following Friedrich Schiller, called "the disenchantment of the world" and the advance towards modernised life where rationality trumps belief.

In canto 2, "Feeling Freed," Francisco Goya, Johann Wolfgang von Goethe, Ludwig van Beethoven, William Wordsworth and Charles Baudelaire exemplify a new sense of liberation from the perceived bonds of society. The artists here emphasise emotions and individualism. In the Romantic movement there is a turn towards humanity and nature where the sublime replaces the supernatural. Later, there is a preoccupation with urban complexities and moral ambiguities. The Romantic genius is set apart and demands that our human emotions shake us out of the straitjacket of rationality.

In canto 3, "Labyrinths," the five who illustrate this phase are Richard Wagner, William Butler Yeats, Pablo Picasso, James Joyce and Franz Kafka. This is a reaction to Romanticism, or maybe a further rebuff to rationality in an interiorised extension of Romanticism. There seems to be a withdrawal from society, a proud turn towards perfect pasts—the mythic ur-German or O'Leary's Romantic Ireland—or a retreat into the labyrinths of the artistic mind or the unhappy self.

Canto 4, "Breaking Out," features Fyodor Dostoevsky, Gustav Mahler, Rainer Maria Rilke, D. H. Lawrence and T. S. Eliot. These fervent artists reach beyond ideal pasts and break out of the maze of self. They search for meaning in staunching human suffering with compassion, for perfection in music, mystical love and solitude, in sensuality and religion. Yet none of them seems to yield completely to the intense joy of embracing in astonishment the sheer richness of our human lives.

Canto 5, "Abundance," gathers in fifteen poems some of my great guiding lights: Dante Alighieri, William Shakespeare, George Herbert, Matsuo Bashō, Johann Sebastian Bach, Wolfgang Gottlieb Mozart, Samuel Taylor Coleridge, Robert Browning and Elizabeth Barrett Browning, George Eliot, Paul Cézanne, Willa Cather, Marc Chagall, Patrick Kavanagh, Olivier Messiaen and Brian Friel. All of these artists I find not only seek to illuminate the meaning and poignancy of our lives but embrace in amazement the dazzling profusion of being. Their gift blesses the glory of existence with its counterpoint of joy and tragedy, welcoming *the swing and sway* of the world.

The other four quintets, "Dealing," "Steering," "Finding" and "Meaning," reflect the broad phases in a similar fashion and trace them through the economy, politics, science and philosophy/theology. As in "Making," in the three quintets "Dealing," which concerns economy, "Steering," which concerns politics, and "Meaning," which concerns philosophy/theology, the cantos chart the general phases through individual lives. The phases can overlap so that the life stories are not necessarily in chronological order. On the other hand, while it may seem an injustice to see Margaret Thatcher appearing between Adolf Hitler and Osama bin Laden, this is due to the fact that, within the cantos, the personalities are in strict chronological order. In the case of "Finding," which outlines changes of perspective through science, the five cantos are structured by themes and stages in the growth of science. It moves through the shift from an earth-centered cosmos to the solar system, the passion for exact laws and measures, the sense that almost all was tamed and tied down, the surprise of the subatomic world and the realisation that all matter is in motion.

What, in broad brushstroke, is the vision for the future that emerges? Do we have to relearn the humility of not being in control? Science, which epitomised the mastery of the world and linear progress, now offers a new model in the dance of the subatomic world. We are no longer in charge of a universe which we are part of and where we, too, belong. We need to re-examine overarching certainties, dreams of excessive individualism, isolation or fixity of borders, ideologies and -isms. Our world is interwoven for good as we learn to cope with plurality of every kind.

There are no shortcuts. If we want to better the world, if we want justice with compassion and generosity, if we want democracy with rule of law and accountability, we begin as best we can from where we are, in the here and now. We try to find our way with wisdom and discernment, and the world remains a work in progress. Instead of demanding perfection, our ambition is patience, determination, and the courage just to keep making the world a little less imperfect. We are beckoned onward by the thinkers, the artists, the theologians, and the philosophers who through time embrace the whole opulence of being, the entire giddy kaleidoscope of our humanity.

The idea of writing *The Five Quintets* emerged slowly. I know that it may not be a popular view these days, but I do believe that poetry belongs in the public sphere. I love the lyrical and hope as long as I live to continue dealing with life in lyrics. At the same time, I believe that poets have a part to play in shaping our public discourse. There is a tradition behind this. Dante Alighieri's *Divine Comedy* in many ways catches a world picture as the medieval began to slide towards modernity. John Milton's epic *Paradise Lost* and *Paradise Regained*, another great public poem, is in turn a justification of *the ways of God to man* and of the Protestant Reformation.

I read the philosopher Charles Taylor's *The Secular Age*, where he traces, across four centuries, how a society where God was taken for granted changed to one where the default position in the academe of our time, in what he calls "the Atlantic culture," is secular. This is a history of ideas. I was fascinated by the range and sweep. Though my focus is somewhat different, I began to wonder how a long dramatic modern poem might take stock of our way of thinking, as our stance in the world seems to be in the process of change. Would it be possible even to hint at some vision?

Dante was the key. A history of ideas has its purposes. Yet history, however it moves, is changed by the actions of flesh-and-blood humans with all their gifts and flaws. I wanted to try to tell what happened, at least where possible, through lives and personalities. Certainly, a person's character and background affect how he or she acts in the arts, economics, and politics, and in philosophy and theology. I am sure it's also true, if perhaps to a somewhat lesser extent, in science. I like the way Dante could encounter and engage his characters, and there is something fascinating about his trope of hell, purgatory and heaven. After all, playing God has an appeal!

The more I looked at the worst -isms across the board, the more it seemed as if our humanity cries out for justice, and Dante's hell intrigued me. Purgatory as a halfway house for those who look towards heaven also interested me. But even more attractive might be the thought that, transcending the chronological order of the processes described, outstanding people across the different periods of modernity could mix or converse in heaven. Is this what "the communion of saints," a term I learned as a boy, means?

Still, Dante's tripartite model was not enough. I wanted two other sections: one for the transitional figures who introduce modernity and one for those who unwittingly begin the turn towards what will become hell. As the work grew, I was often astonished by how the different cantos seemed to parallel one another. The idea of five quintets slowly took shape. Naturally, such a title calls up thoughts of *The Four Quartets*, but that seemed appropriate. Much as I am taken by Eliot's great poem, I always felt it needed a fifth part. He never really gets to the joy and let-go of an imagined heaven.

The poetic form of the quintets varies. The use of a constant form in each quintet should lend a sense of perpendicular unity. The first quintet, "Making," consists of haikus and sonnets, the great classic forms of the East and the West. The haikus and sonnets alternate in a form I like to call a *saiku*. The haiku allows a broader impersonal comment. There are four sonnets. The first and third sonnet address the artist, and in the second and fourth the artist replies. The second quintet, "Dealing," and the third quintet, "Steering," are written in forms I devised for them; "Dealing" has certain rhymes, while "Steering" depends on stress. In "Steering," when the people with whom I am engaging speak, italics are used. The fourth quintet, "Finding," is in iambic pentameter and the fifth quintet, "Meaning," is in terza rima.

I wish to acknowledge the conversation and support given through the Cambridge-Duke Theology, Modernity, and the Arts project.

I want to thank a number of people: Steven Weinberg, who very kindly read "Finding" and made helpful comments; Brian Friel, who responded to a portion of "Making"; Hallgrímur Magnússon, who read and commented on each canto as it was completed; Audrey Pfeil, who read and responded to the completed work; Tom Wright, for his helpful comments on the manuscript; and Tom Greggs, for intensive discussion of parts of the work.

My greatest debt of gratitude is to my late wife, Bríd, who did not see this book completed; to David Ford, who was my first reader and who accompanied me throughout; and to my wife, Christina, whose wisdom and love enabled me to complete the work.

Be with me, Madam Jazz, I urge you now,
Riff in me so I can conjure how
You breathe in us more than we dare allow.

In words and hues and tones, please, Madam, blow,
Play in me the grace I need to know,
How in your complex glory we let go.

Show how an open hand is worry-free,
Spark again your love's economy,
Your generous first words spoken "Let there be."

Enhance our trust in hard-earned betterment,
Humbler world we may in turn augment
In long adagios of increment.

While marvelling at your choreography,
Stars and quarks beyond our mastery,
We still explore to praise your mystery.

Although each sacred book's a lip-read score,
Improvising there is always more;
You jazz on what's our own and our rapport.

Each solo and ensemble of a piece,
Grooves and tempos shifting without cease,
We flourish in a syncopated peace.

In all our imperfections we advance,
Trusting in creation's free-willed chance;
Sweet Madam Jazz, in you we are the dance.

1

Making

Canto 1
Transitions

(i)

Migrant sandpiper,
Both forager and winger;
Wader in between.

Cervantes, I still see you plagued with debt
And roaming Spain half-beggared by its king;
The Jews now banished, Moors are under threat,
Our Europe's sovereigns bent on conquering.
You mock all hankering for a courtly love,
The lost and gone of tournament and lance;
Yet in your Rabelais-like push and shove
You hatch Erasmus dreams of tolerance
Between the Middles Ages and your tour
Through plots and greeds of bungling humankind.
In all the giants and windmills you must fight
For twenty years of silence you endure,
Beside flatfooted Sancho's earthbound mind
Are you still Desiderius's knight?

Wintering southward,
Wanting the best of both worlds;
Seasoned voyager.

Though injured in Lepanto's hands-on fight,
Five years I languish in Algiers until
Redeemed; a score then taxman when, despite

Myself, my failures too will grind my mill.
I know the pimps and backstreets of Seville,
The canons, barbers, ladies of the night
Whose stories too I ink out with my quill
When in the end my life and work unite.
Careers that flop or somehow don't take flight
And each false hope I never could fulfil;
As truth and fiction blend in all I write,
Like interplays of life with God's own will,
In all the wrongs my errant Don would right,
Forgotten dreams of justice echo still.

Low over water,
Burrowing deep in the sand;
Busy dark-tipped beak.

My namesake, I admire your grit and pluck
When under threat of death you'll hold your nerve—
How through the years of exile and ill luck,
Your honesty will neither skew nor swerve.
I marvel at such long-term cussedness,
Although you work in rival Vega's shade,
You trust a story's open-endedness
And history's long-hidden accolade.
I know some lives unfold by fluke and chance—
Yet decades hoarding grain and ballasting
Your youth's mistake and only to finance
Spain's Philip's overdrawn warmongering—
How could you house such thoughts of tolerance
And lose your years in propping such a king?

Remembered summer
Traversing Eurasia;
Long-distance flier.

Though sober now, I know I was obsessed
And quit the coop that I both craved and fled
To hover near an era's watershed;
Look not for this year's birds in last year's nest.
Among my vagrants and my dispossessed
All arguments too easily gainsaid,
So I can cure you I amuse instead—

The truest words are spoken still in jest.
My humanist compassion was hard won
In dogged years of hurt I overwrite;
Quixote and Quixana die as one
Beside his weeping squire and acolyte.
Of course you hear what smarts behind the fun;
Cervantes too was once that saddened knight.

(ii)

Array of coverts,
Spangling flared out green-blue eyes;
A peacock's fantail.

Are you that wanton Jack or Doctor Donne
Or both, becoming every part you play,
A lover chiding the *unruly sunne*
Or preacher warning all who disobey?
Are you the Catholic boy, your mother's son
Whose people still would rather die than stray,
Or Protestant believing all are one,
That all may heare, Lord heare us, when wee pray?
The new philosopher whose sun must stay
And bid the passive earth about it runne,
Or wooer whose *sun's motions* trace a day
To thwart lovemakings only just begun?
In showy puns, in each fantailed conceit,
Your actor's role and you conspire to meet.

Cries for attention,
Black-blue flapping and gliding;
A peafowl in flight.

Why can't you fathom all my reasons why?
My tortured brother gave his chaplain's name,
Then died in jail of fever and of shame—
A strutting youth I didn't want to die.
Why can't you see the whys that underlie
Why Jack and Doctor Donne are both the same?
I underwent travail and overcame
My youthful self, my overweening I.
So what if now the sun commands the sky?

Philosophy can claim and counterclaim—
To ask God's mercy is the preacher's aim,
Heare us, weak echoes, o thou eare, and cry.
My words take up each mood and moment's cue;
No player has our playwright's overview.

Courtier of God.
Such extravagant display;
Wooer's flared plumage.

Although your thought takes words and words take wings,
There's still some self-absorption in your tone
As, brooding on your life's imaginings,
An inward mind makes every world its own.
A time so full of angst and hankerings,
Of reason not content with what's unknown,
Your God becomes the *workeman* of all things;
You too have stepped beyond the hallowed zone.
Whilst our Physitians by their lore are growne
And we don't hang from old wives' apron strings,
That selfsame faith in reason will dethrone
A God who trusts to sacred-righted kings.
Enchanted worlds begin to disappear,
Once you have walked outside the sacred sphere.

Proud pavane dancer,
Straying from its habitat;
Bright-hued wanderer.

No Shakespeare hiding in a bigger cast,
I strut the stage of my dramatic mind;
You too were once a young iconoclast,
Determined, self-assured and flying blind.
A later self our youth's own counterblast,
Again like me you leave act one behind
And in one woman's love rewrite a past
That childhood's flaws and hurts had undermined.
My poems are moods I wanted to outlast
Myself and catch the thrill of thought refined;
For all our likeness, so much to contrast—
I bless your Dantean sweep of humankind.

Three-personed God is battering you to see
What was and is now shaping what's to be.

(iii)

Swaying side to side
To compensate refraction;
A lowlands angler.

A painter envoy extraordinaire,
You Rubens craved the black hole of success,
A driven man the top and nothing less—
A Michelangelo? But why stop there?
A global citizen and *homme d'affaires*,
Your endless energy still can't redress
A father's shameful fall that you suppress
In brushes hued and stroked with manic care.
The best and greatest, yet so self-aware,
Compeer of prelates and of all noblesse,
You're banking on a new assertiveness
That Europe's bourgeoisie are soon to dare.
You feed the maw of hungry self-esteem
And chase a shadowed fame from dream to dream.

Cosmopolitan
Whose long neck retracts in flight;
A zigzag heron.

I keep a deep and sensuous self in check;
An Antwerp burgher never second best,
I zig and zag yet don't stick out my neck
But work to lay my father's ghost to rest.
Whatever drives me I will never tire;
A business sense still wants me to be free
To pick and choose the work that I desire,
Portraying clients who can pay my fee.
Both under church and monarchies I knew
An artisan would have to tack and trim
But wealth achieves what guilds can never do
And frees an artist from a patron's whim.
I preen my gift and, steering my career,
I'll match Italian masters I revere.

Downy canopy
Of wings darkening water;
A patient fisher.

Careerist dreading scandal or disgrace,
You marry steady Isabella Brandt
With ruff and busk and whalebone carapace,
So primped and passionlessly elegant.
No carnival or slip betwixt the cup
And lip, no risks of love's come-hither row;
For all your genius still so buttoned-up:
One perfect husband and his teenage Frau.
What flashes through a mind is best unknown—
Assent an eyebrow raised, dissent a stare;
Such self-control and no emotion shown,
New stoical sangfroid and savoir-faire.
A youthful hurt and trauma's stains are in
Your dream a burgher's ordered discipline.

Now upright, now crouched,
Its wings either flapped or spread;
Shape-shifting wader.

But have you seen my young Hélène with fur?
Ambition's push and drive have acquiesced
In her, and now for her, with her, by her,
With nudes and landscapes, see how I'm possessed!
The Eros bred in bone will out in flesh—
Her fifth child sired just weeks before I die—
In old age my desire and spirit mesh
Undressing her for every naked eye.
Once diplomat and youthful arriviste
I angled for church work; a man of means
I'm artisan become my patrons' peer
And second wife's besotted lyricist,
Outsider painting Flemish country scenes.
The moods of Europe shift in my career.

(iv)

Sad unseeing eyes
And scornful smile half-suppressed.
Disapproving bird.

John Milton, I admire your self-belief
That you're another Dante London-born
To set the ways of God in high relief—
I know the cost and what delights you scorn.
Although fame-spurred you live laborious days
With Providence still in the common grain;
To want to prove God's ways itself betrays
Enlightenment that thinks it must explain.
Rebirth all earned, for you no grace comes free,
Afraid you'll hide your talent in the earth
While your taskmaster watches from above;
Your judging carpenter from Galilee
Keeps measuring in virtue and self-worth.
How could we justify a God of love?

Swooping here and there,
A bird in love with grandeur;
My sad-eyed eagle.

But look how my adventurous song takes aim
And *with no middle flight intends to soar*;
For me all knowledge turned to metaphor—
Copernicus or Ptolemy the same.
Is science too an art in its own right,
Describing well beyond its imagery
A room where God has staged his comedy,
His drama's plot revealed with fresh insight?
I didn't catch as clearly as I ought
Things unattempted yet in prose or rhyme
And so reflect a shifting paradigm;
Or was my cosmos narrow and too caught
Up in the past to shape a coming time
And wake the mind and heart to deeper thought?

A sublunar vault
Flown now by outdated charts.
An eagle straying.

Though Galileo's glass can well observe
Imagined lands and regions of the moon,
Though Raphael sun-centres us, you swerve
Between such new and older modes that soon

Lose currency, a trawl and lucky dip
Of medieval lore which in its day
Had served but now your age and times outstrip;
For Robert Boyle and Co. a world passé.
Heroic verse with nothing of the chime,
Each battle fought in grave Miltonic tone
And yet, for all your sense of what's sublime,
A cosmos still within your comfort zone.
No Dante in the foregleam of his time;
You do not touch the edges of the known.

Skywriting soarer,
Dipping, at long last turns and homes,
Easy on the wing.

You're right, my friend, in what you say:
I was my father's Virgil still to be;
When I was yet a child, no childish play,
My days *love virtue, she alone is free.*
I did God's will for fear we might in turn
Lock up an English Galileo too;
But blind and broken in my Christ I learn
To say *who best can suffer, best can do.*
In Christ's temptations see how I've explained
My need for power, my Stoic stock-in-trade,
The Plato loved while still my father's boy.
But I too change. My *Paradise Regained*
Resists mistakes I know my years have made.
At last my God *brought on his way with joy.*

(v)

Over all borders
As sailplanes soar in thermals,
A gliding black kite.

Impatient, he's yawing through each regime,
Proud Handel, London's impresario,
An artist crossing lines which others toe,
The boy who'd shunned his father's lawyer dream.
God's word in plays for some is to blaspheme,
So maestro of the oratorio—

That halfway house of musical tableau—
Your singers now can stage a sacred theme.
Extemporising, on the wing you seem
To let your chorus soar above the gap
Between the church and concert room, as though
For all your failures still deep down you know
How in the end such music reigns supreme;
You glide above where eras overlap.

Plunging angle-winged,
So dark-shafted and fork-tailed,
Busy bird of prey.

You're right! I never let things get me down.
I swoop on work, yet nothing is ill done;
I have such endless patience and yet none;
You see it in my jowls and close-browed frown.
I still imagine God. *Thou art my son*
This day have I begotten you—I stun
With my *Messiah* all of Dublin town.
I want both recognition and renown
But failures win out in the longer run;
There is no put-down I won't rise above;
Though rivals see me as some Saxon clown
I work and work and know I'll be the one,
Whom Hayden, Mozart and Beethoven love.

Canny adapter,
An opportunist hunter,
A city settler.

As every year new pieces come and come,
Behind your brusqueness and your bursts of rage,
A down-to-earthness, equilibrium
Of Milton, Dryden and that reasoned age.
Impromptu genes unwilling to succumb,
With sections added or left out, you gauge
How best to beat the impresario's drum
And pay your hired musicians their due wage.
Such grand Italian divas you engage,
Though opera outsoars its solos' sum;
As *Faramondo* struts Haymarket's stage

And music shifts now to the concert hall,
Still pouring out each chorus you become
The greatest improviser of them all.

Buoyant forager
On the move and ad-libbing,
A migrant raptor.

The fireworks of my mind I can't refine—
My patience is for work not self-control—
I don't fly off the handle by design,
My raw nerve ends just rush from role to role.
But have you seen a manuscript of mine?
My flair refuses any pigeonhole:
Italian, French and English I combine
As humours trace their passionate creole.
I only want to hold the music's line,
A flighty psyche focused on its goal
So every voice can shine but not outshine,
From all the woven parts create a whole.
The spectrum of my moods played pole to pole;
I did my work, then rendered up my soul.

Canto 2
Feeling Freed

(i)

A cool-eyed dauber
In his red-braided jacket;
Earthy torero.

So knowing, Goya, as you turn and stare,
Pot-hatted matador still stabbing paint,
Your streetwise eye declaring, "I'm no saint;
I love this world with all its earthenware."
You're carnal as the heavens you've portrayed
In frescoes painted on Antonio's dome;
No God here tipping Adam's hand in Rome,
Just people crowding round a balustrade.
Your cherubs caught in life's own push and shove

Gaze down at us below where now instead
Seductive angels pillar up the sky;
Your brush must never see beyond the eye:
Baroque's high heaven stood so on its head,
A world looks up and sees itself above.

So plunge deep into
Life's fiercest spectacle;
Glory's picador.

When I look up I only see the sky—
Both hell and heaven lurk within the mind;
I want them both so turn my sceptic eye
And daub the plainer face of human kind.
For me no wispy classic lines redeem
The man, the rogue, the whore, the thief, the nark;
We're close to nature in our most extreme,
The blots and scribbles of our light and dark.
I've seen the greats but never can look back.
I want to show the cruel Spain I know:
Garrotte and war, the whole unholy show;
Though in the end such immanence turns black.
My ears are sealed, my head a padded cell,
I paint dark murals in my deaf man's shell.

Swished fancy footwork,
Cape-trailing feint and dodge;
Cunning bullfighter.

Ambition got you there, your inner drive,
And though you never chose to fawn or shirk
Some artist's bullish instinct to survive
Just shrugs as if to say "all work is work."
O yes, a sharp enlightenment critique,
But you're still painter to the royal court;
Despite your fiery independent streak
For forty years you live by their support.
A Bourbon leaves and worse then comes to worst—
But one king gone another reigns supreme—
You paint Napoleon's José the First,
You're ribboned portraitist to each regime.

For all your moral rage and posturing,
A trimmer who survives from king to king.

Beyond bravado
Sorrow glanced in the bull's eye;
Ruthful matador.

My witches and my scenes of sin or crime,
Caprichos with their pointed wit and dart,
All *banderillas* in the neck of time
Which shifts now towards a new Romantic art.
Though I am called the first great modernist,
A future movement's distant lightning rod,
My best is still compassion's unclenched fist,
The shining eye before the firing squad.
Beyond the portraitist and royal hack
Or any darker world of deaf caprice,
My testament to you the *Third of May*
Where fusiliers have turned their nameless back
And bend to execute their point-blank prey;
My lamp of pity lights the victim's face.

(ii)

Conjurer of selves.
Smoke and mirrors of passion;
A quick-change artist.

With Werther's death, you, Goethe, hit your stride,
Young *Sturm und Dränger* come into his own.
One jilted girl acts out a suicide;
In grief you carve her monument in stone.
Although you never wanted to betray
Old friends, you shed a few as you advance;
All lovers your dramatis personae,
A Faust who conjures poems from each romance.
"Along unsure meandering passions" path
We're drawn again by your exquisite lines:
Dann zog uns wieder ungewisse Bahn
Der Leidenschaften labyrinthisch an.
Precise, upright and dressed up to the nines,
A steel-haired, fastidious polymath.

Round and round the tent
Somersaults between all horses;
One circus rider.

The empire died, Napoleon came and went;
Through eighty years of Europe's arcs and loops
The circles turn in all that's transient—
I jump through each of history's hoops.
With time and age I cast my Stoic's eye:
Beginnings like ends and lives spent in between
Must all *sich in Eins zusammenzien,*
"Contract into one point" as you rush by.
I ride the storms and whims of my time's *Geist,*
My Kant-like God both outside and within;
No smokes, no bugs, no garlic and no Christ,
I love and lose and take it on the chin.
Though some sleep off their moods like late-night drink,
My life a whole I lived and left in ink.

Toeing balanced lines
Above the applauding crowd;
Lofty rope-dancer.

Proud Goethe craving order and control,
Napoleon fan, yet always hand in glove
With fate you play your mind's heroic role,
A tumbler falling in and out of love.
Prometheus of overview and art,
You turn from folkish ways to ancient Greece;
When Germany reverts post Bonaparte,
The timeless eye sees history's caprice—
Your God a trace in nature's harmony,
A disembodied king of things sublime
Whose distant eye refuses to engage;
The braver souls you dare to come of age
And stand outside the silhouette of time.

Showing what you will,
Now you see it, now you don't;
Love's illusionist.

"Our lot seems beautiful, our human fate"—
Des Menschen Leben scheint ein herrlich Los:
Der Tag wie lieblich, so die Nacht wie groß—
"The day so lovely and the night so great."
Detached from all the fugitive regimes
My poet's classic eye surveys the scene;
I love a sense of poise and am serene
Despite the passing circus of extremes.
Though I eschewed the zealot's black and white,
And radicals would mock my hard-earned *von*,
Once entered in the German pantheon,
I'm then embraced by hard-line left or right.
Buffoon or alibi for every mess,
I pay the cockshy price of timelessness.

(iii)

Changes of heading,
Luffing up as the gusts blow;
Determined sailor.

Proud Beethoven, you come to make your mark
As rhythm by sullen rhythm your will begets
A gentler dove that flies the coop of dark,
and rage subsides in beautiful regrets.
You struggle to endure—not just to please—
To navigate all whims and psychic states;
A music veers and tacks through distant keys,
Detours and ponders, dreams, then ruminates.
Beyond the measured zones of reason's grace,
Each squall a palimpsest of elbow grease
That earns a calm above a grumbling bass,
An inner seascape's deep and hard-won peace.
No craftsman here: creator of your art,
A genius truculent and set apart.

Zephyr or tempest,
Reaching, running or beating;
All-weather seaman.

So much, so much I thought I once would do:
To wife, to settle down *cantabile,*

14

But somehow deeper down in me I knew
My muse would storm again and I'd obey.
I meant to travel but never reached the sea.
Instead, like Shakespeare, every human mood
Must find a voice and bear its melody;
In one man's soul all lines of latitude.
As nature ekes its dawns from satin nights
My notes transverse a still unplotted chart;
Beyond polyphony or court delights
I sound the depths of unbeholden art.
I mean to shake what logic has confined,
Let passions stir up reason's sleepy mind.

Mare's-tails gather,
Cat's-paws trembling still waters;
Uneasy helmsman.

Through all my churning youth I was a fan—
I never could repay the debt I owe—
Yet swarthy, head-bent, testy Ludwig van,
Why is it that you never quite let go?
Your brothers' wives you always sought to blame,
Those servants you so suddenly dismiss,
A nephew your own smother love will maim;
Your shadowed self a semitone from bliss.
Such hurricanes of phrases scratched and quilled
That grope the dark before the light can break;
Each anchorage achieved by odyssey,
The swaying song of some desire fulfilled
That riptides of your temper sweep away;
Deep currents still unease serenity.

Long tacks and trimming,
Slow years of windward sailing;
A sailor havened.

Long gone my pride, that youthful mutineer,
And now my deaf-sealed years will rub and fret
Farewell discourses I insist you hear,
My close-knit criss-cross chamber tête-à-têtes.
All hauteur shed and yet *hot blood begets*

Hot thoughts which scud inside my silent head,
A voyage logged in five unheard quartets
Where all that's said leaves just as much unsaid.
In closing lean and inward traffickings
No bravado now or flourishes decoy
The rumbling conversations of the strings
As resignation climbs at last to joy.
A note comes home, a final tonic kiss.
Applaud, my friends. Remember me for this.

(iv)

*Fitful teenager
Among his rocks, meres and tarns;
A lone fell-walker.*

Tall Wordsworth orphaned in your fourteenth year,
Hill-rambling inward Cumberlander boy,
A presence still disturbs you with its joy,
Fostering both by beauty and by fear.
Between what's real and thought's own vanity,
In both the objects seen and eye that sees,
I hear in spite of your love-hate unease,
The still sad music of humanity.
Your footfalls echo. *Thither I repaired
Scout-like and gained the summit. It was day . . .*
And yet those plainer lives you try to probe
All lack the stitch and pain of suffering shared;
Your cheerful faith that nature won't betray
Unthreaded through the needle-eye of Job.

*The heady moment
Of a first glimpsed overview;
Cloud-nine clamberer.*

Those years when France and Godwin stepped beyond
The limits of experience and truth,
The dedicated spirit of my youth
Demanded life and reason correspond.
I tramped the inner landscapes of my mind
And scrambled hillsides shelf by lonely shelf—

The man whose eye is ever on himself—
Does nature mend what reason undermined?
Once healed, I then had learned or think I learned
To coax in *hearts that had been turned aside*
From nature's way by outside accidents
The joy and peace that habitude prevents
Us feeling and how nature is our guide.
My world delights in reason's tables turned.

Would-be mountaineer
Balks at edges, smears, fingerholds;
Rappelling climber.

I know your renovating spots of time—
The mind revives again while here I stand—
But what became of epics you had planned,
Those sheer rock faces Coleridge dreamed you'd climb?
You gain a name but soon you will solidify,
The aura of your steadiness a sneer
At Coleridge's old bony mariner;
You fear his skinny hand and glittering eye.
A radical returned to yeoman class,
You change with Latin words and measured speech
The prelude to a work you'll never write;
Those years of safe inscapes and gravitas,
Or feelings gathered with hindsight's delight,
All foothills to the peaks you never reach.

The recalled sublime
In thrill of youthful ascents;
A grounded cragsman.

The laureate in me had grown too tame.
Cocooned by wife, by sister reassured,
My wilder ecstasies so soon matured,
Was I too hooked on opiates of fame?
My first French love I shouldn't have played down
Or let addicted Coleridge thorn my side;
A climber whose base-campers wound his pride,
Was I imprisoned in my own renown?
A glory and a dream were once my youth
But daily farther from the east I mused

On first-hand joys and tranquiller reruns,
Hints sanctified by reason and by truth
Of something far more deeply interfused
Whose dwelling is the light of setting suns.

(v)

Risk-taker maudit,
Fire-eater courting applause,
A haughty stuntman.

Pale Baudelaire, so gaunt and Catholic,
A desperado, sui generis,
Both dandy and bohemian maverick,
At forty-two you die of syphilis.
Your angel chides his strayed anathema
Commanding you to love and yet you don't;
Le damné répond toujours: Je ne veux pas!
"The damned always replies: Oh no I won't."
Expelled schoolboy still craving *maman*'s praise—
Your womb-to-tombing mother, Caroline—
You never learn how in love's twofold blaze
Madonna and Delilah both combine.
Your double need and vented spleen inspire
Nostalgias of glittering desire.

Spins and barrel rolls,
Dives before inverted flights,
A loop-the-looper.

Monsieur, you judge me glibly even though
You too have known the clap of young despair
And craved a mother's praise those years ago—
So much of you could be a Baudelaire.
We both have loved the lamps of perfect rhyme
That light the turnings on each line of thought;
For me, my lust and things sublime don't chime—
Desire is pure, the animal is bought.
My life fulfils the fate I prophesy,
A cussed derring-do that shuns the crowd,
Or that hauteur of wounds you too once shared
But which one woman's love in you repaired.

Was I too long guilt-ridden and too proud,
To hear my guardian angel's eagle cry?

A steep dizzy curve's
Accelerated circles;
Wall of death rider.

Outsider poet spending garret years
To eat your misfit opium of dreams,
Is there no role for prophets and for seers,
For vision which both steers us and redeems?
But round and round the bowl of failed desire
A Jansenist is arguing within
And so you court the *proud priest of the lyre;*
The only pleasure possible is sin.
Your life a blossoming of *fleurs du mal*
With mistresses you scorn but can't elude,
Performer of the bitter kiss and tell;
Ironic, urbane, both tender and banal
In inner shifts of thought or whim and mood,
A harrowed self still climbs the walls of hell.

Lifelong cliffhanger,
Cascadeur désespéré;
Aware daredevil.

In each street-walking Parisian scene
Did I not show the broken and the poor?
I made their cause my own *affaire d'amour*—
God knows I tried to reach beyond *le spleen.*
You know in every line I ever turned
I kept my childhood sense of right and wrong;
A Catholic in me has always yearned
For grace beyond this hell where I belong.
Remember. Souviens-toi! Esto memor!
The law-court moralist misunderstood—
I praise the angel as I praise the whore.
My evil flowers have grown among the good;
The self-deluding choose the perfumed slope,
The would-be damned exude a sweated hope.

Canto 3
Labyrinths

(i)

Dispersed from the pack,
Hankering for approval;
A hungry lone wolf.

Renaissance beret tilted to the right,
Herr Wagner, still your worn outsider's face
Demands the fame for which through life you fight;
Your exiled loner years will leave their trace.
The world, you claim, now wants your German heart—
Not just what's tuneful but what's also true
Must sanctify the altar of grand art—
For all that's French is frivolous for you.
Such unfulfilled desire and failed control,
A fiery wheel, debt-fleeing Lohengrin;
Strange mix of self-conceit and outcast's role,
Some broken Wotan fuels your will within.
A misfit craves approval from his pack;
A Siegfried stealing treasure stolen back.

Home-hunting prowler
That repossesses a set;
Underworld game dog.

I turned to legends from the fatherland,
Utopian dreams in tragedy's rebirth;
My mission was to make all opera grand,
Regain the ring and rule the underearth.
An epic mind demands pure truth again.
I seek deep myths within our Teuton soul
And am the hero daring Fafner's den
To gut the dragon in his glory hole.
Too long we've borne our music's Latin yoke—
That play and levity which I deplore,
All comedy and lightness à la carte—
The artist of the future is the Folk.
I craft my language from our German lore
And build my Bayreuth temple to our art.

Evolved as top dog,
Barking out a territory;
Lupine arrogance.

Your vision of high art yet nonetheless
For das *Volk* a mythical decoy;
Your Niebelheim a narrowed earnestness
Where there's less lack of hope than lack of joy.
You may become the master of your art,
Yet every note you add you answer for;
You conjure with an aftercomer's heart
And never know with whom you build rapport.
The unafraid should rule the underling—
The dog-eat-dog you dreamed of bringing back;
Blond Siegfried, hero for a blonder race,
Can murder Nibelung Mime for his ring.
Der Führer stows your Tristan in his sack.
Your phobias will scar our human face.

Alpha insider
Howls deep in his wilful den.
An omega cries.

I want no truck with trails they say I blaze,
Commending me for movements I'd begun;
To praise my Tristan chord is damned faint praise:
For me, the muse of art and life were one.
No phrase of mine was made to entertain—
Of course my music can't just stand alone—
I knew the green-eyed hate I helped engrain
As I weighed up each word, each line, each tone.
My Teuton worship turned against the Jews
As hate became a long-held leading note;
No need now to explain or to excuse,
The *Ring* must stand or fall on what I wrote.
My loathings haunt my offspring's offspring still;
This hell a hell of overweening will.

(ii)

The churring digger
With its nose close to the ground;
A scenting badger.

21

It's you, grand Yeats, our poet fantasist,
Who blurring woman won with woman lost,
Still craves Byzantiums that can't exist,
No matter what remorse such shadows cost.
Right from the start you struck your Byron pose,
Your sailor-knotted tie and Hamlet stride,
From London's rainbow dream of nine bean-rows
Till Plato sings and you're dissatisfied.
Things argued in the head, self-tête-à-tête
And verse which *only wasteful virtues earn*;
Yet scenting any change of scene or ground,
Careerist who can shift from set to set—
Romantic, patriot or squire by turn—
Still W. B. and proud archpriest of sound.

Nocturnal hunter,
Grey elusive dreamlander;
Burrowing mammal.

Between my mother's low-church merchant truth
And father's freer-thinking disbelief,
Old tales, emotions, figures from my youth
Became my faith, my life work's leitmotif.
This spur then turned with time to lust and rage;
My love of lofty things and towering speech,
My necromancing make-believe in age,
All like O'Leary's Ireland out of reach.
You say I couldn't countenance what is—
Why look for what you want not what you find—
My questionings, my introspective quiz
Dug music from the chambers of my mind.
Seek out reality, leave things that seem.
What be a singer born and lack a theme?

Dim tunnel-visioned
Hierarchical animal;
A black-and-white brock.

But Yeats, a world you want is dead and gone,
That perfect past your mind's own cul-de-sac;
Retrieve best thoughts once shed and then move on—

A future cannot bear such turning back.
Though scorning base-born products of base beds
A pride condemns modernity's nightmare,
Your brew of folk and noble thoroughbreds
Now seems more self-absorbed than self-aware.
Utopian still opting out of time,
Old lecher with a love on every wind,
For all the great perfections of your art
Or faith in how from age to age we climb
By laws of time that turning gyres rescind,
Your blindsight can't repair what falls apart.

Its scent beyond sound,
A badgering pipe-dreamer;
Striped somnambulist.

Abhor the counting house and cinder heap
That mars an older quality of mind!
I follow signs but still refuse faith's leap;
Where are the captains who can keep mankind?
I pace upon the battlements and stare;
Was I Byzantium's unburnished sage,
A soul still summoned to the winding stair,
To voice my vision for our tunnelled age?
For all my talk of time or turning gyre
Between eternities of race and soul,
My cold eye cast, I play the horseman squire;
Yet every role I play remains a role.
Damnation is to know that, in the end,
The curse I rail against I can't transcend.

(iii)

A cunning hopper
Zigzagging, shifting viewpoint;
A nimble rabbit.

There at the counter *au Lapin Agile,*
A clown among Montmartre's lone and racked,
Among the demimonde and down-at-heel,
You ask how art keeps pace with artefact.

Picasso, anarchist and wonder boy
Who'll shun perspective, nature's light and shade
To stress the form within what you destroy,
Collaging bric-à-brac our hands have made.
Your dared *Les Demoiselles d'Avignon*
Becomes those spheres and cubes for you and Braque
Where all things are a process undergone
In shifting inner shapes which you unpack.
Possessed, a rebel genius set apart;
You'll turn romantic king of modern art.

Swift warren dweller,
Now you see me, now you don't;
A rampant buck.

Whatever willed I had the power to pull
Out of imagination's magic hat;
A saddled handlebar becomes a bull,
I am the harlequin and acrobat.
Like sex desired or song I am all now;
Each period a pedant's shibboleth,
No past, no path or no explaining how
Duendes still cry out at age and death.
And winning each young woman I pursued,
In blue or rose or classic parody
I'm on the hop, I'm watchful and aware
That even though we cubists caught a mood,
The moment I submit to what I see,
I trust my own eternal youth and flair.

Underearther,
Holed-up, insulated
Coney Islander.

The Spanish anarchists have left their spoor,
Your youth in you refuses now to grow,
Allow your mind to broaden and mature;
And you, Picasso, just become more so.
Bohemian and Midas out of touch,
A famous-for-being-famous millionaire,
Gone underground and self-engrossed, you clutch
At whims and hunches fetched from anywhere.

You're painting lovers trapped in lust's machine
For decades filled with cravings mixed with fears
Or lone obsessions with your sinking light;
A dwarf still doting on a beauty queen,
An old man anguished by your appetite,
A wizard none the wiser for your years.

Dazzled unawares,
Caught in too bright light,
A rabbit freezes.

I searched in my outsider Paris years,
When fellow feeling for my demoiselles
And passion's conversations with my peers
Had made me think, although my heart rebelled.
Give me élan! For all our cubes achieved,
I do not want to search—I want to find.
To hell with thought and all things preconceived;
I will not work the warren of the mind.
Duendes sparking me now damn my soul.
I crave the favours that my fame now grants
And paint the jokes that please and play my role;
Have I become a king of sycophants?
Enclosed in both my fortune and acclaim,
I can't outgrow the icon I became.

(iv)

Sensing a pursuit
Its sweep switches direction;
A fox turning tail.

O one-eyed Joyce so proud and so obsessed
With inward-looking Dublin left for dead,
You traipse through Paris, Zurich and Trieste,
Both turning from and into what you'd fled.
Half-blind and hoarding burrower engrossed
In weaves of mind, yet posed and self-aware;
Become your feckless father's punster ghost,
You cock a snook at years of dons you'll snare.
A peeping Tom with skittish schoolboy thrills,
Your life less lived than held by words at bay;

You thimble-rig each mood to grist your mills,
All others walk-on parts in your world's play.
Betrayed betrayer, guilt's *poète maudit*;
Forever fleeing nets you never flee.

Wary of humans,
Opportunistic feeder;
A pouncing reynard.

I'm proud but have no pride whatever way
My meanest means are justified by ends;
All serve to delve my mind's soliloquy—
My patronesses, rivals, faithful friends.
A willing exile with my town within,
A modernist I'll make a day stand still;
Although I don't believe, I love to sin
And thrive on each taboo and furtive thrill.
Confess the contradictions, even doubt.
Of course, in all the cast of selves I mime
My own distrust, my impulse to betray;
An in-depth guilt that I turn inside out
Wool-gathers up a world I warp in time,
The criss-cross mindscape of one Dublin day.

Long-snouted mammal
Retracking through its tunnels;
A remembered den.

I love your language burbling up in fun
And am as good a reader as you'll get
To understand your punning riverrun—
I know the charge of words, and yet and yet . . .
Such Proustian compulsions to detail
The dreamlike doodling of an introvert
For me a microscope too small in scale,
The Hades of your endless blab and blurt.
You grub around the psyche's secret lair
Of daily reverie and riddled night
To lay a haunted mind's meanderings bare,
But in the end does anything take flight?
O Mister Joyce, I fear your joyless gaze,
That inward stare involved in its own maze.

The allure and scent
Of a yea-saying vixen;
Single-minded fox .

I too was of my time and so I fled—
I couldn't bear an ism's golden calf—
I chose the loner's monologue instead;
Have I become too clever now by half?
I pun, I joke, I dig and I lampoon
Both friends and foes as long as I can freeze
My Dublin town's cuckolded day in June—
Yet satire somehow lacks love's joy and ease.
For all the wit and fun at Finnegan's wake
And martyred Stephen D. within his maze,
Still once at least, though in a woman's voice,
I didn't pun or try to be opaque
But spoke my shortest playful word of praise:
And yes, in Molly's yes I did reJoyce.

(v)

Underworld digger
Worrying up heaps of clay;
A hill-raising mole.

Herr Doktor Kafka, your lack of faith has foiled
The light; guilt-ridden ghosts perpetuate
The mother you despise because she spoiled
A father all your life you love to hate.
An outcast in your castle of no hope,
Deep underground aggression feeds your ills;
Upscaled by your neurotic microscope,
All details make your mountains out of hills.
Still threatening and enthralling from above
Your upstart father and your fallen god,
That you still loathe although you crave their love,
Remain your inner ethic's measuring rod.
You're doubly bound by duty and by doubt—
Prague's Janus opting in and opting out.

Earth underminer,
Bad-sighted unremitting
Furry soil-tosser.

Some cared for me and yet I didn't dare
Because of fear or feeling no concern;
So moling out the depths of my despair
I kept on tunnelling at every turn.
A stunted son in me still tried to please—
For years a bureaucrat I'd strive and strive
But all dissolved in ambiguities;
My life this life that never came alive.
I'm teller of the poisoned fairy tale
Where human rhyme and reason are at strife;
Distrusting heir, I'm Hamlet, Prince of Prague,
Who faltering believed love had to fail—
My doubts condemn me to my death-in-life,
My slipped-in grave a cosy sleeping bag.

Double-thumbed delver
Scooping out the ground we walk;
Underhanded boar.

You're icy as your idolised Flaubert,
Your inner terror cold-eyed and detached
From all around you as you word despair
To haunt us with those dead-end plots you hatched.
Your head can't bear to yield to honeyed sleep,
Your left brain quarrels with its limber right—
Some unforgiving backward look can't leap
As breathing underground you brook no light.
What wounded logic in our Western mind
Concocts your penal colony's machine?
A manic burrower, you've undermined
The ground we walk with such begrudging spleen.
You feed the wizened dreams of minds withdrawn.
Your nightmare's broken trust denying dawn.

Sunless labourer,
A clawed shovelling groper
Forepawing the dark.

Though saintly Rabbi Amschel's great-grandson,
I'm neither German, Czech nor shtetl Jew;
A mole in every tribe and trusting none,
With words I coped—the only way I knew.

In every circle I can see a null,
My dark forebodings I forestall with dark;
Some saw a face, I only saw the skull;
Do I belong alone where black dogs bark?
Uninterested in other humankind,
All Ks and Karls and Joseph Ks are me
Awry in my own reason's padded cell;
I'm cursed and cannot quit my delving mind
But, gouging out my loner's trilogy,
I slide with ease into my sleepless hell.

Canto 4
Breaking Out

(i)

Plumbing an ocean
Of dolorous melodies;
A whale's plangent song.

F. Dostoevsky, diehard of extremes,
The torrid gambler, convict serving time,
Who'll ravel dramas of such broken dreams
And catch the tragic in cold-blooded crime.
Romantic realist, your plots explore
Endangered souls as carefully you sound
Each sea of cries and tears from crest to floor
To fathom depths of lives both lost and found.
Though you regret the vision of your youth
Still deep in you, you'll never deviate
From your desire to staunch life's sufferings;
No truck with any cause but moral truth,
Intricate lived-in lives and real things
Where you depict the Russian people's fate.

World's largest mammal,
A submarine carrier
Changing direction.

Such plans we made, utopias explored—
Idealists, we'd grope the Holy Grail;

But bungled youth gone overboard—
I've been inside the belly of the whale.
As Jonah tried the opposite extreme,
In Omsk I U-turned, thinking it all through;
However stubborn or against the stream,
Like thoughts that change, *the whole man changes too.*
My heart has known the sum of humankind—
Dmitri's flings, Alyosha's dreams are mine—
In turn each passion has possessed my mind
And all my life I've crossed the final line.
Idealist or lapsed iconoclast,
A giddy gift lives in my stories' cast.

Vertical yearning,
A quick celestial stake-out;
Moby Dick sky-hops.

Your mother's son, so talking you'd console
Your father's sick, you fathom as a boy
The secret theatre of a human soul.
Did childhood angst choke off all adult joy?
To love each other as we love ourselves—
Distrusting revolution's draft regime,
Your mind a purgatory muse who delves
Dark lives that skew your sky-aspiring dream.
Roskolnikov redeemed in Sonya's heart—
Repented sin and love's self-sacrifice
Or saints encaged by their dark counterpart;
I don't know how to build a paradise.
Those lives still lunge at skies you can't achieve—
Your unbelief keeps yearning to believe.

Gleam of emergence,
One breathing heavenward lunge;
A humpback breaches.

In Omsk I learned to love the plain muzhik
Whose faith and soil I thought could save our land;
I feared revolt and vengeful rhetoric,
A sterile force my Russia can't withstand.
And I foretell how fortune's wheel will turn,
That communism too will come and go;

The sway they'll hold, the bridges they will burn,
Another thrust of power will overthrow,
No matter whether I am right or wrong
I strove to try to understand and cope
With human pain—and pity was the price
Of handling childhood angst my whole life long.
Perhaps not joy but still a leap of hope:
Compassion is a glimpse of paradise.

(ii)

From the dark-wine depth
Skyward surge of porpoising;
Half-glanced emergence.

Romantic maestro, modern pioneer,
In halting steps and leaps you play the stave;
But billowed tunes turned suddenly severe
Drum up from underneath a tidal wave.
In twilight worlds you're moving in between,
Knowing gaiety will side again with grief;
In every joy a darkness unforeseen,
Your deep belief undone by unbelief.
Idealist too long misunderstood,
Still arguing the moral force of art;
Your youthful hurts confer outsiderhood,
And each mood ends in its own counterpart.
In sways across a gentler sea of sound
Your breathing hops in fourths so heaven-bound.

Between sea and air,
Ocean and wild blue yonder;
A porpoise breathing.

My whole life long I'm homesick everywhere,
My mind conducts, my mission to compose;
Both Jew and goy, a Judas here and there—
I'm Mahler. Music is the world I chose.
The darks and bounds to light are both my theme—
Let music-making deal with doubleness—
Each movement can contain both gloom and gleam,
Perfection is my faith and nothing less.

For friends concessions made, for music none.
A klezmer band or barrel-organ ground,
Bohemian refrains, a concert hall,
The waltz or *Ländler* dancing all in one;
My symphonies embrace the depths I sound.
I live to work; my work's my all in all.

Even as it jumps,
The wave drag of surfacing;
Mereswine losing faith.

Your buoyant spirit flirts with its despairs;
A youthful lover you could leave or lose,
Delighting in the wake of love affairs
As on the rebound you arouse your muse.
In folktale tunes your *Wunderhorn* reveals
A liquid mystery, a line that roams
In breach of staider harmonies and steals
From key to key but never fully homes.
Eternal love and *Lebens trunk'ne Welt*—
But life's besotted world concedes its doubt
In final melodies that rise to melt
Back in the stillness where they'd started out.
Behind your brio, every leap or breach
A yearned-for sky that vaults beyond your reach.

Over and over,
Still dreaming the perfect leap,
A porpoise plunges.

I cannot tolerate the second-rate,
So every posting ends up in a row
Or headstrong rivalries that turn to hate.
But am I arrogant, I wonder now?
My baton summons up a pleasure-ground;
For all the rancour of my stern regime,
In concert after concert I astound
The audience with dreams they feared to dream.
Aufsteh'n wirdst du, mein Hertz, in einem Nu—
Those five iambs of Klopstock I reset,
My second symphony's one great amen—

You will, my heart, in no time rise anew.
I yearn for resurrection's joy and yet
Each surge to heaven seems to sink again.

(iii)

From take-off to plump,
Predicted trajectory;
A dolphin leaping.

My troubled Rilke angels can't transcend
Such angst inside your mind's abandoned boy,
Whose every new beginning bodes an end;
In love with absence, all your loves will cloy.
You court the things you then begin to shirk—
Another dream, another driven lunge—
But wavering between your life and work
Each playful jump's a sudden madcap plunge.
The hearts you win you break in fallen waves;
Each woman wooed until, ensconced in joy,
You flee again the gift your passion craves.
Tormented by this double-minded call,
Your history each leap's inherent fall.

A tension released,
Ponderous arrow in flight;
A bull scuds mid-air.

Creative angel, can you hear my cry?
Just working—*il n'y a que travailler*—
Rodin's austere advice I still obey
And labouring I live and cannot die.
O sweet and magic spurt the moment when
Excess existence builds up in the heart,
A surge within I freeze back into art;
In every line my Eros dies again.
Seduction dares transform its own unease
And pleasured well beyond our afterplay
We find God's fullness deep in everything.
Consider Stampa, selfless Heloïse,

Whose loves were stations left along the way.
An arrow overcomes its anguished string.

Mistrusting heavens,
The outsider of the pod
Thuds into water.

Each lived-in question like a foreign tongue,
Where you are riddling through the doubts you raise:
On what stroked instrument are our lives strung?
O tell us, poet, what you do? I praise.
Instinctively you try to understand
Whose hand both holds and bows our violin—
Und welcher Geiger hat uns in der Hand?
A loner still you stalk a God within.
Then gravity begins to second-guess
And craving bluer depths you double-cross
Each leap of joy to label happiness
Your too-soon profit from approaching loss.
A prodigal, you choose to praise and yearn
But balking at being loved you can't return.

To glitter aloft,
Then arcing downward, submerge;
Dolphin's double need.

How we *avoiding fate must yearn for fate.*
I know how things can thrive and I've
Delighted in those loves I celebrate;
Yet even as I leap, I long to dive.
Did childhood shape my falling shibboleth?
When lurking in each other's light, the price
We lovers pay is never nearing death,
But side by side would we glance paradise?
Yet if the endless dead still can uncoil
A simile awakening our surprise
Where empty hazel catkins hang and all
God's rain is spilling down on dark spring soil,
Would we who reckon bliss must always rise
Then find we're startled that such bliss can fall?

(iv)

Out of the ocean
Soaring, yet somehow aware;
A ray's conscious flight.

It's you, Lawrence, bearded collier's youth
Whose every story goes on straddling both
A mother's soul, a father's so uncouth
But lived-in self; two worlds you love and loathe.
Madonna Jesse, daring Frieda's sex;
Both son and lover sucked by undertow:
Your mother's inner chapel boy still checks
Your passion's leap in every letting go.
You celebrate the body's sacrament,
Refuse to blur the things the blood has heard;
Creation's surge must surge in us afresh;
But you're, for all the sweat of your consent,
A burnished lover standing back to word
The fleeting sweetness of a pleasured flesh.

Bursting from the deep,
Pitch and yaw as fits the air;
A fish on the wing.

Against the tide of this ungodly time,
When we've become mechanical and crass,
Though sick of English Midland soot and grime,
I clashed with all that's snug and middle class.
And then I seemed to drift but heading south,
My creed a richer life, my pen my crook,
A Moses for our age, and hand to mouth
I worked to change the world with every book.
From leap to leap each glance of sky was new
And chronicles a shifting mood in me;
But yet no vision, no one point of view,
Just making heavens move as needs may be.
I strike red angry seas with Aaron's rod,
My life a search to find my fallen god.

Caught in cross-currents,
Between light and gravity;
Glittering fish-plane.

Still toiling with your mother's piety,
Your father's ghostly rage won't let you go;
You're living out your own Lord Chatterley,
A cuckold for your Frieda's captain beau.
Despite yourself, in fiction you conspire
With her, as though in Mellors' guise you must
Become her captain to recall desire
And lapse back into sweats of younger lust.
I hear a chapel sermon's ecstasy,
As giddy with your Eden once again
You rail against our reason's narrow gauge
And, still insisting that each self is free
To feel the blood's mysterious amen,
You swim in counter-currents of an age.

On reconnaissance,
A broad-winged devil fish buoyed
By an airborne dream.

I long with Frieda to befriend a male
In some Atlantis of free love I've planned,
But all utopias I teach now fail
To conjure my incarnate promised land.
I wonder watching ocean fish in flight,
Both daring in their leaps and in their dives,
Will those who balk at thrusting into light
Be resurrected to their richer lives?
At least I leap and though each leap seems bound
To let me down, I dare the upward thrust
And even in an Eden never found
My heaven is a dream I hold in trust.
A ranging wide-spanned leaping manta ray,
I graced the air, I glanced the greater day.

(v)

Under the surface
A great white shark nerves itself
To venture a breach.

Your tone impersonal and passionless
As ruling your own roost in Russell Square

36

You turn, our pained superior T. S.,
To wonder, "Do I dare" and, "Do I dare?"
Your grandfather engrained in you, an Eliot
Commands a Hamlet you're not meant to be
With chilly politesse and touch-me-not,
More English than the English care to be.
And yet, however steely and astute,
Aware how waste lands of the self can slide,
Your temperament demands an absolute
To order seas of doubt which rage inside
The toothed gullet of an agèd shark.
And will you dare to leap out from the dark?

Tailfins flip upward,
Fuselage gravity drawn
Belly-flops downward.

You know the fear I barely hold at bay,
The littered waste that lines the ocean floor,
My dreaded void, our cultural decay—
How I by will belong to rite and lore.
Tradition I must bow to and then bend;
As even in my leap I ease my arc
So each beginning gestures towards its end,
As I both dare the light and hint at dark.
How strange that I who struggle to avoid
What's personal despite myself must feed
On inner history; tradition's king
Without forebear or heir I birth a void
And move in measures still unpedigreed.
My everything becomes its counter-thing.

Volt-sensitive shark,
A lumbering torpedo,
Falls below the mark.

Your lone *"Who then devised the torment? Love."*
O Thomas Stearns, a thrift-taught uptight boy,
You're dodging cutting loose. Although the dove
Descending breaks the air, it brings no joy.
A static view, maybe some stoic lack
Regards the present with opprobrium;

Your absolute keeps tending to look back
And shudders at the shape of things to come.
In mixing reminiscence and desire,
The soul's sap quivers, brief sun flames the ice;
Unless restored by that refining fire
Your daring must fall short of paradise.
And yet Old Possum your quartets entrance,
When from the still point you still stir the dance.

A frolicking fish
Light-hearted in the shiver,
Leaping heavenward.

My driving will, my mother's driven son,
My artist's cold both Brahman and urbane—
Was I all things to all and friend to none?
To be a poet cost me too much pain.
Although to thaw my ego I had learned
To woo a God with prayer and discipline,
Surrounded by a sense of grace discerned;
Yet even hard-won faith was honed within.
But wait! Once for *delete* instead write *stet*
And let my lover's voice just soar to life;
A fifth quartet—or should I say quintet?
One carefree *dedication to my wife*
To whom, God knows, I owe my leap's delight.

Canto 5
Abundance

(i)

Still underground bulb,
A deep and dormant thriving;
Lily in waiting.

My Dante, tend *nel mezzo del cammin*
Forgotten bulbs your times again unearth;
Your gift to see a flowering unforeseen,
To rake the soil for Europe's lush rebirth.

A rich premodern mind allows you mix
Rife thoughts retrieved with things so up-to-date
In science, art or purse and politics,
The cosmos in your seedbed city-state.
You're lily-signed Firenze's exiled son—
Why is that place assailed by so much strife?—
Who'll name and face dead figures one by one,
Descending and ascending afterlife.
By conscious metaphor and fact combined
You parallel the purpose of God's mind.

Overwintering,
A year's adventitious roots;
Lily emerging.

Ah yes, the middle of the way and yet
Recall the years I yearned, a troubadour
For Beatrice since Mayday when we met
One fateful moment in 1284.
I break new ground and graft a *Comedy*—
I'm politician, poet-citizen;
Though love can shape a tongue in Tuscany,
I end an exile, never home again.
With Virgil I will climb hell's deepest ice
To reach the doorway of the dead and weep
Till Beatrice unknotting nerves in me
Redeems my guilt and, braving paradise,
I dare allow my sacred poem to leap
From where we are to where we're made to be.

Six luscious tepals,
Rich indelible stamens;
Lily unseaming.

You're polymath and eager pioneer
Who doubling back becomes a daring scout,
Defining our modernity's frontier
By summing up what somehow opens out.
A fluke of birth, a lucky *floruit*,
As banished and uncoddled by soft fame,
You blame defectors' sham and counterfeit;
Unhampered your cold hell will name and shame.

But more! As certain as the second thief,
This day in paradise you too are shown
The smile whose warmth unzips the lily's leaf,
The light eternal in itself alone.
You're stretching still my mind and my desire
To walk our daring God of love's high wire.

Spotted and brushstroked,
A glorious flourishing;
Stargazer lily.

But seven centuries beyond my theme,
You've chosen to pursue the selfsame path
And summing up an era work the seam
Between the modern and its aftermath.
You've climbed from hell to heaven's vertigo.
I'll be your guide! Though dazzled in that gaze,
Allow flawed words their spill and overflow,
For God delights in lily-gilding praise.
Imagine all we've done or left undone,
Our broken longings longing still for more,
Completed in the glory of one glance
And, as both stars and atoms dance and dance,
Our lives unreel around one loving core
Where all our wills and all desires are one.

(ii)

Unbudding to praise,
An infinite unwinding;
O rose of the world.

The parsons, clowns, the porters, dukes and kings,
A sexton, jeweller, servant, witch or queen,
All playful, loving, tragic, lived mood swings
And battlefields our fantasy has seen.
Such wonders bred from such a fetid womb,
That plague-thronged London, city of disease,
A bloodstained hothouse where your plays will bloom
To entertain the hordes or even tease.
This cockpit holds *the vasty fields of France.*
Will Shakespeare, you rehearse our human kind

Which in your wooden O you will entrance
And *eke out each performance with your mind.*
In heavens of our spirits' empty space
All breathe in your compassionate embrace.

Abundant species,
Our climbers, trailers, hybrids;
A lavishing rose.

I mix and match each burgeoned metaphor
And break the rule of unities, as rife
With words I let the highbrows I abhor
Confuse confusion with profusion's life.
I'll lift whatever line or theme I will—
Soliloquies, asides, a quip, a pun,
Styles merged—Macbeth is hiring men to kill—
His porter fuses tragedy with fun.
Let paradise and earth run parallel,
This venal world a play within a play;
Inventing words I break convention's spell,
Speak what we feel, not what we ought to say;
Extravagance of heaven on the ground,
My rowdiness creation in the round.

Bud to bitter hip;
Blushing at such falls from grace,
Our five-wounded rose.

A player rooted in the fetid Rose
Too busy to debauch, too wise or shrewd,
Exploiting ancient plots that you transpose,
You're master of our every shifting mood.
Such rancour star-crossed lovers rise above
To bud before the summer's ripening breath,
Before ambition blots out heaven's love
And makes of Juliet a queen Macbeth.
Like Eves whose guilty flaws have eaten fruit
Your queens, who for their crowns have double-crossed
With falseness which should not find ground to root,
Must learn how hells are always heavens lost.
Some sell eternity to get a toy;
Your lovers know how joy delights in joy.

Enfolded red core,
Symbol of our blood and love;
All-embracing rose.

I weep the dust of all love's waking cries
And grieve myself to guess at others' smarts;
A rooted voice at once both wild and wise,
Am I the pardoned sum of all my parts?
Reality's a manifolded heart;
The forms of things unknown a poet's pen
Can move because he knows he's moved himself.
I am all things to women as to men.
My role both Juliet's and Romeo's,
In my renaissance mind all opposites meet;
What's in a name? That which we call a rose
By any other name would smell as sweet.
Our life's kaleidoscope a paradise.
I never sign my name the same way twice.

(iii)

After the leaf fall,
Trusting winter dormancy;
A vine lying low.

Though shape and substance in your work are one,
The learned savour puns or turns of line;
George Herbert, poet-priest of Bremerton,
So few dare savour word-fermented wine.
For some it's faith, for some it's wit; both fail
To cross the zeal and art your gift creates,
And wines that maderise are stained and stale,
The tannins soft, the taste disintegrates.
Quite underground to greet your mother-root,
How thou dost dwell and linger here below
Preparing green the sap still plots to grow;
When times are right you'll bear the ripest fruit.
Our paradise a love we lose and find;
Your fresh return both *feeds and fats my minde.*

More than highest grapes,
Sweet sap of broken berry;
Cana's best bouquet.

God's work has worked his juices through each vein—
As you too intermingle lines of mine—
I let my words become his work's refrain,
I take and taste what he doth there design.
I know my worth; I know power's thrill and sheen;
For me sour grapes don't hang there high above,
I know too well what mirth and music mean,
I know the ways of learning yet I love.
But can he want the grape who hath the wine?
I don't despise in pride a pride acquired,
As pleasing kings, I too once played with power;
Ambitious grapes can be both sweet and sour.
But Christ has crushed the juice my life desired;
Such love that liquor sweet and most divine.

Old wines, intense grape,
A new sapling grafted on;
Deep root renaissance.

Your times like ours such times of shift and change
When ships of our desires sail new-found seas
And maps unfold a globe we rearrange
To room both new and old discoveries.
Both testament and manna you approve—
The soul doth span the world, and hang content
From either pole unto the centre move—
You want to live both word and sacrament.
Discerning well the year and vintage you
Embrace in what is old what's still alive
And savour tangs and taste of old and new
To love whatever best allows us thrive.
Amazing paradise of middle ways;
My poet-priest and secretary of praise.

Bud break to harvest,
A precisely tended vine;
Voluptuous wine.

A verse may find him who a sermon flies.
Whatever I have learned and live to share
Reflects my conflicts with my God, those cries
And hopes that prose can shirk and proverbs dare.

If wise erred not it would go hard with fools—
My thoughts could stray, too strained or undefined,
But proverbs teach me density that schools
Such thought to churn and thicken in the mind.
Each poem I write to praise *his swing and sway;*
To graft my thoughts I choose an epigram,
A short refrain, a sudden shift of pace
To join two words that sparkle and enjamb;
The dense both-ands of pliant thought and play—
This heaven we both earn and win by grace.

(iv)

As for one spring night
And the dawning cherry trees—
It has disappeared.

The twenty-seventh morning and third moon,
I see you, Bashō, as you step on board—
The sakura you know will blossom soon
But you can't leave new lands yet unexplored.
Tradition greets and echoes everywhere—
What Sagyō said of Shiogashi pines;
You're following his footsteps so you share
His island haunts and visit hallowed shrines.
Each moment rides an image's caress
As real and random somehow here unite
And you combine both wit and wistfulness
In linking renga poems with such delight.
Mount Fuji's mist a morning haze that shrouds
A wanderer still drawn by windblown clouds.

How I want to see
In the blossoms at daybreak
The visage of God.

The locust's trill is stinging in the stones;
My thoughts still come and there is loneliness—
I drop out from all dreams of my success
To live my travelogue of weathered bones.
Go sweep the yard, another year is gone,
The month's last night now moonless I depart;

A pilgrimage within keeps moving on
To find my full bloom in another part.
I tramp from place to place, an escapee
Who has to risk the narrow heartland road,
Uprooting time and time again to roam;
The thought of settling down is death to me,
My make-up balks at any fixed abode—
Each day a journey, journeys now are home.

From what kind of tree's
Blossomings I do not know;
Yet such a fragrance!

Apprentice samurai whose master dies,
You're tempted then to toy with love of men,
But seeing nothing yet quite satisfies
You learn philosophy and turn to Zen.
Your students build your hut which later burns,
A sign that somehow elements approve
The lavish wanderlust that grows and yearns—
You're most yourself when keeping on the move.
In tune we're interwoven all in all—
A pilgrim both must know this and obey—
In four great sweeps of travel till you fall,
Your *haikai* once-off stations on the way.
Creation's home is one coherent whole;
Your words define a geography of soul.

Cherries in blossom
In this world; for them also
All hail to Buddha.

My lines no learned courtier's half play
Or butterflies that flit in fields of sun;
I work my deepest inlands day by day—
In all I do my life and art are one.
I started tight; relaxed, I finish loose.
My years now try to let each word ring true
And, paring down allusions that seduce
The mind, I let May sigh its honeydew.
Five petals sing quintets for paradise

And ah! the umbels fresh and pink and frail,
With vaguish fragrance in their v-nipped wings;
My syllables are blossoms so precise,
A cosmos sized to such a tiny scale,
Delighting in the strange alas of things.

(v)

Five blooms on one cyme.
Perennial, taut-woven;
Heaven's carnation.

Just as your father's great-grandfather Veit,
A miller-lutist, played while his mills ground,
You, Meister Bach, like him take huge delight
In criss-crossed lines of layered woven sound.
Five generations so deep-rooted in
A love of German Lutheran chorale
Your contrapuntal God can underpin
With joy—*Nun freut euch, Gottes Kinder all'*.
As Veit's lute played against the grain he'd grind,
Each line must make its own melodic sense
Or chase one theme hot-heeled a bar behind
To weave a music that's both one and dense.
Such joy in what freewheels and intertwines;
Incarnate heaven held between the lines.

Year by year seed pods
Hue their practice dreams of sun.
Red, yellow, white, pinks.

My spirit spilled its tears in hard-won art—
Cantata turning week by week to years—
As from a honed and faithful cantor's heart,
I offered God the music of His spheres.
Long practice finds impromptu forms of prayer,
As prayer in turn is processed by its form;
A carelessness attained by years of care,
Serenity that takes the ear by storm.
To rid my favourite hymns of rust-like spores,
Cascades of colour suddenly astound
In point and counterpoint as I unpod

A seed of dormant melody that soars
In ruffled blooms to coruscate around
The *cantus firmus* of capacious God.

Unseamed cultivars,
Red rockets, laced Romeos;
Boundless show of pinks.

Inveterate reviser, you amend
To near an Eden you're reminded of;
A need for flawlessness that in the end
You know can only hint at heaven's love.
A rich and careful cast of mind can sprout
An endless growth engraved in simple germs,
Motifs that flower in tunes turned inside out,
Traditions you transpose beyond their terms.
Such flourishing is where all musics meet
As in perfection futures spring alive—
Romantics cry in moody cello suites,
And jazz feeds Brandenburg concerto five.
Is God's precision bursting at the seams
In music ripe with tautly ravelled themes?

A tight bud's outburst
Meticulously scalloped;
God's flower. Dianthus.

My own taskmaster, matching work and flair,
A thoroughness became my theme for life;
My tour de force *Well-Tempered Clavier,*
Those six carnation plants to please my wife
Or sending her a linnet that would sing,
Partitas, passions, minor Mass in B,
The six-part fugue I coaxed for Potsdam's king—
The same painstaking flared intensity.
Two centuries before my work's refound.
Did my perfection cause a fashion shift?
Eclipsed by chords, a rage for cleaner lines,
As roots dream up their flowerings underground,
I'll serve my God and neighbour with my gift
And hold my bloom until a heaven shines.

(vi)

Seedless eyelashes
Surround a risk-taking bloom;
A sunflower opens.

Son Mozart, father's migrant wunderkind,
A curiosity all courts admire;
Your talent's seeds are fed and sunned by dint
Of memory and exercised desire.
Young sunflowers seek the light's magnificat
And prodigies will try each vogue and trend;
So learning on the hoof you copycat
New styles you first absorb and then transcend.
At twenty-four a broader field of view
Demands you leave your father's smother love—
That once had warmed but now is stunting you—
And dare the sun outside his puppet's glove.
What father knows the solo seeds he's grown?
Your opened bloom will flourish on its own.

Loop-throwing florets
In arithmetic spirals;
Astounding sunflower.

I manage well but fail to woo court cliques—
My *Figaro* falls foul of the regime;
Yet all my life an alter ego ekes
In me a father's *Kapellmeister* dream.
My melodies all spiral a surprise;
As golden-angled patterns intertwine
In florets coiled inside the sunflowers' eyes,
I vary lengths of phrase to turn a line.
Imagination needs no fulltime post;
Composing in the mind I pour each note
And stretch the known as far as newness dares;
My heaven still the grace to live engrossed
In tunes that ripened in each bar I wrote
To lull and catch my listeners unawares.

Tall, vulnerable,
A sky-reaching gravity;
O Sonnenblume.

As sunflowers seize their yellow petal light,
Long yearning childhood's keyboard years invade
Your consciousness and notes have taken flight
To soar in music you've more heard than made;
And each allegro's playful discipline
Subsides to send a gentle but precise
Legato Meister's loving violin
Adagio-ing up a paradise.
Delight in longing longs for full delight.
Good Wolfgang! Einstein wants to rendezvous.
It's Bach for praising God but Barth was right;
The angels en famille must favour you.
And none but you can pitch such poignant fun
Where joy and grief seem woven into one.

Great sun-imaged disk,
Light-loving inflorescence
Blooming just to bloom.

Bach's counterpoint and yet a pioneer—
My sense of fun will keep the seraphim
Awake and blaze a sudden wild frontier,
A yellow flare around a sunflower's rim.
Although I can still fill a concert hall,
At court I rank as number four or five;
In trills and flighty runs I trust my call
And live foreshortened life in overdrive.
In skies a million mobile phones relay
One serenade, a little *Nachtmusik,*
And consonance of noise you can't mistake
Which never takes the answer no will play
Sound ratios of God's arithmetic—
So hear my music made for heaven's sake.

(vii)

Overshadowing,
Sticky with honey-dewed leaves;
A dreamy lime tree.

Dear prince of preparation's castled air
And master of great schemes drugs undermined,

Sad Coleridge so acutely self-aware,
Imprisoned in your lime-tree-bowered mind.
A mother's stern upbringing stinted praise
And you play Hamlet numbed by reverie;
Youth's promise lived in opium's malaise,
A baffling preface to what once you'd be.
A wholeness sought, you risk a prophet's role;
Then, turning second-sighted Highgate sage,
A tortured mind that swings from pole to pole
Can still reveal the story of our age.
You coaxed that sunny dome, those caves of ice;
Now drink the mother's milk of paradise.

Deciduous lime
Defying a late spring storm;
Profuse re-leafage.

You only ghost-write shame, my wedding guest,
That guilty trail of friends and loves betrayed;
Though I'm to blame, can self-despair be blest
As when I praised the water snakes and prayed?
As serpent roots keep raging under earth,
Dreams ramify and spread soft lime-tree leaves;
I give my word for what my word is worth,
Yet every breaking promise self-deceives.
Out of my need to start and start again
I face the healing failure of Christ's cross;
Dare I believe such pardonings uplift
A heart to hope for love beyond all ken,
Whose amnesty unnecks the albatross?
My craving for forgiveness turns to gift.

Heart-shaped linden leaf
Scythian diviners touched;
Truth-unearthing tree.

How blandly any age assumes carte blanche
To tear up deeper roots it needs to tap;
But you embrace the whole tree, root and branch,
In wonder at the oneness of its sap.
Then, though you lust for Edens lost, you find
The dazed sublime Romantics rhapsodise

Rings hollow when there's nothing more behind.
Are Wordsworth's shepherds Wordsworth in disguise?
In chemistry you're keeping up to date,
Improving still your stock of metaphor,
And racked imaginings still recreate
The secrets in your veins that juiced can soar.
Your range of thought a sap-divining rod
To dowse the lavish mind of dazzling God.

Rich-sapped foliage,
Furcated trunk ramified;
Abundant lime tree.

My father showed me fathomless night skies,
A world where large and little all cohere,
Where stars are dewdrops of a different size.
And am I still my father's faithful seer?
We ride a universe inscribed in rings
Of love that yearly bind both branch and bole;
In all this thick community of things,
How gropingly I integrate the whole.
But yes, he prayeth best, who loveth best
All things both great and small, for saps of grace
That soar within can summon up grand schemes;
But this I tell thee, thou my wedding guest!
Although so much eluded my embrace,
I drank dew buckets full of God's own dreams.

(viii)

Opposite matched leaves,
God's gift for purging longing;
A pomegranate.

I want to parley with you as a pair—
Elizabeth and Robert Browning, both
Of you, so deepened in each other, dare
C major of your matching double growth.
Both guessing God's soft presence out of sight,
You hanker still, or what's a heaven for?
Yet loving to the depth and breadth and height,
Both pour out gratitude for such rapport.

As pomegranates poise opposing leaves,
Your conversation's endless node renewed
For love's own sake, in such love's strength believes—
A pledge of beauty in its plenitude.
The infinite in sixteen nurtured years,
As love endures from life that disappears.

Fertile and bleeding,
So sweet-tart-juiced and thin-skinned;
Fruit of Granada.

While hanging poets' portraits I admire
And sticking to my penny-stamped affairs,
Some pink-flushed pomegranate of desire
Keeps fleshing out my words half-unawares.
My pale mistrusting paper-self transformed
Finds love that's larger to enlarge my worth,
That far beyond my childhood's faith has warmed
And breathed on this my heaven-brimming earth.
Now everything I dream I can become
And I, who once was so obsessed with death,
Am poet, lover, mother. *Me voici!*
In spite of spirit-raps and opium,
My Robert soothes me to my rapt last breath.
Thou mayst love on, through love's eternity.

Ancient rebirth fruit,
Many-seeded and flawed sphere;
A punic apple.

You dare *the dance of plastic circumstance;*
Though falling short in all you do and did:
I live and die a man and take man's chance
That imperfection means perfection hid.
The once-loved Byron lyrics start to wane—
Too grounded in the self such minds regress;
The world as stage you, Robert, still maintain
Lets drama mend Romantic innerness.
Why must a single of the sides be right?
You turn trailblazer and ventriloquist—
A heart can house the seeds of every plight
And guess the words of God the dramatist.

That heart will nurse and lose Elizabeth.
I will but love thee better after death.

Embroidered emblem,
Desert Israelites' food dream;
Fruit of paradise.

Without a mask Elizabeth felt free—
My monologues, dramatic stratagems,
Mix sound and sense and thought in poetry,
As bells and pomegranates bound priests' hems.
From roots comes fruit that growing ripe succumbs
And so evolves; eternity is rife
With arils at the core of what becomes
A heaven in this shut-up house of life.
When facing time I'd left, my sonneteer's
Love mimed my future's epigraph for me—
The pain in parting was our love's sweet price.
Our conversation kept two dozen years
On ice as I won fame you'd wished I'd see,
We're picking up the threads in paradise.

(ix)

Colour-changing bloom,
Clematis of mind's beauty;
Supported climber.

Some friends name you "clematis," Mary Ann—
Your sap climbs towards a sun you're dreaming of,
Someone to be your all in all, a man
To lean on, bloom you to the full with love.
A pietistic time you soon abhor
And fallings for already tied-up men;
The long sad years of youth worth living for
The sake of middle age, to gaze again
On life unfolding plots of gain and loss
Among the pots and pans of daily facts,
To grind by slow degrees and mill the Floss
Of choices made in mundane sleepwalked acts.
You live with Lewes, godsend's Lancelot,
And ostracised become George Eliot.

Clinging, tremulous,
Delicate separate flowers;
Clematis in bloom.

My heroines unbed a bittersweet
That's rooted deep in memory's rendezvous,
Where Dorothea and young Maggie meet
To share my feelings and my failings too.
My novels delve a lifetime's residue—
Poor Dr. Lydgate's hopes sold out to house
Blonde Rosamund, whose charms he comes to rue,
A fable seeded in my sister's spouse.
We all can house such ego-clinging elves
And tales can turn on one such tragic flaw,
Till Dorothea's waking window gives
On to a world of other-centred selves.
I learn to see as Feuerbach once saw
A trembling love in everything that lives.

Unfolded leaflets
Among intertwining stalks;
Criss-cross clematis.

The moods and scope of your wide-ranging mind
Still loves our clay and makeshift daily mess;
In every fate your plots unfold I find
I hear that voice friends heard as your caress.
All history spreads out under heaven's arch
In lives both intertwined and singular;
A cosmos woven into Middlemarch,
We're in the thick of things just as they are.
The wise to be, the silly well-to-do
Or artisans with narrow jealousy;
Such sags and weaknesses all ringing true,
Your heaven rooms our frail humanity.
A mind and heart in love can coalesce
To tell God's honest truth with tenderness.

In cool, moist, drained soil,
Thriving under a full sun;
The traveller's joy.

A traveller's joy will trust what's new and strange
And dare to go beyond the diagram;
Of course from book to book the readers change,
My voice evolves within each self I am.
Yet criticised I'm seized by nerves or doubt;
Unloved I know how little I'd have done
Or dared to trust and travel on without
My Eden's journey under George's sun.
I know my marriage to John Cross has miffed
All those who thought that I'd rebelled before—
How covertly to know becomes to own.
Close friends are never shocked although we drift
Or change and so by chance may fall once more
In love. I never could have stood alone.

(x)

Candled leaves, bare limbs—
Insatiable seasons turn;
Indian-red spheres.

Cézanne, still dauntless on your daily treks
To paint Mont Sainte-Victoire from day to day;
You clash with all your friends, recluse of Aix,
Return to childhood's chestnut-lined *allée*.
Distrustful, trenchant, unpraised banker's son,
Both full of doubts and fed by complex pride,
Your best-loved paintings, paintings not yet done—
A falling short that's never satisfied.
Your father's trees unleaf each falling year,
Turn arabesques both bare and angular;
Your eyes in love with luminous ripe spheres
Keep glorying a still-lifed ginger jar
And unities of tone-dissolving bright—
Long live the sun that grants such stunning light.

Ambitious catkins
Seeking their place in the sun;
A chestnut's striving growth.

As boys, Zola and I both learn to dream
In words and paint, refusing to conform

To bourgeois norms; while still at school we scheme
How we'll take Paris and the world by storm.
My father's disapproval salts a sore;
A prodigal and guilty breakaway,
I can't just call myself a *refusé*—
I'll dare keep knocking on the Salon's door.
Courbet and Delacroix imbued my youth,
Pissarro taught me much and fathered me;
But now I fall in love with light and shade
And learn to trust myself to paint the truth
Of sailors, fruits and skulls—the things I see;
My art's creation's ardour rearrayed.

Furrow-trunked, widespread,
Prickly burrs cream-fleshed inside;
Open pelicarpus.

Zola reneged, Monet, Degas, Renoir—
Outsiders all—by now well moved inside;
Though you're rebuffed, a critic's bête noire,
Yet such neglect self-faith somehow defied.
So long an outcast, loner blunt and brusque—
Still younger men get under your thin skin;
You change and open up, a spiky husk
Whose wariness conceals its seed within.
"A line's a meeting place for coloured planes"
 or "light and shadow angles should concur."
"God's sun," you say, "paints all the world contains"—
And leave for vespers at Le Saint-Sauveur.
Your heaven reached still layer by painful layer—
Was every stroke a slowly entered prayer?

Firmly set, dense-crowned,
Full-coloured candelabra;
A grooved sunlit nut.

I learned to let the colours draw for me
To soak my senses in each liquid zone;
Although I seek Poussin's calm clarity,
Nuancing shapes in tight mosaics of tone.
I still refuse to kiss the fashion's rod—
Our insights turned to blotchy in-betweens—

Once a certain age, there's only God
Whose reds and blues and yellows, blacks and greens
Reradiate from rocks and chestnut trees
Or waistcoats, plums and smokers' playing cards,
A millstone, bathers in their bare delight,
The caves near Château Noir, a man's chemise;
There's nothing God's hued glory disregards;
All beauty's light within a greater light.

(xi)

Endless prairie vista
As far as west is from east;
Lonely bluestem grass.

I see you, Willa Cather, as you watch
Your grandma's turbaned gold-skinned slave's return
From Canada, where she'd decamped; you notch
It quietly up as grist for memory's quern.
Transplanted to Nebraska's beard-grass plains,
You root your teenage Red Cloud prairie years
Among Bohemians, the Magyar, Danes
And Swedes, the Poles and Czechs—O Pioneers!
And youth's outsider love in you will grow:
The ousted Pueblo peoples' history,
French missioners who plied New Mexico,
Quebec's old settlers' lifelong constancy.
A tune's persisting memories can taunt,
Each story hallows childhood things that haunt.

On wine-stained ground,
Stems sway like water;
Determined settlers.

You can't both eat the cake and keep it whole—
I choose devotion's cost and sacred call,
Though sacrifice puts iron in the soul;
My life and work and love are one in all.
My models were the grass-roots minds I knew,
The frontier folk, my friends, a diary
I burgle; yet I know how I imbue
My men and women with so much of me.

Yet sagas don't conform to our design.
When artists love their art above all things
So much it seems seeps through ambition's sieve;
Both Thea Kronberg's thoughts and dreams are mine:
A married nightingale so seldom sings.
My stories only know the life I live.

Pioneers sow corn;
Longing aeons of prairie
Recall old homelands.

Yet music's your life's passion and delight
And every word a tone and tact you chose;
Your lover Edith Lewis was so right
To praise the riffs and rhythms in your prose.
For you the New World's yearning largo sees
Night-scattered lights of settlers' lives that part
In miles of maize and beard grass symphonies
And hum the songs of Europe's homesick heart.
Another novel seemed to want to brew
But Wolfgang Amadeus dazzles most,
Those final infirm years he balms you too—
Will Barth and Albert Einstein both play host
And welcome you beyond the wailing wall
To paradise regained for good and all?

A blue-tinted spring
Rusts autumn's boundless heartland;
A spectrum of praise.

Once art for art itself or so I thought.
Unfolding people's souls at story pace
I fell in love with them and found I caught
God's glimpse of glory in each human face.
The little-bluestem grass in spring that grew
Turns gently red once autumn has begun;
I learn with years to bless both red and blue—
For me both faith and art would merge as one.
The patient bending trees, the patient lives,
The sum of small and daily things we do
More than the plot or grand dramatic parts;
Our now that neither passes nor arrives

Finds wholeness under heaven's overview;
All histories begin in human hearts.

(xii)

Gray magentas merged
In cordate opposite leaves;
A fragrant lilac.

Chagall, determined in your second sight
To prime God's dream in us at any price,
Your eye allows an airborne trust delight
In gravity's suspended paradise
Where lovers in their lilacs float above
A naked moon reflected underneath
And recklessly enjoy in timeless love
The breath of prayer and mourning paintings breathe.
Flirtatious hues and tints of mauve conspire;
A wooer tends his woman's playful pose
And purples merge with satin pink desire
Where climbing sap is seed and lobes are clothes.
As heart-shaped leaves in pairs can counterpoise,
The lilacs and their lovers match their joys.

A sun-loved sapling
Daring its fragranceless years;
An earned flowering.

I left Vitebsk, there was so much to learn;
But more at home the more I was away,
Its fiddles, cocks and goats and carts return;
I'm rooted still in Belerusian clay.
You reckon I'm the first surrealist?
Each ism by ism I know I'd slowly grown,
But schools it seems by nature I resist,
A carte-blanche sapling on my carefree own.
To know I'd been my mother's wonder boy
Would room with love my almost century;
I paint my witness now for all I'm worth
To life's own jazz of grief and chosen joy
That Bella and my Vava bore with me.
Such loves can move a heaven here on earth.

So timelessly layered
In dreams of a Persian park;
Eden's bluish shrub.

A fresh imagining in us now frees
Our safe arrangement of the world, unseams
And blooms unbounded by old boundaries
To drift between reality and dreams.
In heaven's overview all things converge,
Upsetting our too-careful apple-carts;
So lovers in their lilacs seem to merge
And pig-shaped farmers feed their counterparts.
Time too is layered in your intensive gaze:
Your folk can watch the fall of Icarus
Or Satan's plunge replayed in our own days
While Christ redies amidst the Exodus.
In all the leaps and overlays you've dared,
Our paradise imagined and prepared.

Brief-bloomed syringe,
Flourish to delight and grieve;
Generous shining.

I loved this playful topsy-turvy world,
My dreamy inside-out and outside-in
Where sweethearts and the silent angels swirled
And Vitebsk figures bowed their violin,
Or loaded carts and three-branched candlesticks,
A hut in flames, another fleeing Jew,
A menorah and fallen crucifix—
Is Christ now crucified for shtetls too?
My lifelong work this chosen way that fetes
The sheer fertility of all that shines
Through all and leave the signs of my belief
In colours as a grace that integrates
The light and shade that shape my God's designs
On love that overlaps both joy and grief.

(xiii)

Dense understory,
Thriving in acidic soil;
A startling bluebell.

But Kavanagh, anarchic and thin-skinned,
Did you rely on love's own IOU,
A kamikaze trusting in God's wind
To blow each mood and counter-mood in you?
Capricious prophet, your hand-biting gene
Keeps on undoing any debt that binds;
Ezekiel has come from Inniskeen
Demanding God surprise angst-ridden minds.
Such troubled years before the bright stick trapped,
The couple-kissing seat's third-party breeze
When you in your new-woven world enrapt
Retrust the bluebell angel glanced through trees.
In hungry times, you pay the prophet's price:
A peeping Tom who lusts for paradise.

An angel's carpet,
Overbearing groundcover;
Bluebell nodding praise.

It's Kavanagh's comeback now to you, my friends,
Here after angst and satire's letting-fly;
My trade I'd learned absorbing all the trends,
Yet had the bluebell angel bid goodbye?
But sit and watch a nesting water hen
And heal here sinless on canal bank seats;
Let Jordan's waters wash your soul again.
Reborn I choose the bebop ease of Beats.
Ambition's bells are always false alarms.
No-caring jag. The jazz of unconcern.
Abandon now all thoughts of poetry biz
And stomp once more in Kitty Stobling's arms;
Like Ibsen's Terje Vigen we return
To praise the way it was, the way it is.

Careless, lopsided
Under the dim canopy;
Heaven-coloured bell.

Our green and peasant poet, forlorn Maguire—
So many might-have-beens your spirit fled—
The sour-tongued satirist's unholy fire,
Each sponged up role at first espoused, then shed.

You search like any probing self-taught man
And tunnel every modern mood in turn
To find again the light where you began;
So much unlearned we need once more to learn.
Some kink, a cussedness in you transcends
Each dark impasse, a third eye seeing through
To open up to daylight our dead-ends,
Reshaping older things we thought we knew.
My scathing prophet dares a scapegoat fate;
In wounded light the bluebell angels wait.

Lowly and sublime,
An ancient woodland prayer mat;
The common bluebell.

So folks, let's leap into the blinding light.
Picasso, Kafka, W. B. et al.
Too dour or mad, don't dare the giddy flight
Where angels bless what's ancient and banal.
My theme anonymous Lough Dergs of need,
The girl who's won a lover, girl with none,
Half-saints or souls as black as bluebell seed.
Was justice God until he saw his son?
I'll take this faithful father at his word,
Who means to show me still no matter what
The fabulous and commonplace unfurled
Into the light of love's audacious plot
Of death and wake-up to the dancing bird
And laughter loosed across a broken world.

(xiv)

Pendulous branchlets,
Turn Autumn's brown and gold;
Babylon willow.

I hear the bells and singing stained glass birds
As, Olivier Messiaen, you shift the scale
Of chirps from semitones to tones or thirds
For tawny owl or tenor nightingale.
Time weighed with what endures you interwove
Among the sounds you sense as gold and brown

Or blues lit up by ruby, red or mauve
And dazzling tones of rainbows upside down.
Your two great loves are Mi and Loriod,
Who share that jazz of freedom faith enjoys
Where limit modes allow the heart to flow
Its giddy praise and prayer—Chagall in noise.
Our spirit's here and there both correspond;
Here in this earthly life our life beyond.

Shimmer and shadow
Through caterpillar catkins;
A mystery's presence.

My poet mother's pulses in the womb
And I become her music-making heir;
I bless the rhythmic genes in me that bloom
To celebrate *mon Dieu et sa mystère*.
Let harmonies and rhythm both share one root
In riots of creation's rising prayers;
In modes retrieved or borrowed I transmute
Polyphonies of beats and patterned layers.
Renewing metres in what's old and new,
The spirit fanfares up eternal fun
And double-dotted crochets shiver as
The brass blows red, the sighing woodwind blue.
Is music pleasure, prayer and praise in one?
The horns and harps of paradise play jazz.

Fuzzy yellow blooms
Where of old we hung our harps;
Notre saule pleureur.

Your music's where the sacred intersects
With camp or college; worker by routine,
Precise and private, steeped in hallowed texts,
I see you planting trees at La Sauline.
He held a small scroll open in his hand—
Hope's angel fires your end of time quartet
For cello, upright cast as concert grand,
A violin and clapped-out clarinet.
The kestrel calls as angels come and go,
St Francis and his chatting birds both buoy

Us up with clarinet, *ondes Martenot*—
Where there is sadness may I bring a joy.
In wonder at the glories of the word
You dare to celebrate the sacred bird.

Drooped over water,
A weeping willow glories
In flickering light.

How everything is God's, who's everywhere:
The Greek, Hindu, Haikai or Balinese,
And all of life, both *son et lumière*,
Brown-headed cowbirds riding on the breeze.
And then the last *Éclairs* with all my themes
Assumed in one long fluent genesis;
Four years to shape and yet somehow it seems
A whole life's timbre pointed towards this.
My God will wipe each tear from waiting eyes,
The salty tears we wept, the teeth we gnashed;
I'm sure I've caught *Éclairs sur l'au delà*
And seen the dazzling love of paradise
In lightening glimpses of a glory flashed,
A Sabbath of beyond, the soul's aha!

(xv)

Demure grove lover,
Fine-haired blades and petioles;
Shy nemophila.

You're sucking a cigar that Friel has lit
As Brian private shows his public twin;
Your mix of wistfulness and impish wit
Both shy and sharp-eyed taking us all in.
Such laughter and chagrin both leaven tears
Through fine-haired plots of families explored
In Donegals of loves and doubting Lears
And gardens guarded by a flaming sword.
The planter in his lodge, O'Donnell Hall,
Grandees that time has taken down a peg
Still eking glistening Edens of recall
In interwoven worlds of Ballybeg.

Your gathered myths a sociology;
In glints of lives a global filigree.

Overlapped petals,
Reticent paradise eyes;
Hardy annual.

But hold on, friend! Am I in heaven too?
I think you're skating here on thinner ice;
There's double-mindedness in all I do—
My debut was *A Doubtful Paradise*.
Friel private canonised: world première!
Would Dante rank me in his upper rings?
My Ballybeg's no city of despair,
And yet I see the poignancy of things.
A language still a homeless dialect,
A trade that hovers near an ego trip—
Confusions that both fascinate and lurk.
No plan. My life and plays all intersect
To shape a craft without apprenticeship.
Is it enough to grope from work to work?

Five broad bell-like blooms,
Low-growing ground-coverers
Ringing silently.

Your father's maths grinds fall to rows and tears;
A son unpraised, your fragile self-esteem
Will come to raid a bank of praise arrears
To understand your women's stifled dreams.
"You're my nemophila," her father said—
Blind Molly Sweeney places trust in men;
At home in dark, half-willingly misled,
She buys two men ambition's oxygen.
Your Kate and Maggie, Agnes, Rose and Chris—
Five half-remembered aunts whose dreams and might-
Have-beens are teetering towards a precipice
As Henry Hall's *It's Time to Say Good Night*
Still sways a dancing tableau cheek to cheek;
This wordless rite, their silent way to speak.

Stars of semi-shade,
Moment of unwintering;
Spring's baby blue eyes.

New modes to waken you to what I mean—
Yet less a meaning, more like any art
That hears the cries of history's overseen
And lets compassion rearrange a heart.
The hedge schoolmaster Manus's chagrin,
Life's strays and changelings, chance's afterthought;
Five sisters holding down the dance within,
A pier become the pilgrim island sought.
I sound the dark and private in each soul—
A boy with wonderful but windless kites
I fail and pay my faith's still blue-eyed price
For hallowed time when I again am whole;
That one in ten of Harvey's healing nights,
A sword of light absorbing paradise.

2

Dealing

Canto 1

Mechanisms

(i)

You enter here a taut quintet
Where theorists can shift or shape
How we make sense of market flow;
How men, and how it's mostly men,
Explain the ways our commerce works.
No flash of insight, more a slow
Encroachment that in turn creates
Our understanding how by stealth
New certainties of common sense
Construe the weave of life and wealth.

But what had been the bond before
That held our frail household as one,
Before new earthbound seers unfold
How money and a market cause
Each flux of goods, our loss and gain,
The double bind of bought and sold
That guides and thrusts our give and take,
So drive and rivalry ensure
By willy-nilly laws a world
Of push and pull can still endure?

The Pharaohs cracked a failsafe whip
And built their tapered sunray tombs;
Of course the odd and jealous Cain,
But certainty was tasks retaught

And sons must follow fathers' suit.
No interplay, no need explain
Where meaning is a pyramid
Cohered by king or czar's whip hand
Or government by caste or guild
In measured custom and demand.

Though travelled traders pitch their tents
For taffetas and silks and furs,
To offer these exotic wares
That titillate the manor's lord
And ladies eager to collect
Such merchandise at marts and fairs;
For most their life and work are one
In every task they undertake—
Still strangers to commercial strife,
To worlds of gain for gain's own sake.

And yet the charge of creeping change
In double entries, balanced books,
The paper mills and printing press,
A merchant class who'll manage gain
To drive God's glory in his goods,
What once was stained reward's success,
As slowly all absorb the seeped
Street wisdom of the well-to-do;
Despite the groan and pain of growth,
A passion now to risk what's new.

For wool all common ground is grabbed
And England's paupers pack the towns,
Their web of custom worn too thin.
Kings stumble towards nation-states
Of measurements and currencies
Where wonder workshops soon begin.
The soil all once had worked to eat
Now land that's bought and labour sold,
The bargain struck, the business done,
The dealer's will and drive for wealth,
Our new concern with number one.

As Pole Copernicus had done,
This shift of mood has shaken us
So nothing now can be the same;
A process never standing still
In Western worlds that learn to deal
Our gambling beggared-neighbour game
And mills and looms accumulate.
Does no one know what's driving on
This shared machine of scrambled wealth?
Here comes one Richard Cantillon.

Wigged oval head,
Arching eyebrows,
Bird-in-flight mouth
Over pointed chin;
The shrewd eyes smile.

> *So few remember me. But for a don*
> *I'd gone for good into oblivion.*
> *I sparked political economy*
> *Show quantity's relation to demand—*
> *A butcher and his buyers' synergy.*
>
> *I came from Ballyheigue where meat is meat*
> *And understand a butcher's balance sheet;*
> *I live in London, mon Paris and Spain,*
> *A banker who has learned to speculate,*
> *But leaves strict laws for others to explain*
>
> *Enough to know a cause and its effect*
> *Beyond the mercantilists who protect*
> *Trade balances with bullion they purloin;*
> *I show a simple cyclic flow of goods.*
> *For those who risk their capital I coin*
>
> *"Entrepreneur" as now I separate*
> *a market's mechanism's steady state*
> *From sentiment, allowing reason see*
> *The inner workings of both goods and gain;*
> *A science of surmise my legacy.*

You'll die in debt, your London home
Burns down and no one knows the cause.
Some think debtees have done for you;

Some say you set the house on fire,
A stage-set debtor's suicide.
Once famous then you fade from view
Until Will Jevons talks you up
As founding student of this field;
The tracked circuities of trade
A market's modes you'd first revealed.

"The soil the source, man's work the force
That yields our riches," you'd begun . . .
Quesnay and so Turgot regard
The land as all, since labour's power
Is eaten food the land has grown.
But work becomes wealth's trading card
And we will fail to balance both;
In mapping out this age's myth
Of flawless clockwork measurement
We're adumbrating Adam Smith.

(ii)

Heavy bulged eyes,
Under weighty lids,
Aquiline nose.
A jutting lip
And headshake tic.

> Of course some know my skin but not the pith;
> My parents' line, a little of my kith
> And kin and how my mother cared for me.
> Two books will stand, so burn my papers, please—
> I pride myself on guarding privacy.
>
> I'm not some Newton of the marketplace.
> My work a fathoming and interface
> Where ordered sciences of man can meet;
> Our politics and tax, our thought and art—
> A planned compendium I won't complete.
>
> Quesnay too knows supply must match demand
> But still too bound he doesn't understand
> The skill and higgle-haggle of the mart;

Kirkcaldy-bred I've watched how deals are done,
How human science mixes mind and art.

Our discipline at best a paradox
Where each man's betterment unlocks
The door to opulence; each stock a stall
To meet demand and ups a nation's wealth
In competition's tempered free-for-all.

A hidden hand ensures each dealer's gain
By mechanisms the markets preordain,
Serves only good, so never speak of need
As rivalry in trade keeps down the cost—
Trust in your baker's and your butcher's greed.

I call Pascal a whining moralist;
Why must Descartes and Mandeville insist
On such dark souls? What's wrong with trade?
Like language, commerce loves exchange;
Our nature needs to bargain and persuade.

The rich accumulate and reinvest
And wages rise so workers too are blest
With progeny who live to propagate
More labourers who lower wages to
Allow a business world self-regulate;

Unless the crafty dealers are in league
To fix a price and profit by intrigue
Against the public good, or breaking trust
The lending banks permit malicious runs—
My times have seen the Ayr Bank's boom and bust.

But Adam, though I apprehend
Your trust in markets' flux and truck,
Your faith in dealing's benefits,
Why you don't rail at children used
And harnessed in black holes of dark
Deep down in Durham's shafts and pits
To pony-cart full tubs of coal
As victims of the hidden hand
That guides a nation's flow of goods,
My modern mind won't understand.

Oh no, a nation with such sores won't thrive,
Though I believe free trade's lift-off and drive
Will raise all ranks; the labour we divide
Allows our universal opulence;
But some must drone the duller underside.

No skill can separate the pith and skin—
Our moral sense a self that sees within,
Our conscience our spectator counterpart;
All progress must be based on prudent thought,
So our best head is joined to our best heart.

With lairds and greed's monopolists
Who stop the flow, you fault the state
Which interferes with laissez-faire;
Yet those whose dealings you condemn,
Whose mean rapacity you taunt,
Adopt you as their first forebear.
So you become the merchants' man,
Embracer of the creeds which brand
All governments that tend the maimed
As maimers of the hidden hand.

While government must guard what each one owns,
All states should deal with states in free-trade zones;
But don't infer that welfare interferes
Or that I think we'll endlessly expand—
My hazard guess about two hundred years.

Admirers only want me as their myth
And followers become more Smith than Smith;
Deny my moral stance, don't understand
We grow imagining each other's need—
Our sympathies another hidden hand.

Friend Hume's and teacher Hutcheson's
Disciple you'd evolve and so,
Epitomising your epoch,
Your rage for order has arranged
The unplanned jumbled marketplace
By laws of balance like a clock
Whose weighted wheel ticks time away

Or pendulums that equipoise
Each countervailing value's swing
To metronome the market's noise.

Like Newton now you too seem set
To undergird our thought for good.
You're both discerning and reserved,
Ambitious yet a modest man
Content to know that times will change;
You serve a world that you've observed
In laying bare your hidden hand.
But even epochs disappear
As markets soar in cyberspace–
Enough to help one age cohere.

(iii)

Almost six feet,
Curls, red-whiskered,
Bright dark-blue eyes,
Fair complexion,
A cleft palate.

But let the parson's son appear,
The Malthus many come to hate
Who'll check the cheerful certitude
His father friends and fashion share
By telling optimistic times
How faith in progress without food
To feed expanding masses spawned
Would end in epidemics, war
Or famine—nature's laws enforce
To find a balance as before.

A parson too in turn he'll teach;
His college students call him "Pop";
He's mild and yet he speaks his mind,
Opposing Poor Relief because
They'll breed their broods for poverty,
So crueller first but far more kind,
Much better nipped in early bud
Than left to nature's ruthless law

That holding folk and food in step
Won't fail to feed its hungry maw.

> Some things I think I safely can conclude:
> If for existence everyone needs food
> And sexual desire will never wane,
> We'll double and redouble till we're more
> Than Mother Earth's stocked cupboards can sustain.

> The poor must starve or steadfastly abstain;
> The only strategy is to restrain
> Our urge to multiply, and marry late,
> Or else it's sickly seasons, war and plague;
> We dare not keep on doubling at this rate.

> My view may have a melancholy hue—
> Utopians despise me and pooh-pooh
> A vista they will see as too severe;
> My sombre theory will say what all
> Naive pipe-dreamers never want to hear.

> For all their refutations they're in awe—
> In such an age of clockwork thoughts they saw
> How nature's mechanisms balanced food
> And population by its hidden hand;
> My dismal science damped an era's mood.

And you were neither right nor wrong.
How could you ever know how now
Planned parenthood would so take hold
And stall exhausting our earth's stock,
Or how the fossil fuels hoard
The sunlight stored like sunken gold,
Deferring dearth we yet must face?
And though our minds have grown immune
To risk, your writings were the first
To prick our progress's balloon.

Strange how your strictures seem to brew
Across two centuries. You sensed
A flaw in laws of how goods flow;
You name a glut, predicting gloom
Of boom and bust. Although gainsaid

As Say and friend Ricardo sow
Their seeds of doubt, half-mocking you,
So you are classed iconoclast;
Yet seen with John Keynes's kinder eye,
We'll see the cycles you forecast.

> *My malt can mellow slowly in its brew;*
> *I'm neither eloquent nor quick and few*
> *Agree but still I know my know and worth;*
> *I've tumbled to a vital system's fault,*
> *Where surplus damages the same as dearth.*

A generation and times change
As Smith's great family rings false;
Once lulled by gentle large-scale laws
And fonder hopes of harmony
We'd all grow perfect by degrees;
Instead, we're stuck between the jaws
Of human lust and hungry mouths—
Your thesis bites so near the bone.
Malthusian views now haunt our thoughts;
These times will know a darker tone.

(iv)

Sleeked-back black hair
Recedes at temples;
Short, trim sideburns,
Large nose, V-chin
And bowed cravat.

His name is Jean-Baptiste but known
By surname Say his market law
Will enter economic thought,
Opposing Malthus and his angst
About a glut across the board;
Self-regulation is inwrought,
A good that's sold will buy a good,
Each ware paid by another one;
A surplus soon is evened out,
The market mends each overrun.

How soon? A later Say admits
It's in the longer run things right
Themselves; his steely sanguine view
Supposed that people wouldn't hoard
But spend all gain on other goods.
So slacks and slumps he thought he knew
Could not turn up as in due time
Gluts balance out and markets bear
One ware's production overdone—
All slumps are fixed by laissez-faire.

Agnostic Huguenot who'd been
A revolution back-room boy,
Both watched by Bonaparte's police
And still suspect when kings resume;
Enlightened liberal, his trade
Twice crushed by taxes that increase,
He'll turn to teach economy.
Admirer of all middle-class
Advance, how could he conjure up
A global glut's complete impasse?

> My youthful years in England stirred in me
> A dream of steam machines for industry;
> John Stuart Mill and Bentham both my friends.
> Ricardo's theory appears too cool,
> Utility explains both worth and ends.

> Though claiming Smith as master I'm no clone;
> My view of what is value is my own:
> One line's worth more for some, for others less—
> Smith saw all value as its labour's sum,
> For me each ware is worth, is usefulness.

> Smith knew divided labour's great advance,
> But venturers and newly found finance,
> Machinery to shape all nature's force
> Must count, and mental work that we segment—
> How management is too a deep resource.

> But Malthus gluts in general still jar,
> His double-think I find indeed bizarre;

Though he's dismayed how surpluses amassed
Could stall a market lacking in demand,
He worries that we multiply too fast!

Though Adam Smith's digressions grate on me,
I'm his disciple wanting still to see
How sciences of man should intermix;
I didn't write as I had meant to do
My book to teach the art of politics.

Your legacy your market law,
La loi de débouchés, that leaves
Divided schools who either skew
The market's fix to fit their stand
On how it's false to intervene,
Or veering towards the other view
Abhor how laissez-faire allows
For lazy optings-out to let
Things go. Your later goalpost shift
Both sides to suit themselves forget.

But whether markets mend at once
Or in the longer time it takes
Which you concede, it's your work still
Attests across the continent
To markets as an oiled machine
Whose gearings both for good and ill
Self-regulate by laws and rules,
A mechanism that we can mar;
Its beams and cranks and balance wheels
All certain as each sun and star.

(v)

Dark-eyed; waned hair
Grey-edged and brushed
Forward; broad-browed,
Full-faced, clean-shaven;
Sensible smile.

I have no bugbear, no great bête noire,
And yet I like to speak my mind and spar

With true economists—but Malthus more
Than you, poor tongue-tied Jean-Baptiste,
Your halting conversation's such a chore.

In you, dear Malthus, I had met my match;
We trade our heedful letters where we hatch
Our lines of thought that parallel and cross;
Although we do lock horns we're lifelong friends
Behind our argued public pitch and toss.

And as for how you, Adam, dazzled me!
Like Say, your work my first epiphany—
You wonder how our wealth should be defined;
I ransack distribution's laws and rules
To satisfy my own methodic mind.

Your views, Ricardo, cool and calm,
Sephardic Londoner whose line
Of Amsterdam's shrewd moneymen
Has shaped your steely sharp left brain;
Your father stockjobbed faithfully,
But zealous Jew and denizen
Condemns you when though young you dare
To woo a Quaker girl and wed
Outside the tribe; alone you'll seek
To follow both your heart and head.

In stockjobbing it's time at stake,
A wager on how markets move
Between the deal and closing date;
You sense a panic in the pack
Unnerved at talk or rumoured news;
By selling soon, rebuying late,
You are the man of means who'll keep
Your bonds till Waterloo is won;
Though Malthus balked, you multiply
Your wealth—all thanks to Wellington.

You worry that banknotes aren't worth
The gold that once they guaranteed
And advocate a curbed supply
Of paper notes, propose a piece

Soon called "ricardo" to restore
Again the gold that notes imply;
But government's last-minute move
Rejigs your plan and so disjoins
All banknotes from their bullion base—
Ricardos melt to sovereign coins.

> What worries me much more than gold is how,
> Although our wealth will grow, it won't allow
> Employers gain their proper place; instead—
> Unlike the landlords or the working class—
> The more a nation booms, the more they're bled.
>
> If rent is the return from fertile fields,
> The more fecund the fields the greater yields;
> When business booms and everything expands,
> You'll notice how the workers' wages rise
> Because to meet this growth they're in demand.
>
> They'll spawn and spoil their market once again
> And as more mouths demand more grain;
> When poorer land is put to seed the cost
> Will rise and so the landlords stand to gain,
> Which means the business man once more has lost
>
> For workers' wages climb to pay for bread.
> You see how manufacturers who led
> The growth machine and gradually laid
> The ground for wealth must lose as grain costs soar.
> We need to trust in open-bordered trade . . .
>
> Ricardo! I'm of course at odds with you!
> You share my much-reviled Malthusian view
> That we'll outbreed the world on which we feed
> And yet my goals and yours are so unlike.
> I'm sure that in the short-term you'll succeed.
>
> I want a social science that adjusts;
> As parson and a parson's son who trusts
> That thoughts adapt to circumstance I see
> How economics change with changing needs;
> Lived lives are thicker than your theory . . .

But Malthus! geometric ratio
Proved how we breed. I bring my skills to show
Our science is pure science where each cause
And its effects adhere to logic's routes;
Our economics need both rules and laws.

And you, Ricardo, rule the roost
In moulding Smith's enlightenment
To your own mathematic mind.
Although you die still fairly young,
At fifty-one you've shaped a field;
A century remains resigned
To economics' noiseless laws
That most won't dare to countermand,
As mainstream pure economists
Pay homage to the unseen hand.

Canto 2
Visionaries

(i)

This science seeks to understand
Blind laws it trusts and lets control
The fractious to and fro of trade,
As smutty factories rear up
To crowd across a skyscape blurred
With chimneys' smutch, and men self-made
Churn daily shifts from dark to dark,
Where child or grown-up both must graft
For sixteen hours from six to ten
And greed still drives on overdraft.

Then in the wake of Waterloo
Malthusian gluts and gloom occur;
In England sheer machinery
Means labourers are then let go
And phantom figure Captain Ludd
Burns mills that soot the scenery;
A bread or blood rampage erupts—

According to Malthusian thought
The multiplying masses starve
To answer nature as they ought.

For some there's been more heart than head,
Some dreamers making common cause
With racked, defrauded rank and file;
Aristocrats or risen poor
That fellow feeling deeply moves;
But stargazers can lack the guile
To graft their visions with the grain;
In addicts' self-indulgent fizz
Their pipe-dreamed futures once more fail
To wean a world from where it is.

High bare temples,
Questioning eyes
And beaklike nose;
Half-cheek whiskers;
A portly frame.

Your eyes a shifting quick-fire quiz,
Arrive Henri de Saint-Simon;
Defying your own father's voice
You turn against the great and good,
Embrace the third estate instead,
Rejecting privilege rejoice
In how the high and mighty fall—
Noble houses, hangers-on;
I want the world my father feared,
The day of good-for-nothings gone.

> I'm born before you, Monsieur Jean-Baptiste,
> Ricardo and Malthus; you all dismissed
> The workers, I, the one with bluer blood,
> Know les industriels *alone are due their wage;*
> For me the idle wealthy are dead wood.
>
> Those least deserving still will seize what's best,
> And earning nothing feather their own nest;
> While those who work are worth their golden weight
> And serving us deserve their wage and gain.
> Unfairness need not be our human fate . . .

Like you, Ricardo, and you, Say, I come
A late vocation sage and cult for some;
Though you read Smith, when jailed by Robespierre
My phantom Charlemagne foretold I'd make
Another philosophe extraordinaire . . .

But, Saint-Simon, your mind must surely see
All things are underpinned by theory,
Though nature's laws like nature aren't nice;
For science's sake from facts I argue facts—
Though some will call it yet Ricardo's vice—

But you just chop and change at will,
Keep shifting terms you use until
To follow what you mean I find
Defeats all fastening down;
You fudge the words that you'd defined . . .

Although I change from cahier to cahier,
In every switch one thought holds sway;
Society is not the sum of single wills
Or just a chain of hap and hazard bits,
But every part both functions and fulfils

Another to nudge us on and play a role,
Engage in one superb organic whole—
Contributing in various modes to move,
Each according to one's cast of mind,
The grand machine of life along its groove.

You father's face commanding you,
My radical aristocrat,
You wake each day to words you teach
Your own valet, Rappelez-vous
Monsieur le Comte—Recall that you've
Great things to do! You'll overreach
Yourself but still you serve us well;
At first you'd run with laissez-faire
But seeing then how dog eats dog
Your lifetime's passion is repair

And all your scrambled schemes and plans
For government by merit, not by vote,

Where skills can serve society,
Entrepreneurs and engineers
And artists all cooperate,
Derive their dream and surety
From one great axiom that we
Are born for service and are bound
To give again what we receive;
What goes around will come around.

I know your anger at your class,
Your struggle with too strict a voice
Within that inched you to the edge;
But like the man you half-admire
You too in turn can dominate
As childhood hurt not conscious choice
Can steer the stances that you take;
How winding up in want you fail,
And kept by servants or by kin,
You'll end frustrated, poor and frail.

For Marx, a mere utopian;
For Engels, though in embryo,
A socialist; for Lenin you're
A guesser who had got it right;
For all your sad and darker sides
One daring insight will endure:
That markets' frenzied free-for-all
And rivalries are both akin
To anarchy's chaotic greed—
But interwoven all can win.

(ii)

Long-faced, high-browed;
Prominent nose,
Persuasive eyes
With glints of charm
And canniness.

This story waits for you; step in
New Lanark's Robert Owen raised

In Newtown, Wales. You quickly work
Your way, a wonder boy who's bound
By pluck and luck to make your mark;
McGuffog's clever young shop clerk,
Then, cotton-milling manager,
You'll marry up to run a mill
And make your fortune by your mix
Of governance and earned good will.

A stern regime with judgement books
And colour-coded conduct signs
Or random search so nothing's nicked,
Sobriety, your tight ship run
By night patrols, all spick and span,
A low-cost store where loans are ticked
And goods set off against a wage;
All children under ten are taught,
A sick fund too but still the gains
Finance associates had sought.

Perhaps your Severn Valley home
Where nature and trade's busyness
Could mix, or your own turn of mind
That local vicar Drake unveiled,
Inspired in you some special faith
In how an atmosphere defined
Behaviour and in how each man
Is such a child of circumstance;
So all we make we can remake—
In change we venture, we advance.

I marvel at so much you do—
A pioneer who sees the need
To cut excess, to curb abuse;
And though at first you mostly thought
How stockholders would stand to gain
By what such well-oiled works produce,
Yet paragon philanthropist
You're king whose education moulds
Your subjects to conform, and fears
The mind that marvels and unfolds.

Both chosen and endowed deep down I knew
I had to spread my vision, my new view
On how our factories demand reform;
And there's no way to shape the shapeless poor
Unless New Lanark now becomes the norm.

Ricardo, as revered committee man
You will review my model village plan;
Although you like best abstract thought, I am
A man of action and I have designed
A clean and perfect parallelogram

Of houses with two rooms in careful rows
For paupers furnished with both food and clothes,
A common kitchen and a dining room,
A school and shop. Presuming they'll produce
A lot more profit than their lives consume,

The surplus will be duly sold to pay
The costs and wipe what we at first outlay.
For five years it is best that there are fines
When rules aren't kept. And yes, so all watch all,
I know we need these parallel designs . . .

But Mister Owen, this worthy case you make—
Committee man or not—I want to take
An interest in, at any rate at first,
But sadly soon grow sceptical and cool.
Although you're overweening, what is worst

Is not your arrogance or that you're no
Economist but more the fact I know
The contradictions lurking deep in you;
A sorely ill-at-ease philanthropist,
Your gifts remain a debt you feel you're due.

Like me and many other self-made men
You think old ways should always work again;
New Lanark's deeds you never really leave
You have your paradigm and can't adapt—
I fear your would-be schemes will all unweave . . .

Ricardo, parliament's committee kept
On grilling me, then graciously I'm swept

Aside by verbiage and raw veneer.
My blueprint works and, though a while it's blocked,
I blaze my virgin trail, I persevere.

Oracular celebrity,
You're chasing phantom fame—
New Harmony will come to naught;
A visionary arriviste,
You take attention for assent,
But you have nothing new that's thought
Completely through. All full of plans,
You found trade unions that too fail.
Grown old, a spirit rapper you will spin
The fabric of your fairy tale.

Once cotton miller who demands
Both bartering and back to spades.
In your strange mixture I admire
Your wanting still to change the world.
While others better understood
The theory, a rapt desire
Still overdrives elusive dreams
Which deal with data in the raw
On schooling and on ambience
That later on pass into law.

(iii)

Broad high forehead,
Blue eagle eyes;
Nose crooked leftward,
Lips thin and tight.

Charles Fourier, both faith and awe
Demands of you one mantic thought,
That God who gave his human race
Such passions and instinctive zeal
Foresees relationships of love,
Where all our ardour can embrace
What suits ourselves and serves a whole
Society that should in turn
Display this God's array of gifts
In subtleties of co-concern.

You balk at talk of liberty
As long as labourers must slave
For wages at some boring work;
Industrial attraction means
To give us tasks as suit our gifts
So all can shine and none need shirk;
For humdrum jobs the highest pay
Or let our children help with chores
And, reaping riches by desire,
New wealth will open wider doors.

Your make-up shapes your flights and flaws.
You're shocked when parents punish you
For blabbing truths that blow a deal,
And hearing rice is dumped to hike
The price means commerce at its core
Is false, will feed your lifelong zeal
Defending your phalanstery,
Your grand hotel with graded floors,
And finding patrons who might fund
Your noble plans the world ignores.

Besides concern and sympathy,
Your childhood's tense obsessive side
Amassing globes and charts and maps,
Designing notes each named the same
For all of music's instruments,
Becomes compulsive later, saps
Your common sense, as you conceive
Our growth from Edenism in grades
Until our saltless seas will turn
By nature into lemonade.

> *As boy and man I loved to botanise;*
> *In every plant I see God's playful eyes*
> *Where unity is never uniform*
> *Or monotone but more a myriad*
> *That blooms and ramifies around a norm.*

> *As only nobles can be engineers,*
> *I toured in Europe, then became for years*
> *A travelling salesman while my mind had tried*

Imagining our moving on a stage
To climb the scale of growth I've classified.

I calibrate unfolding humankind,
Gradate and group our varied casts of mind
So best to formulate my phalanx schemes,
Reflecting God's own flawless order in
Communities of well-selected teams.

My phalanx favours outcasts and the weak
And growing by degrees we'll slowly peak;
Our women will be on a par with men;
No homophobes, a hotel card index
To mix and match for those in need of sex.

Cat-loving bachelor, I live alone.
Each afternoon I wait for the unknown
Rich benefactor who may fund for me
My model for humanity's advance
And found my planned phalanstery.

And Owen, yes, I'm silly sending you
My book revealing my new point of view;
I thought that, Richard, maybe you'd break ranks
And heed my phalanstery scheme; instead,
Your secretary's timid note of thanks . . .

I daren't deal with you, Charles Fourier.
I am engaged with schemes, and anyway
I know I'll never understand that stuff
About the saltless seas and lemonade;
More business pressure than a meant rebuff . . .

How could you ever comprehend such hope?
Reform's paternalist, you lack my scope.
I lost my patrimony when Lyons
Was sieged by demagogues who twice had sought
My head; from then a dream will drive me on

To find a fairer world where spite and hate
And class divisions all can dissipate.
And Saint-Simon, you too I tried to mend—
While Richard wanted barter, you rebel
Against the goods and gain that I commend.

You're dead when some at last do dare.
New Jersey's phalanx first tries out
Your fable but then splits and fails;
A phalanx in Ohio fades.
But though your schemes now skew and die,
A boy once shocked at shady sales,
Concerned for fairness, you insist
A grub's engraved with dreams of skies
And want to give our world its wings;
From caterpillars butterflies.

(iv)

A lanky frame,
And bald sculpted head;
Fair tufts, sideburns;
A twitching eye.

You're Mill both made and self-made man—
John Stuart, hothouse child of James;
A home-schooled genius you are skilled
To think not know; a Benthamite
Utilititarian and yet
A stern self-will that James instilled
To analyse, in turn allows
You leave our nature's narrow choice
Of pain or pleasure's reasoned plan
To find a newer nuanced voice.

Most happiness for most amount
Of men—a creed your crisis lost
At twenty. Wordsworth's poems wooed
Suppressed emotion, moving you
With time to turn to Coleridge's works;
But, wedding guest, you miss the mood
As still you stick to the sublime;
In later life, when you explore
How prayer outreaches prose, you can't
Unlock your logic's iron door.

When following in father's steps
You're acting boss of India,

Colonial from London's core,
Your surplus energies are such
You write on logic, liberty,
As cause on future cause you pour
Your life—an ardent Francophile,
Reformist, prophet feminist,
Cooperatives' oracle,
Political economist.

The man your father made is Greek;
Athenian democracy
Learned people rule and liberty,
Begins the process government
Must be—a rich ambivalence,
Harmonious disharmony,
A daily thriving cut and thrust
Where most have half a truth and miss
How summits slope so many sides
And see no need for synthesis.

> Yes, Malthus, though your theory is right,
> At seventeen, I found one summer's night
> A child some parent choked and left aside.
> I pamphleteered the poor on birth control;
> A sponge and bobbin beat infanticide.
>
> With you too, Robert Owen, I remonstrate,
> You counter-punishing the poor whose fate
> Is shaped for crime and mock this stricter Mill.
> Society as well as they themselves
> Can surely both reshape a misformed will?
>
> You, Say, I know and was a week with you,
> And Saint-Simon I made my own your view
> Of history and how what's right and good
> When countered will dissolve in something new;
> What's now must one day too become dead wood.
>
> But you, Ricardo, you're my friend and guide;
> A boy you mentored me and when you died
> I'd learned from you those economic laws
> As fixed as nature's strict and firmest rules,
> Which fighting is to fight a hopeless cause.

We both well know the soil can bear so much
And labour's more or less of use as such;
Hard facts we have to face no matter what
That, like the rules of gravity we learn,
The laws we're given, liking it or not.

But as for wages, profits or raised rent,
These belong to human management;
Ricardo, you and Smith have both combined
Producing goods and how we share our gain
And so our sharing seems all predefined.

What galls or chafes us we can rearrange,
The things we do not like are ours to change;
Some wealth is earned and some I call unearned,
Some slave while others gain while still asleep.
This is unfair as far as I'm concerned . . . .

John Stuart, you are still my wonder boy,
In my Ricardo struggle to destroy
Landlords who only live on others' rent;
Though sure you've severed share from gain,
I want to make a counterargument.

As profit and assignment intersect,
High tax on gain is going to affect
All profit and of course depress new growth,
So there'll be less for us to circulate;
In even touching one, you're touching both . . . .

Such income levies I would like to axe;
It's pluck and prudence we repress with tax
And duties on the goods that we produce.
Instead skim off from all the stuff we buy
But spare the moneys put to public use.

We need a tax on land and luxuries,
Inheritances too—but let's not squeeze
What's earned or saved; yet seeing how
There's income tax, we'll free from tax
Allowances for living just for now.

That "seeing how" is so much you—
At least for now until we near
Millennium; enlightenment
Belief in linear advance.
Yet you're a pragmatist whose tack
And thought now seems so prescient;
The gains from soil are nature's gift,
All "private" property is earned,
Not owned; an open-mindedness
Means things once learned can be unlearned.

And economics need not boss
Our lives, its task instead to tend.
Your father's ghost still force-feeds you,
Which means you, Mill, put freedom first
From tyrannies of need or vogue.
So much that's modern you pursue:
The dole, PR and city parks.
Dubbed Mill-stone and misunderstood,
For you the yearned-for happiness
Is passion for the public good.

Those things we think of now as rights
Still stunned and angered staider times;
The absent landlords you resist
And thinking through how communism
Holds up you fear the despot few.
Your causes fill so long a list:
Mass education, smokeless cars,
How foreign dealings must be fair,
An international police.
Your heavened earth, *le ciel espéré*.

A Mill your father made still lives in you.
White-burdened you'd arrange the Raj;
Both Welsh and Scots you wave aside—
Less civilised and best absorbed.
The working classes weren't yet fit
For mass democracy; to guide
Unlearned sorts, your loaded votes
And clerisy would seek to keep

For now mob rule or rage at bay,
Until with time they take that leap.

> O yes, although, Ricardo, you're my guide,
> Like Adam I too want to spread it wide;
> Economy must blend with so much more.
> Engaged in life my model is Turgot;
> Both words and works so long as one can score.

> In everything I've done I owe a debt
> As half of all belongs to Harriet,
> Who eighteen yearning years for me had been
> A loved one shared with her own loveless spouse,
> Then seven years of bliss my sage and queen.

You're half-detached and half-high-flown,
A cool prophetic fantasist,
A bridge between the golden gate
And how it is the world must work
With parliaments and public bills,
A harder-hitting heavyweight
Utopian who's toying with
The best Athenian rebirth.
Stern progress now the primrose path
As still you hope for heavened earth.

(v)

Slight and handsome
Curls over ears;
Moustache, pointed beard;
A loose-tied bow.

And here's the New World's Henry George,
A Philadelphian, you ditched
Your schooling, skipping off to sea
At fourteen as a foremast boy;
So print apprentice fool's gold finds
And wanderlust's elusive joy.
You're twenty-two, she's seventeen,
When you and your young love elope;
It's soon two sons and still odd jobs—

You're strapped for cash and strive to cope.

In San Francisco your first piece
Now sees the light and launches you
As Henry George the journalist
Who probes land-grabbing deals and graft
For railroad land and local trusts,
Evoking an evangelist
Against this gambling on land's worth.
Your paper folds, you fail again;
A metre reader makes ends meet,
While lecturing on your life's campaign.

> *Vocation, vision, name it as you like,*
> *It haunts me how when cities grow they hike*
> *Land's worth with workers working all the more;*
> *This cleft can widen steadily by stealth—*
> *Advancing poverty, advancing wealth.*

> *But J. S. Mill do you remember me?*
> *We corresponded once and we agree*
> *On much; how landowners rely on gains*
> *They never earn while others earn by sweat.*
> *I've been a down-and-out and don't forget . . .*

> *Indeed, I well recall what we discussed.*
> *And unproductive earnings are unjust.*
> *Of course our unlike backgrounds are the key:*
> *Your leanings mean you tend to labourers,*
> *Where I would tend to think of liberty.*

> *Yet in so many ways we're both at one*
> *As nature both belongs to all and none.*
> *We both can trust frontiers in trade that's free;*
> *And guess that communism would narrow down*
> *And easily then turn to tyranny.*

> *From you I learned the need for tax on land.*
> *But still I wonder if you understand,*
> *Or you, Ricardo, fully comprehend,*
> *Though manufacturers may feel the pinch,*
> *The weight is born by workers in the end.*

But even more as you, Malthus, too know,
The giddy economic stop and go
Of growth and slowing down now due to rent;
Land speculation gone too far will lead
To value crashes we could well prevent.

A single tax absorbing all land rents
Would mean we'd purify our governments,
So wages rise and capital by rights
Must too, abolishing all poverty,
Then hoist our culture to yet greater heights

And stop the cycles of our boom and gloom.
One tax will guarantee a world that's just;
What change may come no mortal man can tell;
We tremble on an edge—how will it end?
Is it an upward leap or lunge to hell?

Economy and social science teach
The same as what the One was sent to preach
To poor and faithful Jewish fishermen;
And laws of progress lay it down for us:
If morals fail, a culture falls again.

Though human laws are moral laws,
One tax is pure utopia;
A messianic mission feeds
Your once bestselling book and if
Your panacea now seems strange,
Land tax met many nations' needs
To even out economies,
Yet cannot cure the blooms and glooms;
To speculate on land alone
Can't play the role your plan assumes.

Your labour party falls apart,
Some want free trade and some do not;
Your work advanced the secret vote.
Though Fairhope, Alabama, fades
From Georgianism, your instincts know
The rich whose fathers underwrote
Their wealth in land they never worked

Should pay. You worry for the poor—
The steel mill drudge, the stevedore—
And for this daring you'll endure.

Canto 3
Poles Apart

(i)

Model frame to hand,
Astride your chair;
Wigged, haughty-eyed;
Striped waistcoated paunch.

So Richard Arkwright, barber's boy
Made good, a rags-to-riches boss
And hell-for-leather cotton lord,
You're father of the factory world;
Sir ruthless Richard, when you die
You'll leave the mean half-million hoard
You gather as you guard your hold
On patents for half-pilfered claims;
Your game a game of zero sums,
A fortune spun on spinning frames.

Before you handmade fabrics reigned—
A cotton weft, a linen warp
On wheels and loom in Lancashire,
But flywheels turn two weavers' task
To one man's work, yet spinning yarn
Still takes such time that all desire
To find a way to speed up work.
One Paul now thinks of rollers, though
He'll miss the mark, soon Highs and Kay
Will both succeed, or nearly so.

Then you manoeuvre Kay to make
Again High's failed machine to show
How rollers work. You change the weight
So pushing on their counterpart
Top rollers stop the twist's quick run

That backing could well implicate
The draft; then you line up the length
Between the roller sets to suit
The fibre; near it snaps, too far
The roving tends to lump en route.

The horse gives way to water power;
The Derwent's flow near Derby drives
Silk mills and so your partners move
To Cromford where a water wheel
Will spin by day and dead of night,
Propel your patent's frame to prove
You're time-and-motion's tyrant now,
Commander of both thread and thrift;
The local lead mines' wives and young,
Your weavers', pickers', piercers' shift.

The spindle yields to spinning wheel,
So too in turn the wheel to frame;
But there's a change of space and speed
As water too gives way to steam.
All workers working now by piece
Where warm machines keep shuttling greed;
But warp and weft of power ignore
The shape of lives, the river's gift;
It's empires where the sun won't set,
The cotton barons' culture drift.

> *I am a saddler's son, the thirteenth whelp,*
> *Collecting women's hair I learn self-help;*
> *Inventing dyes for cut and bob and curl*
> *I shape my wigs from ladies' tufts and locks;*
> *By work I made my wheel of fortune whirl.*
>
> *I winkle out of Kay how rollers work*
> *And mending Kay's near miss I didn't shirk*
> *The deals that got my Derwent mill to run.*
> *What's all this gentle talk of shape and gift?*
> *The winner in this game's the one who wins.*
>
> *Are you so pitiless you'd stop the poor*
> *From earning bread by work? And I am sure*

97

Child scavengers who do a twelve-hour day
Fare better than those others who don't earn
But making mischief waste their time at play.

I license out my patent, let some learn
To work my weaving frame and in return
Become lord cotton mill supreme who blazed
An economic trail and as all know
Great Britain is enriched, all standards raised.

But hasn't Highs a hand in this?
And Paul's first thought? Although both miss
The mark, just inches from your frame,
Do rags-to-riches ghosts still haunt?
You keep on fencing in your fame
And suing those you think have thieved;
To ruin their mills your muttered oath.
A poacher from the past keeps game;
You burn with pride or greed or both.

In Manchester the merchants envy me
Because I guard my patent carefully;
Each vies with me and thinks of number one.
It's me who taught those millers how to spin;
I will compete and I must always win.

A cotton lord monopolist,
Still scheming other ways to win
And looking down from Willersley
You're paying out three thousand pounds
For boulders grubbed to build your fort,
So what you own you'll oversee.
Your new built castle soon will burn
Before your complex calls your bluff
And dares you face your demon self
To ask when is enough enough.

My first lived till my son's delivery;
My second, Maggie Biggins, jilted me;
Before I went, I made up with my son.
My motto multa tuli fecique—
Plain English: much I've borne and much I've done.

I push from five a.m. to nine p.m.
It's gouge all others or be gouged by them;
To win demands both graft and brazen will.
I'm damned if I will listen to your likes!
I'm sliding if I'm only standing still.

I treat my workers well by housing them—
Some other merchants maybe you'd condemn—
But at my candle-lighting feast each year
Five hundred workers march around my mill
With bands and dance, free buns and fruit and beer.

Though asthma-riddled you've arrived,
Replacing older landed lords,
Yet lose the chance to change the mode
And let the working weavers share
Both risks and gains, so lives they give
They'd also own; instead you stowed
All gain and wove the conflict gene,
A need for more, the moguls' gripe
So deeply in their DNA.
Sir Richard Arkwright, archetype.

(ii)

High-browed, rough beard,
Dark-skinned, deep-eyed,
Thick-set, haired hands;
Boils and smoke stains.

Karl Marx, though wrathful and enraged,
You see as no one else had seen
Where market laissez-faire could lead.
Four hundred billionaires can hold
Just half our wealth and you see how
That wealth and want divide as greed
Demands, the way that we could move
Through constant gyres of boom and bust,
To dismal ends that you predict
For capital's fierce cut and thrust.

So well your thorough work sees through
A system's self-delusions, yet
The communism you forecast
But don't develop still unveils
In your own traits its tragic flaw,
A know-all coldness at your core.
As Dante's traitors damned well know
Infernos hold both ice and fire,
And both can burn though poles apart;
Extremes that freeze or spark conspire.
At seventeen such certitude
As your school essay yearns for good:
The perfect One we work to be
Was sacrificed for mankind's sake.
Your start intentions' paving stones
A social framework that could free
The waged to realise their worth
And analyse material laws
That rearrange relationships
Accounting for the workers' cause.

Your messianic Midas touch
Means you must always rule the roost,
As you lay down the party line;
Suspicious, spiteful, putsch by putsch
You fall out with your former friends—
All swindling bastards, rats and swine—
And no dissent—you plot and plan,
Or simply spoiling for a fight,
Put down all those who disagree;
All-knowing Marx, you know you're right.

Throughout your London years you live
In debt and squalor squandering
Whatever money Engels sends,
While holding bailiffs just at bay.
Though indigent a gentleman
Disdaining poverty depends
On wine and smokes and wants the best.
You keep your brood a cut above
In case denied they can't become

The bourgeoisie you loathe and love.

> To hell with hearing you explaining me!
> A Christian Jew who joined the bourgeoisie,
> My father wanted law. I fell for thought
> And Hegel's history at first gives me
> The sense of wholeness I have always sought.
>
> He read how change and history must fit:
> Despite itself thought spawns its opposite,
> With which it then is merged to make what's new;
> What's new in turn will hatch another thought,
> So history is conflict through and through.
>
> As academe's small doors have shut I turn
> A journalist and find I have to learn
> That life is lower than Herr Hegel's brow
> And things beget our thought not thought our things;
> Our histories are lived both here and now.
>
> Just look what mass production mode demands
> And how its products too in turn change hands,
> Decide society's whole form and shape,
> From which derives our order, castes and ranks
> And how we build and bond our culturescape.
>
> Our history is not in minds of men,
> Or in our mode of thought, our mise en scène,
> But in our human harsh reality
> Where economic shape can also shift
> And conflicts bring their own brutality.
>
> The landlords huff in rage when merchants rise
> And masters of the guilds don't compromise;
> They rage but history won't stop at that—
> Dislikes or likes don't count in winds of change
> Which tend to lift the proletariat.
>
> And soon, my friend, is sooner than you think.
> The base and superstructure out of sync
> And factories' production rudderless;
> We need to plan and private property
> Restrains the way the world must now progress.

Each boom and slump a bitter cul-de-sac
Where bosses cut a rod for their own back
And plants create a class with discipline,
So manufacturers must face defeat
As time matures their enemy within.

For years you cooked *Das Kapital*,
Distracted by your struggle with
Split movements that will melt away
Indulging in vendetta's rage;
Your deadlines slip from year to year.
In every library dogged day
While Engels pays your debts you delve
The economic end of class,
Anticipate the tipping point
When workers will awake en masse.

Ricardo, you and I concur if price
Means value; what's involved if we're precise
Is that amount of work commodities
Contain. A worker's worth's a living wage;
With this I think our Adam Smith agrees.

Supposing no cartel can hike the cost;
If fair is fair the barons would have lost
Their gains; but workers work beyond their wage
And so give more than their subsistence worth;
Yet caught inside the owners' iron cage

Their surplus time will guarantee a gain.
But bosses too are under stress and strain;
Beyond their greed they know that they must grow
Or fail; you gobble or you're gobbled up—
It's competition's blow and counterblow.

As owners bid for workers' wages rise,
Low profits soon will threaten enterprise;
According to Ricardo and you, Smith,
As wages rise the workers breed much more
But I like Mill want no such Malthus myth.

Instead there's new machinery installed—
It's labour-saving systems that are called

For now to sink the wage so profits soar.
But gains turn on the workers' excess time
So profits fall from what they were before.

The further now the profits fall the more
Machines and fewer on the factory floor;
Consumption sinks, small firms are facing ruin.
As goods are dumped and workers are let go,
The fatter boss becomes a world tycoon

Who—cheerfully by buying on the cheap
Machines the bankrupts ditch—now both can keep
The workers' wages down and invest less
For more; as profits once again emerge
They suck from others' loss their own success.

Mesmeric Marx, ideologue
Who bridles when we speak and brooks
No antidote or answers back,
You can't conceive a compromise
Where conflicts could be reconciled—
For you the tactic is attack.
No time to keep, no time to heal,
No baron bargaining like Mill;
All government their instrument.
A time to tear, a time to kill.

Much more than J. S. Mill I hate Proudhon
And foolish Fourier; such carry-on
Delays our revolution's ripening;
Instead of stirring up the working class
All wishy-washy eldorado-ing.

But Marx, you mellow out with age;
A little less enraged you nurse
Your dying baroness and dote
On children's children while you wait
In vain on violence to down
Your bugbear bourgeoisie, to gloat
Exultingly as worlds break up.
Your know-all coldness casts its spell
And in your wake such wanton pain.
How dreams of heaven end in hell.

(iii)

Reddish-gold hair;
Sharp-chinned, tight-lipped;
Twitchless taut face;
Cold, unblinking eye.

Come pirate king of kerosene,
Each muscle mastered so your face
Shows no emotion, stony-masked
And fearless Rockefeller you're
Both business shark and thoughtful boss—
Consensus sought and questions asked;
A pious Baptist and home bird
In love with ledgers, balanced books,
Your cool control still keeps at bay
A childhood time on tenterhooks.

Your conman father came and went;
Big Bill the frontier bigamist
Said, "Trust me, son, just lose control
And fall—I'll catch and keep you safe."
The fourth time he will let you fall—
"Trust no one, son, with all your soul,
Not even me." Your mother copes
But leans on you so you're a boy
Too soon a man, a spirit maimed,
A jilted son who loses joy.

And John D. you can justify
All means by ends; you're mortgaged to
The heaven holding company
God chairs, where chits and dividends
Will risk no jazz or lavish riffs
And money has strange majesty
That signals God is satisfied
With secular and sacred ways;
Though not predestined you're still due
Both heaven's prize and worldly praise.

Some venture Pennsylvanian oil,
But wild cat rushes are bad risks,

So you refine for paraffin
At home in Cleveland. You might hear
A gusher spurts more dark thick gold
And prices slump and profits thin
Or sparks might fire refineries.
Too free-for-all for you, John D.—
Smith's weeding out is slow to work—
You mastermind monopoly.

> A boy when playing chess I brood and bide
> My time till every move considered I decide;
> Some try to fuss me but I still refuse
> To move before I've figured countermoves;
> You do not think I'd like to play to lose?

> God-called I light the dark with kerosene;
> In keeping with his order I recoil
> From all confusion as a form of sin—
> Cooperation cuts out so much risk—
> My mission is to see that we all win.

> I need to bring the crude up here by train:
> Refined, I route it then by rail again
> Or ship by lake and shaving costs begin
> My covert cut-throat games and start to play
> Each one against the other so I win.

> I need the railroad as they too need me.
> I'm one but they are weaker as they're three;
> My secret railroad rebates undercut
> Competitors that I with time will crush
> To guard against the risk of slump or glut.

> Some sages call my schemes a rope of sand,
> Despite a crash I play my hand as planned;
> I hear the jibes but I'm a tight-lipped Job
> Who names God's ends and knows the day will come
> I'll gloat, the richest mogul on the globe.

> Instead, by stealth I raid the powers that be
> And buy New York's own big refinery,
> The largest company in kerosene

Who still will feign to fight our Standard Oil
But quietly prove to be the pawn we queen.

I do a deal with all the railroad heads;
Our company will keep its word and spreads
Between the fractious railroads all our freight,
So we get tolls for others' oil they take—
Of course we keep our preferential rate.

All hell breaks loose, the pact then falls apart
But in the meantime men in Cleveland start
To badger them, to sell out now is best;
Soon twenty-five refineries are ours.
A mercy mission God no doubt has blessed.

So one by one we pick them off and squeeze
Them out with graft or palms we choose to grease,
Till eighty-five per cent of kerosene
At home is ours; abroad we're honing skills
To keep our rival Russians off the scene.

All other things are safely under thumb:
Transport, the spin-offs of petroleum,
The pipeline, spigot, lighter, longshoreman;
We can control the golden conduit,
The whoosh from well head to the jerry can.

John Archbold and scarred Dan O'Day
As lieutenants eliminate
Your need to deal in dirty games;
You float above their bullying—
Such underlings use undue force—
A strategist who guides the aims
Each branch committee then must meet.
You're precedent and paradigm
For corporations yet to come,
The model other kingpins mime.

How wanton waste makes woeful want
Or pride will come before a fall—
Proverbs your mother's mother taught,
A thrift and thorough self-control
That you now teach your children too;

The bicycle you and Cettie bought
They all must share to show them how
Your mother learned to make ends meet.
No drink, no dance, no cards, no dice;
Your backlog on God's balance sheet.

> *I had retired before Ford's Model T*
> *And bulbs retrack the whole oil industry;*
> *Imagining the way it might have been,*
> *Those ducks and dodges John D. Junior learns,*
> *I'd like to play the game of gasoline.*
>
> *Instead I turn a stern philanthropist,*
> *Unable to assess my lengthening list;*
> *There's some I want to aid but all the same*
> *I'm anxious my appellants apprehend*
> *That learning self-reliance is my aim.*
>
> *I do not give to gild ill-gotten gain,*
> *All gained, give much—God's economic chain;*
> *Whatever means my ends are surely just.*
> *Remember then how rosy all things were;*
> *Why were so many traders antitrust?*

It's you, rapacious pirate John,
There clad in brighter clothes for golf,
Selecting lavish memories,
Your hell a laundered monologue.
The ill and dying you will dodge;
The food you eat, your routine ease
All yearn to live a hundred years;
John D. still wants the winner's role
But two years short you'll shuffle off.
A lid has blinked. You lose control.

(iv)

Short-necked, shine-bald,
Combative eyes;
Right top lip raised,
A furrowed smile.

You do not know your father's name—
A Greenberg, Greenstein, something Green—
But know he took the Friedman name
When still a boy in Budapest;
At sixteen settled in the States
And met your mother, who too came
From Hungary, to hunker down
To live their New World lives and leave
All roots behind, to rear their brood
And drive the dreams you must achieve.

You're Milton Friedman, man of facts,
Dynamic, certain, self-assured;
Robust debater, you'll wear out
Adversaries, as squat and vigorous
You argufy, lay down the law,
With rigour that will room no doubt;
Your mind demands all black and white.
No fellowship, we're fancy-free
To choose how we achieve or fail,
Unless we hinder liberty.

A boy you'd been a pious Jew
But by bar mitzvah you will balk
At what pure logic won't allow;
In student years John Stuart Mill's
On Liberty your guiding light.
The nineteenth century still reigns
Supreme, and much named progress since
Is interference not called for;
Both-ands faze libertarians—
Let everything be either-or.

> *I stress the actual, I don't abstract—*
> *We must not merge mere values with what's fact;*
> *Such half-guessed mixed-up thoughts leave me aghast.*
> *I step back to predict, not understand;*
> *Our science only worth what it forecasts.*

> *We need to tighten state expenditure.*
> *Although my rootless parents' lives were poor,*
> *They didn't need a rife bureaucracy*

But worked their way by dint of sweat and grind.
Let's keep America a land that's free.

At thirty-six I think equality
Can too go hand in hand with being free;
But governance now seems a juggernaut
That single-mindedly I seek to halt—
Our freedom my recurrent framing thought.

Your rugged views now polarise—
Chicago can't keep you and Cowles—
So, teacher of free marketeers,
Your facts and figures want to prove
How Keynes' belief that savings caused
The crash and cramped depression years
Had underplayed how right supplies
Of money would have mended more
Than Roosevelt's New Deal's three Rs
That played a role your creed deplores.

Although you serve neglected thoughts,
Your monetary focus means
Keynes' one defect now justifies
How you oppose all state support.
An unemployment rate that's right
Will moderate inflation's rise;
All wage or price control can warp
The messages the markets send
And ruin the way they self-correct
The course on which we all depend.

Withholding tax I helped to pilot through;
In wartime we can need quick revenue—
And yet this is a governmental yoke,
Another mean and meddlesome device
I've often wished in vain I could revoke.

I'll bow to logic to the bitter end;
I fight the draft, and drugs too I defend;
All rights states claim I always counterclaim;
Unless it heads off harm from someone else
I, Friedman, will oppose in freedom's name.

Although at first against the zeitgeist grain,
I turn a public man and so campaign
To launch again the ease of laissez-faire,
Where failsafe market forces guide our lives
In ways that governments don't often dare.

In Chile my Chicago boys hold sway
And shape his miracle for Pinochet,
Who backs the plan the boys have now devised:
Deregulation, licensed copper mines,
The tariff cut and pensions privatised.

Our TV programme Free to Choose *will preach*
The Friedman freedom's gospel that will reach
Great Britain's Thatcher, whom I too enthral;
She'll start as Reagan had already done
To nurture economic free-for-all.

You'll see Estonia's Mart Laar will save
His Baltic state from wrack and ruin to pave
Its way to wealth by banishing state dues—
Such tolls abolished, all on flat-rate tax;
His Bible is our Friedmans' Free to Choose.

Just look how China too will learn from me
And after Mao it's free economy
As they embrace unbridled growth and trade;
No more collectives, few monopolies,
The market's mechanisms are all obeyed.

I had a hand in helping to promote
The move we made to let exchange rates float
And wean the dollar from its weight in gold;
Trade deficits and foreign cycles wane—
Less prone to shocks our system's self-controlled.

Free-flow finance gives quick-fix gains
But blows up bubbles that must burst;
Dot.com will concentrate our cash
In risk-free zones, increase the rift
Between the rich and poor, or puff
One currency that soon must crash;
A sudden rush, then panicked sell—

In gaps between we gain and chose
When best to bet, trade in and out;
A worldwide game of win or lose.

Though nothing's done and nothing's made,
Fictitious capital can grow;
Deposits loaned and banked anew,
Reloaned now means sums multiply
And criss-cross in a money maze;
Or loans are sold and so accrue
What at a later date is due;
Some risk the shifting exchange rate,
Buy options to both buy and sell
As prices float and fluctuate.

What is a gift is someone's gain,
Your game a game of zero sum;
The wily then are winners all,
The lazy lose. But we can choose
The long-haul Scandinavian laws,
Where weak need not go to the wall
And care and gain can be combined.
In frenzies of free-wheeling rise
The have and have-not gap still grows;
Your rootless world is short-term wise.

(v)

Assured, smooth-skinned,
Goatee, trilby,
Matched shirt and tie;
Dim, black-holed eyes.

The time our Western world balloons
Before the housing market's fall,
When ragtime greed comes home to roost
And Lehman Brothers' loans collapse;
You're Celtic Tiger Fingleton,
Still bent on short-term deals to boost
A bottom line. A bonus gained,
Already on your way to ruin,
All caution to the winds—who cares?

Ambitious tiger burning bright
And brazen in your riot-run,
You do not know the dust you'll bite.

Three years a trainee priest for you,
Accountancy and you become
A thrifty dairy boss and then
Two years in Lagos handling how
The mission's funds and monies worked;
Returned, you're secretary to
A mutual that working men
Far-sightedly had founded once
To meet their members' needs for homes.
Installed you'll stay for forty years,
Chief keeper of greed's honeycombs.

Now prince of profit you expand,
Attract publicity to lure
The margins up; the media wooed
With mortgages and meaty quotes,
Renamed as Nationwide you spread
A net of agents to include
Both auctioneers and middlemen
Or stars of sports, inspiring all
To borrow so they buy their nest;
Intricate mix, a longline trawl.

You're proud of your pragmatic air
That laughs at old idealists—
The streetwise love the bottom line;
You're hale and heartily well met,
You're Fingleton about the town,
As in the know you wine and dine
To suck up secrets you then leak
And hobnob at the golden hub
Of power, politics and wealth,
In inner cliques, the tiger's club.

Your workers though all underwaged,
Flotation talk still fuels their dreams
Of wilder windfalls that now draw
The carpetbaggers in and keeps

The shareholders' sweet hopes alive.
Small loaners find you'll go to law
To take your pound of flesh to pay
What's owed; for bigger borrowers
You bend or buck or make the rules,
Indulge whatever debt occurs.

> *As for my salary, I fail to see*
> *How I'd take less. My lifestyle's bonhomie,*
> *My flair and flexibility will earn*
> *Our Nationwide shareholders' money's worth;*
> *For what I take that is a fair return.*

> *Reports demand I alter this or that.*
> *I keep my course despite each caveat*
> *And bump up every year the bottom line;*
> *A killing made can mute a doubting voice—*
> *The only way to win I know is mine.*

> *New rules within the rampant Eurozone*
> *Mean French and German banks now freely loan*
> *Me what I then lend on to whom I please;*
> *Among the ten or so who've made it big,*
> *A large percentage now is overseas.*

> *Old navvies figure in my chosen few,*
> *Their nurtured dreams are dreams that now come true;*
> *They buy up plots and build in London Town—*
> *Where once they shovelled soon they'll call the shots,*
> *The tables turned, the order upside down.*

The whistle-blowers, all too blind,
Defend small loaners, fail to see
You've lent too few too large-sized loans.
O'Reilly who should regulate
Believes his lightly touch approach—
And anyhow he hopes harassed
By shareholders you'll float your ship
So he'd be taken off the hook:
A copping out, a kick for touch.
Has Mammon's bishop run amok?

Lord Bountiful who, as you fail,
Are giving gifts to older stars
Of sport or stage, a sponsorship
You shower on former showbiz folk,
So Fingers seems the soul of good.
Just as the game is up again
Your dealing fingers now will dip
Down into Nationwide's dug well
To help All Hallows where you had
Aspired to priesthood—special funds
You lavish on your launching pad.

And as the State is stepping in,
A bonus million battened on
The paying public want returned;
You promise them and then renege
As all you have you want to hold
And why give back what you have earned?
You're Fingleton, the tortured prey.
Assured your paying would cut short
All further probes—they'd promise then
To keep you, Fingers, out of court.

But all across the Western world
Your likes are selling loans that trail
A spider's web of cyberspace
Where figures now are fancy-free
From paper notes or norms of gold,
Just blackening nodes of nought and cross
That can take years to track or trace;
The banks on which we based our trade
Swept up in latticed profit's lust,
Like Dante's forgers deep in hell
Betray our faith and break all trust.

You blame the crash and credit squeeze
But your own faults have caused your fall,
As in the name of business nous
Our home-grown greed alone has greased
The palm of tragedy and pawned
The good name of our counting house.

Our age's spirit aged in you
The wastelands of your windowed soul
With dull and disillusioned eyes;
Your hell is greed's own blackest hole.

Canto 4

Cleansings

(i)

Inverted V hair,
Plumped cheekbones,
Moustache and beard;
A walrus stare.

It all seems right, just common sense,
That in the rat race some will rise,
The lucky and sagacious gain
And by their wealth escape hard work—
Until you, cold-eyed Veblen, come
To highlight how the rich disdain
All labour's grease and sweaty grind
To show what money they have made,
And so consuming this or that
Both rank and riches are displayed.

For you old patterns now repeat:
Like ancients too the gilded age
And baron businessmen, who show
Their lifestyle and their luxuries
To vaunt rapacity and power,
Are beasts of prey incognito;
Their hostile bids are booty raids.
Debunking all glib business talk,
Outsider Veblen, you unveil
How still the hunters in us stalk.

The carved and ivory-handle cane,
Accessory of rank and style,
Is still a swagger stick to beat

Aside the weaker in your way.
The barbarous we think erased
Conceals itself and seems effete;
Our savage traits we hide in trade
And winners take their scalps and taunt
With dangled wealth—their wanton show
An overflow they love to flaunt.

What caused you, Veblen, to review
Belief in linear advance;
To double back and find bare greed,
In signs and symbols of new wealth?
Did business barons' show offend
Your pioneer Norwegian need
For ways more Spartan and more sparse?
Or did youth's failures amplify
Your strange sardonic deadpan wit?
What made you cast so cold an eye?

> I coined "conspicuous expenditure,"
> But no sour grapes—my parents were not poor.
> My father's mind detached by temperament
> I made my own and it has shaped what's me.
> But you've still missed the gist of what I meant.
>
> Society does not cohere in hate—
> All workers really want to emulate
> Their boss—the weak are would-be rich at heart;
> If Marx had not been wrong and me not right,
> The poor would tear society apart.
>
> The workers want their manager's success—
> As anxiously they climb they acquiesce
> In finding labour is undignified,
> And nibble at high lives of privilege
> To simulate the leisure they're denied.

But, Thorstein Veblen, you in turn,
Although you probe the progress myth
And underneath veneer discern
The rougher savage side we hide,
Are still aloof and steeled against

Compassion, pity or concern;
Incapable of love or care
Your guarded sociologist's
Cool mind demands you only see
In velvet gloves your Veblen fists.

But leisure too allowed us much—
A time to think, a time to thrive;
Your straight-from-shoulder too extreme,
Too blunt and coarse and couldn't-care.
Though Marxists push your take on power,
You scorn still Hegel's rigid scheme.
For feminists you face male tricks—
But you philander. Liberals choose
Your business stance but soon they balk
At how you finally refuse

Their vaunted progress and advance.
Conservatives love how you see
That in their hearts the masses hoard
No rage to stir the status quo—
Then riled by how you mock the rich,
Annoyed at how you have ignored
The pomp of power, and undermined
Their caste, dismiss you as uncouth.
All shades of thought will shun your work,
Distrust unvarnished Veblen truth.

As college lecturer you keep
All students bored; they barely hear
Your dry and mumbled words that drive
Them one by one away, but work
On leisured foibles brings you fame.
A lady's man you might survive,
But scorned your wife now settles scores—
You're fired for your philandering.
Once more a misfit you seem both
A libertine and moralist.

> *Again you underrate my scope and reach!*
> *A youth for seven years I studied each*
> *Economy both old and modern, know*

Much more than most the hidden deeper traits
That underpin the barons' passing show.

And maybe, yes, I am a moralist
Who underlines what mostly others missed;
How money-making lust can overtake
The goods we make, so value is a game
And all is money made for money's sake.

Where industry and business both now strive
Against each other some come through and thrive,
But little trickles down to less well-off—
It's profit counts not productivity;
The rich will ride the wave, the rest the trough.

Dexterity and craftsmanship are gone
As shift by shift production's wheels grind on;
Society's a tempered counterpoise—
Machines will never need economists,
Technicians tend precision's oily noise.

So much you saw in hindsight seems
To portend later paradigms,
Yet, Veblen, you are visionless
And turn a sullen saboteur;
An outcast you will live alone,
A loafer in your lazy mess
Of dirty dishes all piled up
So long you have to hose them clean.
Your maimed outsiderness has meant
There's nothing mended, much foreseen—

A chilly heart, a psyche hurt—
And yet half-prophet you undo
The cosy myths and easy cant
Of progress, and explain the splurge
Of loans and money's make-believe.
Observant zealous immigrant,
Your cold mind never can commit.
And yet you purge us and prepare
The waymarks for much warmer minds
Who'll offer visions of repair.

(ii)

High taut forehead,
Deep-set black eyes;
Thick, wide moustache;
Integrity.

Now John A. Hobson, heretic
Among the real economists,
"A crank" they call you, who has come,
Not just to rap pet theories
But more to undermine their line;
Each thought they think an axiom
You're ruling out and they close ranks.
A maverick and furthermore
A tiresome meddling amateur,
Another crackpot best ignored!

You won't infer that if a firm
Should take just one more worker on
That every man-hour bought then must
Re-earn its cost and keep the books
In balance, hold the bottom line.
But cutting jobs is still unjust;
You say there is a surplus that
Is portioned out by power and so
The haves who have too much don't spend,
And labourers whose pay is low

Cannot consume, which means that soon
The market stalls by sticking to
False thrift, and lauding bottom lines
We undercut consumption's surge.
We know we might produce much more
But underspending undermines
The whirl of trade and bustle, which
In turn leaves even less employed.
The same old business cycle spins;
What booms built up, a bust destroyed.

At first you separate the sums
The wealthy simply set aside

And bank from monies made to work,
The surplus that the rich have saved
And then invest so they both gain
And serve empires. By some strange quirk
You blunt this difference and blur
How over-saving is a sump
That drains economies if kept
In hand, and slows things to a slump.

A Benthamite in John Mill's mode,
You search for reason's saving grace;
But Ruskin too enriched your thought
With needs to go beyond the gauge
Of wealth that only counts the cost
Or use; and you believe we ought
To measure more the benefit
For human living and align
Economy and meaning's aims
So gain and what is best combine.

> I knew the workers had been underwaged
> But never was embittered or enraged
> Because the academics downplayed me—
> The Marshalls and the Jevens both removed
> To mathematics all the synergy
>
> Of aims and meanings we discern or sense.
> So I refused to score in pounds and pence.
> No unseen hand can ever understand
> Our needs, and neither can self-interest's play
> Of freedom lead us to some promised land.
>
> That I should dare to doubt the worth of thrift,
> Proposing such a paradigm-like shift
> And finding fault with Say's time-honoured law
> Now means I cannot teach economy;
> Yet later some will see what I foresaw.
>
> But Thorstein Veblen, here's where you are too?
> Just two years younger, yet I learned from you.
> How strange that our two lives should parallel:
> Outsiders both, we see what others can't,

Both branded academic infidel.

"You're Hobson? Welcome to this hinterland.
I used your over-saving second-hand.
From me you got how gilded barons hide
The harsher history of tooth and claw—
Behind their wealth they flaunt their hunters' pride.

I purged illusions, lacked your need to mend
Our imperfections. Look how in the end
We both saw education's balance sheet;
It's best that college teachers toe the line—
Our failsafe academe keeps funders sweet."

Yet I think much of you, John A.
You'd be a politician but
In youth an illness weakened you;
Instead a left-wing journalist,
Reformer fighting causes. Yet
A jaundiced Boer War anti-Jew,
Infected by a biased left;
Behind relieving Ladysmith
The Jewish diamond jewellers lurk—
You milk a global Shylock myth.

I made mistakes, regret much done in haste.
A buried hate I hadn't ever faced,
The fluke of childhood prejudice, a chance
Of history again aroused in me
A hidden fear of Jewish high finance.

And lacking focus, was I too diffuse?
In academic life I might produce
Much less but I prefer a larger range.
Although I know my theory is right,
I fail to change a world I want to change.

Although you chose a limbo life,
A thorn in sides of theorists,
Your clear-sightedness will clean
The slate of orthodoxy's debt
In time. Your insight too will serve
As catalyst for John M. Keynes.

Outsider, you prepare a path
Beyond the dogmas of your day;
You up the stakes so others think
The thoughts you'll shape by ricochet.

(iii)

Oval, balding,
Severe eyebrows,
Steady cool stare;
Collared and tied.

Of course economists are made
As much as born, but more than most
The chances of your childhood must
Have shaped you, Joseph Schumpeter.
Your father dies when you are four;
Your mother moves and you adjust
As she remarries Sigismund
Von Kéler from the upper caste.
Your whole life through you have to play
A part a ghost writes from your past.

Your mother's darling, you will move
Between two worlds: the Schumpeters
Whose bourgeois enterprise and pride
You still admire so much, but then
It clearly is the upper class
You learn to imitate. Allied
With your ambitious mother's bent,
You love both bourgeois and elite;
Astride the two your life will strive
To try to make these two worlds meet.

As professor youngest yet,
Then time as finance minister
And chief of Biedermann's failed bank;
Refused Berlin's professorship,
So Harvard's now your habitat
And Europe you will seem to blank
Completely out, although you play
Aristocrat, arrive to teach,

Undo your cloak before a class
That's spellbound by your entrance speech.

Why should we want a meddling government?
Relief aside, such money is misspent;
Economies are self-sustained machines,
Which means they have an inner dynamo;
If things slow down, the vanguard intervenes.

I know that Smith and Mill and Marx and Co.
Dream up a flourishing and changeless flow
Where competition can remove all gain
Above the share of cost that all have borne,
A steady state that we'll at last attain.

By means of competition workers too
Are paid the daily wages they are due,
For land or property a proper rent;
Investors turn into wage managers
In tame Nirvana where we're all content.

But in that stasis no one stands to gain.
So where does profit come from, please explain!
For Mill it's mostly capital's return,
For Marx the worker's milked as usual;
But neither knows it's pioneers who earn

Our keep discovering methods that are new.
The prescient and enterprising few,
The keener who can undercut the rest;
The faint-hearted swarm then follow suit
Until a torpid balance is redressed.

Then unsung tenders of technology
Disturb what is the new normality
And so this endless enterprise becomes
An engine that upsets inertia,
The lurch within the equilibrium

Which over time allows progressive leaps.
This is the constant restlessness that keeps
Advancing, driven vanguard who'll unleash
More energy, who when they jump-start wealth
Become the much-derided nouveaux riches.

What drives the drivers of economy?
The urge to win or wealth's autonomy?
But, Veblen, you know well this need to vie
And want to conquer all you can and how
Achievement in itself can satisfy.

Your errant knights of enterprise
Are fearless upstart underlings,
Come-lately interlopers who,
By dint of work and daring, can
Become the real aristocrats,
The challenging and chosen few
Whose grit and flair upgrade our world;
The grudging name as parvenu
The one whose talent turns the wheels.
Your heroes meld two halves of you.

The top dogs lead, the rest just tag along
And borrow up a banking boom as long
As they're behind; but then they get abreast
And prices down, the profits disappear—
Late borrowers go bust. Again the best

Among the talented elite must start
Once more and so the business cycles spin
From bust to boom to bust and yet we see
How much the way of life for most improves,
Moves on in step with new technology.

Still such a system I believe is doomed—
Not by the sullen conflicts Marx assumed
Nor for the want of ways we might invest;
Much more because our creativity,
When it succeeds it is itself repressed,

As reason snuffs the once-romantic mood.
A creeping bureaucratic attitude
Infects the few who saw the unforeseen
And so in time an ennui tames them
And creativity is dull routine.

Though sometimes wrong, so much rings true;
Technology now knows no end,

The bureaucrats abound, and you
Saw more than most the left's belief
In immanent success would sag
And how the right wing's bugaboo
Was fake; how Keynes, who you think false,
Despite his faith in aid, won't fix
The world for once and all without
Creative minds still in the mix.

And yet it was naive of you
To think that multinationals
Would soon grow mellow with success,
Like lions lie down with lambs,
Or through a lack of real belief
In cut-throat enterprise we'd press
For some mild socialistic dream;
Although all this has just begun
And we must wait while history
Unravels its own longer run.

Your need for Nietzsche's brave elite
And fear of swarming followers
Conceals a boy still sore at heart,
A waif between two fathers' worlds
Who'll hide behind a Wilde-like wit
Or pose and play your old-world part
And womanise. One would-be child
With your young darling Annie died
At birth and salts half-buried hurts.
Your private grief is masked by pride.

I wonder if your wounds at once
Both gave and took away your gift.
Your straddled worlds insist you see
How creativity renews
The sameness of a steady state,
Awakes a jaded energy;
And yet the wounds in you explain
It all as will to win and miss
The generous yes, the jazz of things.
Your vision cries in chrysalis.

(iv)

Hair split, forelock,
Rimless glasses,
Neat three-piece suit;
Sincerity.

Professor Commons, you prefer
John R., which students used instead,
Or simply John. It's you who said
That egghead academics err
Because they cook philosophies
And do not eat the daily bread
That loves how human lives still grow;
And know enough to know the way
All theories adapt to our
Unplanned and shifting passion play.

A pragmatist, you tell us too
The antipole is those who act
With practical no-nonsense pride
And strut their own untrue extreme—
A sort of downrightness that dares
So little, yet its rules deride
All others who may understand
The kinds of patterns that succumb
To shifts that in their turn take shape;
Crude doers think by rules of thumb.

Your logic learnt from C. H. Peirce
Prefers to find another way
Where thought and practice both combine.
So you send students out to see
How theory and real life
Can push and pull and realign
A drama where a third way drives
A thickening plot which weaves its themes,
Enfolds philosophies and change
Beyond the yearnings for extremes.

Returned to Malthus scarcity,
You see how conflicts can occur
When both the workers and their boss

Must press from profits gain and wage.
So you now want the union heads
With bosses face-to-face across
A table where their give and take
Can learn to deal collectively;
Constructive talk, a bargain struck,
So neither grabs and both agree.

> *My father's failures all disastrous,*
> *My mother's roomers' rents supported us;*
> *A summer student sub I learned to see*
> *How in non-union presses you could earn*
> *Above the norm; one personality*

> *Could dole out more among his chosen pets.*
> *When unionised each of the workers gets*
> *What's fair; the fathers of the chapel share*
> *The surplus so the strong and weak both know*
> *This institutional paternal care.*

> *And yet it's fifty years before I'll name*
> *These tactics which we've learnt to use to tame*
> *Our greed and serve some broader greater good*
> *"An institution," and so usher in*
> *An economics of lives' livelihood.*

> *At first an academic failure who*
> *Could shift and change, I never really knew*
> *My mind—I found myself quickly dismissed*
> *From Wesley where I worked a term or two;*
> *In teaching I'm an indeterminist.*

> *I know the shame, the sense of being shunned*
> *When told how funders have refused to fund;*
> *I learned how wealth and assets weren't the same;*
> *Not only what you hold but may withhold*
> *Can also gauge your part in this power game.*

> *Wisconsin's Madison became my base*
> *And here my students hone the commonplace;*
> *I send them out to see the push and pull*
> *Of economic institutions' norms*
> *To feel the rub of conflict to the full.*

This state's a kind of lab for labour law,
A microcosm where we clearly saw
To tend each worker's safety we will need
Some compensation for a casualty
To balance out the gilded barons' greed.

For many Marx is more attractive than
A radical transaction where we can
Agree a scheme of things that doesn't skip
The facts that won't conform to theory.
But all of this is shaped by leadership.

We need those leaders who can deal and dare
To compromise, the captains who're aware
That bargaining must mean both gain and loss;
The union chief who's risen through the ranks,
The make-no-bones-about-it company boss.

I got the boot for being far too red;
In work disputes I always would instead
Of strikes or lockouts look for compromise,
Whatever give and take, whatever could
Improve the ways of worldly enterprise.

Wisconsin labour law becomes
In time a template for all states.
Although thought out by you in spite
Of Europe's years of fascist growth
Or Marxist glow, it still remains
The reasoned line you underwrite.
Economy is never now,
Futurity is at its heart;
It links our ethics and our laws
In each new chapter which we chart.

Like Veblen, you too veer away
From narrow economics which
Deny the notched complexity
Implied, returning to include
What first economists had called
Political economy,
Before the figure-mad cut out

All sociology and so
Unwove the oneness of the whole,
Where threads above loop round below.

> In pragmatism ideals are tempered by
> The limits that in practice always lie
> Beyond what we control; the way that we
> Administer can count as much as rules—
> Our laws are locks but we must turn the key.

> Commitment to the working through of things
> And pushing my compulsive questionings
> Unravelled me and, often overwrought,
> My nerves broke down; and yet somehow I know
> My labour always lives in those I taught.

John R., your life's an open rhyme;
Empiricist, you purged the harsh
And gilded age with labour law
And compensation, chose to side
With plans to practise price controls;
Protectionism too you saw
As trammelling a too-free trade.
A desert prophet you will prime
The generous pump of paradise,
Compassion's shifting paradigm.

(v)

Pale-skinned, clear-eyed,
Moustache over
A smile starting;
Honest bearing

Pigou, your gift to us we name
Pigovian, an adjective
That all economists must keep
In mind. I know, an older man,
An academic anchorite,
You couldn't take the Keynesian leap—
At least at first. Yet what we learn
From you will serve a century

That to survive now needs to tend
Our honeycombed ecology.

Born on the Isle of Wight, you won
A scholarship to Harrow School;
Then Cambridge and King's College where
You start with history and read
Philosophy and ethics first,
As taking pains you now prepare
To enter economic thought.
Your mentor, Alfred Marshall, too
Had been an ethicist and so
Your shared utilitarian view.

For wealth and welfare both define
All economics, and it needs
Concern itself with benefits.
A science not for its own sake—
We learn it not for light but fruit;
This study's finally what fits
The money measures. Yet you want
Your economics to connect
Both commerce and community
And gauge Pigovian effect.

You favour what to you seems fair:
Where some are suffering a loss,
Just willy-nilly, not by choice,
And someone else makes certain gains,
You pioneer another tax—
A novel kind of counterpoise,
To compensate what some have lost.
A factory built means loss of light
And noise that plagues a neighbourhood
And recompense should be a right.

Sometimes it tends the other way,
Where some will get an unearned gain;
Beekeepers' bees will pollinate
Surrounding crops and others reap
Rewards the honey-workers don't.
Our aim should now be to create

A subsidy so keepers keep
On tending bees that benefit
Society and we see how
Our interests can interknit.

> I'm proud I won a Cambridge poetry prize.
> My first book featured how I analyse
> Religious teachings Robert Browning weaves
> Though sometimes too poems self-contradict,
> I still admire so much that he achieves.

There is no good of life but love—but love!
Here is the dream that Browning's dreaming of.
I know in economics how we need
To intervene and take an overview,
So gradually we curb and balance greed.

> Both Marshall and John Keynes keep me in shade.
> With no biography I feel I fade
> Between my teacher Marshall, who in turn
> I would succeed, and Keynes's newer wave.
> Yet from my namesake tax in time all learn

> The ropes, and regulate ecologies
> To penalise polluters and to ease
> The damage done to our environment
> Where few will benefit and many lose—
> I count this as my life's accomplishment.

> Although I sought to tax or subsidise,
> I wonder if the Keynesian way is wise;
> And my effect I feel can well show how,
> Though private banks are primed with ready cash,
> Their rates are still not lowered to allow

> For growth, when systems could just self-correct.
> As unemployment features, my effect
> Explains when prices too in turn subside;
> The real balance then is raised, which means
> Consumption grows, and such a rising tide

> Will hoist anew the whole economy
> To even greater heights, and so we see

There never is a need to intervene;
Instead, we let the system stabilise
Itself and sanction markets' own machine.

All right in theory, at least.
But only time would tell how long
Stagnation needs to last before
The prices fall enough to prime
Consumers' trust as some will wait
Until they tumble even more.
Or what about each deepening debt
And those whose business may go bust?
So much more harrowing and hurt
Before regimes can readjust.

Your schemes to mend communities
Rein in the individual;
Your lavish Browning breadth of view
Remains the legacy you leave.
There is no good of life but love
As in our globe you glimpse anew—
One interjoined ecology
That's loose and yet is so precise,
A fitting choreography,
Prefigured dance of paradise.

Canto 5
Open Hand

(i)

Tall, head stooping;
High-brained forehead,
Bushy brows and 'tache,
Perceptive eyes.

So come quick-witted John M. Keynes,
The Cambridge don who will become
First overthrower of mean thrift;
Though you're no rebel yet you will

Transcend short-sighted ledger minds
That penny-pinch and can't uplift
Or stimulate the latent growth.
The diehards with nest eggs don't dare,
As they believe Smith's hidden hand
Can fix all this by laissez-faire.

And yet that you should be the one!
A single in the Bloomsbury set
Who mocks religion and belief
And chalks up every chance affair
With student or with stable boy,
A seeker of low-life relief.
Yet balanced in the end you'll be
A moderate who, come what may,
Will still refuse to fan extremes—
The one who'll choose the middle way.

Biographer, perhaps you found
Ideas turn so doctrinaire;
A gradualist in your growth
You learn by listening to your peers,
Adapt and change. Not just a don,
For all your learning you're still loathe
To cede hard-headed life outside.
A young man you would realise
The dismal science dares to be
Pragmatic practice of what's wise.

Far more than Marshall, G. E. Moore
Will shape your student mind for good.
Though Marshall taught his take on price,
Moore's ethics set an inner seal
On you and so, deciding how
We choose, we cheat if we're precise—
The probes of probability
Are all. We try but can't control
Our interwoven worlds; we choose
What heeds the goodness of the whole.

> *I had long left my Bloomsbury behind.*
> *Although I match their liberal frame of mind,*

Bohemian in how I love all art,
I'm still by nature engagé I know;
In time without a doubt our paths will part.

Detractors try to paint me fancy-free,
The right may make a bogeyman of me;
My Lydia had borne with Bolsheviks
And, though I come to distrust hidden hands,
Like her I fear extremes and their quick fix.

I've been a civil servant and I know
So much is chance and how most change is slow;
I peak between the crash of '29
And World War Two and, forced to switch my tack,
I think beyond the ledger's bottom line.

Though Marshall and Pigou are both good men,
To sort out prices will solve nothing when
So many are still out of work while we
Just theorise and maybe risk men's lives—
To plan for more employment is the key.

No labourite—it's not my life or class;
Conservatism just seems a dead impasse;
A liberal I still love to move between
A competition's chaos and control—
I always want to gauge the golden mean.

You know that nothing's built by thrift,
While enterprise can warrant wealth;
Yet venture must envisage gain
And gambled business to begin
Demands seed money, which in turn
Will turn on loans it must obtain.
The system does not cure itself;
So maybe it needs money lent
To make it flow and multiply,
Repaying more than monies spent.

But more than any multiply effect,
You know how economics is
In some way too psychology;
Beside a sober calculus,

Your insight was to factor in
Our spirit's spontaneity.
The money-making motive drives
And grooves aggression's ruthless juice
In channels that can change so much,
Creating jobs that they'll produce.

> *We mustn't now confuse transmuting minds*
> *With management of things; a state that binds*
> *Too much can stifle drive—it must leave room*
> *For gumption, guide by interest rates and tax*
> *Propensities of people to consume.*

> *I prize an individual approach*
> *To nurture liberty and not encroach*
> *On choice, but we must change our ways to keep*
> *A lasting room for drive and so elude*
> *The zealot's sway, the militant's clean sweep.*

Soft changer, saint of step by step,
Tradition you'll direct not break;
Free-trader turned protectionist
Because you're both; politico
And don you seek what's best to do
To fine the savers' too-tight fist,
Make them invest. You veer between
Such goals and Smith's get-up-and-go,
You walk the third, the both-and way.
Most paths to paradise are slow.

(ii)

Receding blond,
A deep-eyed gaze,
Jacket and tie;
Integrity.

Herr Wilhelm Röpke, mastermind
Of Germany's renewal plan,
When you return from World War One,
Like many younger men who'd fought
You're leaning toward left pipe dreams.

Aghast at zealots, you've begun
To fear the loss of liberal thought
In sways of flags and fascist swoons,
The manna of imagined states
Where heaven's made of promised moons.

Professor then by twenty-five,
So blue-eyed, blond and Aryan,
A star who would, if standing by
Or playing along, be left alone.
Instead you stir up Nazi rage
Or warn the world and prophesy
How Europe's garden goes to ruin.
The day the Reichstag burns you dare
To scarify all fascist schemes.
Refusing change, you lose your chair.

Four years you're based in Istanbul.
You publish work on boom and bust
And fault the Nazis from afar.
But switching then to Switzerland
You settle where it seems to you
That power can be where people are
And you believe what's local's best—
A nation's nothing to adore—
The cantons grow their grass-roots needs.
What we keep near we care for more.

> I share with socialists a sense of shame
> At crimes committed in the market's name;
> I know the combines' ills we need to cure:
> Cartels and corporations, plunderbunds
> That widen rifts between the rich and poor.

> The communists in love with novel schemes
> Believe in time we'll come to live their dreams;
> In tune with every grievance, every gripe,
> The strong-arm fascists take their stranglehold.
> I weave a way between the dreams both pipe.

> Despotic trends cry out in both extremes,
> Both lure us towards their own illiberal dreams;
> Of course, if markets drift and lose their drive,

The state supplies the needed stimulus—
My third way thinks how polities can thrive.

From Switzerland you launch critiques
Of Nazi policies and power;
Smuggled works in spite of war
Can sow the seeds that will prepare
For Germany's renewal time,
The *Wirtschaftwunder* you plan for.
Small businessmen will build again
The new post-war economy
You name the neo-liberal way,
A market both humane and free.

But there's no turning back to former times:
Nothing is the same post World War One,
When many millions had been mobilised
And mass democracy had first arrived;
To government and market each their role.

Why revolutions where blood's shed?
In such a break, too big a breach.
You're nervous of the nation-state,
Protective of minorities—
Swiss cantons dare your paradigm:
As stubborn realms confederate
Helvetia avoids the mix
Where one must lose if others win.
No need unite and meld a whole
Or integrate as one within.

I'm not for looking back but yet I know,
Though trade may flourish in the market's flow,
We need our bonds and crave integrity;
Without community and ties of trust,
Our hearts become a banker's killing bee.

Economies both drive and nourish wealth,
But I still fear how greed can grow by stealth.
To counterbalance market buccaneers,
We compensate our worst cupidity;
With social bonds our habitat coheres.

When ties untie utopias appeal,
Collectivists unleash their urgent zeal.
There is no flawless plan or perfect place.
All this, all that. My head and heart both chose
A third way we discover case by case.

So broad a man, so many sides;
A linguist and a *littérateur*,
You guard what's best in bourgeoisie.
Your wartime work a lone crusade
That mends your native Germany.
Although a thorn in Nazi sides,
While you're in exile you prepare
The game plan for the *après guerre*.
Too left is hell, too right is hell.
Are third ways heaven's thoroughfare?

(iii)

Sensitive face,
Determined mouth;
Suave globalist,
Swede to the core.

Was Leibniz first with calculus
Or was it Newton? No one knows.
And maybe Gunnar Myrdal might
Have pipped John Keynes just at the post,
Or was it that they both at once
Had realised the time was right?
And with such millions out of work
They could no longer now delude
Themselves and hope an unseen hand
Renews each economic mood.

Though moved to Stockholm, you, Myrdal,
Are still a steady Lutheran
From Dalarna. You'll deal and trust
In right and reason's moral force
To better by unburnished truth.
A realist, you will readjust
Or U-turn any time you learn

By earned epiphany or need;
Like Keynes your double caring gift
Proves daring both in thought and deed.

You study law, then fall in love
And Alva Reimer recommends
You start anew, begin instead
Political economy.
A student of the Stockholm school
Where Wicksell was light years ahead
Because he'd left Say's law behind,
Knew more production would not mend
Depression's workless standing still—
And someone somewhere had to spend.

At first you scorn the classic school
And vilify all laissez-faire
As remnants of raw natural law,
Or blame utilitarians
With net sums of our happiness
For such unscientific flaws.
You want no value-laden laws—
The best economist must be
A rational technologist,
A voice that's always value-free.

> *Perhaps I was naive or had a need*
> *To mark myself as one who would succeed,*
> *And though in later life I knew I came*
> *Full circle, lauding what I loathed once,*
> *That surely is no crime or cause for shame.*
>
> *I'd rather read this as a gift to grow*
> *Through decades, just adapting on the go*
> *And learning how each case must stand alone;*
> *Society and lives are multilayered,*
> *Too thick for any theory to own.*
>
> *The only doctrine I find tried and true*
> *Is Wicksell's warning that effects seep through*
> *Economies and can accumulate*
> *And seal what seems a circle virtuous*
> *Or vicious—both enfold us as our fate.*

I find through life that I complexify.
Our tacit expectations buy;
But gain in fact is not our hoped for gain—
Ex ante and ex post are not the same
When savings and investments sync again.

Together with your Alva you now gauge
Why Sweden's population is too low
And shock your country into caring how
To tend their families and so in turn
To underpin an equilibrium.
You coax and right and left allow
All measures so they don't die out.
These means that raise the birthing rate
Seem innocent; in truth, with these
You weave the Swedish welfare state.

As chosen neutral Swede you're known
For how you helped to integrate
The U.S.A. and your report
Refers back to the founding creed—
All men are equal. You remind
How racist power cannot support
That cherished dream. For change you trust
The moral lift of liberal whites
And courts will cite your summing up
When ruling for black civil rights.

Returned to Swedish politics I made
A treaty with the Russians so we'd trade;
But falling foul of Sweden that equates
This with betrayal, I retreat abroad
To build a welfare world of welfare states.

A decade in Geneva now as chief,
I manage Marshall's deftly planned relief;
Collaborative and collegiate
I'm keeping the commission's conscience clean,
But Communist pullbacks I can't combat.

The Cold War curbed so much that I would do;
Although so many plans I had fell through,
I won't despair. But Third World poverty

Preoccupies me now. How can the poor
Be with us if our world is truly free?

You turn a decade to the East,
Appalled how poverty persists
And find growth models do not fit.
Soft nations don't observe their laws
Or where corrupt the rich grow rich.
You change your mind and must admit
Economies are case by case;
A culture's history can tell
Much more than theory that may
Once work but does not travel well.

In southern Asia it seems best
To better farming management—
Disease-resisting seeds and schemes
To fertilise, term loans to rid
The money-lenders' debt, allow
Escape from sharks and share-crop rent
For local landlords who don't work.
You know that capital won't cure
All ills and industry is slow.
No short-range fix can reassure.

How could you know technology
Might alter all of India?
Throughout your life you cherished change
To tally with solicitude.
Your every shift a sharpened care,
Your history a widening range
Of sympathy that pulls your thought
Beyond the academic dome
To dream a worldwide welfare state.
Is heaven our compassion's home?

(iv)

Huge energy,
Grey, young for years,
Sallow, freckled;
Eyes that know loss.

Amartya Sen, "Immortal" Sen,
"A god"—so named by poet Tagore,
Your mother's friend,—but you're shaped more
By memories of a handyman
Condemned by creed to bleed to death
To settle a sectarian score,
And by a famine in Bangladesh
Which now we know was not a want
Of food but more lame government,
Too laissez-faire, too nonchalant.

I love your learned global mind—
Bengali through and through and still
A cultured ripe economist—
Three wives helped shape in different ways
To straddle worlds of stringent thought,
As seeking fairness you insist
Ideas change and challenge us.
In academe you dare to steer
A wise and middle course that asks
Both where and how we go from here.

In Sanskrit words for justice seem
To sum all up: though those who search
For *niti* need a perfect state
To start, just staying with *nyaya* we
Hone in on how we realise
A justice now that won't await
Perfections we may never find;
By aggregate instead give voice
To likes and preference—in lieu
Of social contracts, social choice.

There's much, of course, statism mends
But here you want the middle way:
Not fascism, not some laissez-faire.
Though keeping Kenneth Arrow's thoughts,
Your much more optimistic view
Would find a course that's sometimes fair,
That's not all equal, not all free,
That's neither nothing nor the lot.
But ought, you say, keep asking all
The while: equality of what?

How carefully we gauge the GNP
Or those below the line of poverty—
All well and good but neither are enough
To tell who'll reach their full capacity;
The measurements we make still far too rough.

Capacity—along with freedom too—
To realise what in our reason's view
We value are the facts we need to know.
It's not just wealth we need to know or count
But all the things we might achieve, although

Such freedom binds responsibilities
And, as Gautama taught, asymmetries
Demand, as mothers love a helpless child,
A care beyond the yoke of contracts' dues;
Asymmetry must somehow make us mild.

Though duties nobble us as Krishna knew,
There are still downsides to so much we do;
As Arjuna unhappy with the hell
A battle might unleash had balked at war,
Let us at once fare forward and fare well.

For most economists self-interest
Is how we humans think, but Smith addressed
Our sympathies and generosity,
How public spirit might inspire us too—
Free marketeers demean his theory.

Each wife who wielded love for you
Did mould the man you did become:
First Nabaneeta's literature,
Then Eva formed a feminist
And Emma enriched your history—
In your attention you mature.
A hundred million women missed
In Asia, you claim, and so declare
How justice must demand we make
The trapped and tramped-on more aware.

Outsiders sometimes bring a broader view.
As Smith could take a neutral slant we too

Require spectators from without who're tasked
To give nonpartisan opinions which
Keep asking what insiders never asked.

To maximise capacities we fall
So short and still we should somehow do all
Within the bounds of freedom to combine
What's best to rate and rank each careful choice,
Yet know sometimes that nothing falls in line.

Economies embrace each charge and chance
To make or break, diminish or enhance.
For fear of failure we cannot afford
To reckon on a lazy bottom line;
We're bound to human life across the board.

For all success I see how you
Still keep that handyman in mind,
That Muslim murdered for his creed
You saw at ten. No stone unturned,
Your reason reaches for what's fair.
So many facts we fail to heed,
Impeding our capacities;
A brother's keeper, your work combs
How best to chart and choose what's fair.
Is heaven where all justice homes?

(v)

Strong steely hair,
Straight back; dark-eyed;
Serious mien;
A smile that spreads.

But time for Kathryn Tanner now,
A cub economist who comes
To grope economies of grace
And find the moves that better fit
The love-dream born in Bethlehem,
Which may yet mend the marketplace—
Not saints alone or jubilees
Or purposed options for the poor,

But cumulated traces left,
Where heaven's gained here spoor by spoor.

That grace is money, money's grace—
Church standing as a status sign,
Prosperity is too a mark
Of favour in God's eyes—you face;
And still you clearly understand
How systems' kernels can align:
For Durkheim how all things cohere
In dominated, dominant;
For Weber status groups that vie.
But is God more extravagant?

What do the down-and-out dream of?
Those goods no one deserves yet gains?
What if, you ask, what if, what if
In giving we gain more ourselves,
So prodigal and profligate,
Our jazz-like gifting riff by riff
Means one hand's giving's all hands' gain?
As light won't lessen when it's shared,
A lavishness can circulate;
In godlike giving nothing's spared.

> My mother's life was brief yet her largesse
> Had shown her girl a giddying excess
> That still permits me now imagine grace,
> God's paradigm so dative and unowned,
> A substantive with no possessive case.
>
> And so my seeming counterculture need
> To plead for fiscal frameworks somehow freed
> From legal modes, to give for giving's sake;
> We too can aid creation's enterprise
> Beyond power games of potlatch give-and-take.
>
> I don't believe each win's another loss,
> Or one subordinate, the other boss—
> I'm hoping for a social overhaul,
> A debtless shift in shared relationships:
> My bottom line what benefits us all.

Is this utopian, I hear you ask,
A heaven here on earth, a hopeless task,
Another revolution run roughshod?
O no! It's here and now we must uphold
The common right of all to gifts of God.

We cannot just withdraw into our dream
Or hide and hedge; instead, why don't we scheme
To meet the system where it needs to mend
And infiltrate its crevices and cracks,
Where we can work as one and share one end.

We decide the system's shape.
At Bretton Woods John Keynes would want
Trade surpluses supporting dearth,
To balance out the burdening debts.
But then we failed to follow through—
Though we are one and on one earth
And all economies now meld.
Post-Fordism's world is mix and match
And means that work can move at will,
As parts are made on any patch.

With neither benefits nor burdens shared,
How can the rich and poor lands be compared?
The creditors' free flow attains more wealth,
While debtors sink into yet deeper debt,
Stagnating into slavery by stealth.

To save a capitalism from collapse,
My vision learns to share our overlaps;
In time no business thrives on built-up hate
That could erupt and rage across our world—
A level pitch demands we regulate.

A system's laws that keep a market free
Are undermined by each monopoly;
When every competition must succumb
The market rate no longer self-corrects,
Allows Smith's basic equilibrium.

Some feared the first remove from gold as base—
Fictitious tender now swarms cyberspace.

It's sauce for geese but ganders don't get sauce;
The rich grow richer, poor remain the poor,
As someone's gain is someone else's loss.

We need another worldwide Marshall plan,
Rebalancing the scales as best we can;
Of course some choose to drift when others drive,
But money's free flow paced could come to mean
A chance for all to live, a chance to thrive.

Your most demanding thought insists,
Just as your God has given all
In pouring out without reserve,
A rich dynamic go-around,
We too must tend to those who lack,
And not size up what they deserve
Or condescend; conditionless,
Our giving must be guaranteed,
A gift that's warranted by want;
The needy justified by need.

Such disincentives then to seek
Out work, the self-made man will say.
But let's acknowledge deeper needs
In all to find fulfilment too,
And offer schooling for new skills.
Has welfare worsened life for Swedes?
So long as aid attends to lack
And well-off do not want the same
Because they pay and play their part.
Your vision wants a win-win game.

Good hearts are good but not enough.
We work within the world we live
To change the structures, challenge all
That holds in check the chance to thrive.
Yet common ends that coincide
And match beyond the margin call
May save a system that we know
Unless repaired could fall apart,
Let's still be signs of kingdom come
Where here on earth our heavens start.

3

Steering

Canto 1

Governance

(i)

Our ancients knew, whatever shapes the ship,
A state is steered. This is a trope the Greeks
Alcaeus and Aeschylus long ago
And Plato in his dream *Republic* would
Refine their metaphor to tell us how
We sailors on such unknown seas that toss
And change must choose a helmsman for our ship.
For him, philosophers are best to helm—
For us the default faring steersman now,
The one that we the common mariners
Elect to chart our course. But those we choose
Abide by laws, and kept accountable
To us, who mandate them, they must return
And face the ballot box or urn when we
Resanction them or seek another helm.

At least that's still for most the default steer.
A state has laws and liability
We have to hold in tension all at once
In order just to helm our human lives.
But how this blend of three so quickly blurs:
To keep a democratic camouflage,
Elections not abiding by the laws,
Or laws enforced or foisted from above,
An out-of-kilter triad breaking trust.

By times an unchecked bid to cheat for power.
By times an inability to change
And so adapt to ward off dangerous
Imbalances of wealth where by and by
We rig the thimble for rich oligarchs.
Unconscious of political decay,
We skew our triple-stranded scheme of things.

The fantasists of left and right both fail
To see how states must ground stability,
How institutions take so long to grow;
Yet like a tree unleafed they too can wilt
And neither Marxists nor free-marketeers,
Despite their fantasies, can find a way
To keep what's brutish, nasty, brief at bay.

And still we came here by no chartered course.
Where did the state first start this move away
From kinship to a country or a land?
Was it in Qin this change began when states
Had warred and legalists had overcome
Confucian faithfulness to fathers' kin?
Or maybe in Mesopotamia,
In Egypt, even in the city states
Of Greece or Rome before a Europe's rifts
Of geography would finally give way
And warring states start fusing into one.
No facile lineage allows us trace
Where liberal democracy shot roots
Or how it first developed here or there,
A cherished triad now our default choice.

But in our comfort we so smugly can
Dismiss the mishmash of all politics
And taking institutions we count on
As given, keep just getting on with life.
Is it Tweedle Dee or Tweedle Dum
We will elect? So little we effect;
Though parties promise much, they're much the same.
But there's no opting out. The thieves of power
Come noiselessly in nights of apathy;

The führer whispers while you're fast asleep.
So like it not or even like it so,
This is the polity we tend, or pay
The price of arrogant indifference.

Though in the broader sweep we see the breadth
Of change and know new chapters were begun,
So loftily and often we allow
A fatalist's philosophy to plan
Our exit strategy. Perhaps the gyres
Of history went round and round again
Through time from what was best to tyranny
And back; or if enlightened we believed
A line of progress from uncivilized
To our sophisticated age would keep on
Happening anyhow. And Marxists were
Convinced our politics were vacuous
As on the past they all served capital.
And now? The global market's juggernaut
Can seem to leave us with so little choice.
Determinism seen in the light of time
Is opting out of muddling through the mess,
Where left to our discernment we must seek
To change a world by choices carefully made.
We near perfection with a nearer miss.

Perhaps we learn a little from the past.
Though paradigms of history repeat,
They also shift or slowly rearrange
The models we assume, so we can know
Something of what's best and so can build
From age to age as wisely as we may.
Let's try to trace our own trajectory
For though we can no longer now believe
In linear advance, we still may learn
From stories of adaption and mistakes,
Aware how we arrived at where we are.
Refining our inheritance, attuned
Anew to what is new, we dare to change.

Then where is poetry in politics?
So many counted syllables in all

The cut and thrust? No more and yet no less
Than lines in our polyphony of thought
That shapes an ambiance in which we act.
Epiphanies occur, thoughts percolate
To shape adaptions we may learn to dare.
And no one knows how syllables are weighed.

We travel towards a star we're steering by
To one imagined harbour's havened dream.

(ii)

Small gestures of gentility,
Conventions, vestiges may spoor
A feudal past. Tipped hats—or how
Our fathers held their hats on high
And bowed to women, walked outside
On footpaths fending off for them
The passing perils—may still hide
The visor lift of vassaldom,
Or courtly lovers so gallant.

A king could give his lands as gifts
To vassals in return for tours
Of feudal duty done at war.
The soil is their resource and lords
Depended still on peasantry
To labour on their lands and fill
Their granaries with corn or grain.
But firstly Europe's feudalism
Will pass, then Russia's and Japan's.
Both times and politics will shift
As various combinations cause
An older feudal world to wane.

Christ's misbegotten missioners
Crusade across to Holy Lands.
And in their wake a widened trade
Brings towns the merchant class will make,
Who renting land near to a lord's
Abode or abbey build up trade,
Where for a fee the local lord

Could charter towns to guarantee
A market for their farmers' yield.
Such commerce meant a major shift
From land to coined economy.

Bubonic plague from Asia's plains
Has raged along the Silken Road;
Black Death now deals a felling blow
To Europe's failing feudal world.
Unknown how many millions die;
A labour shortage starts a shift
Of power and peasants sense their worth
As overtaxed they turn to force,
Revolt in Florence, Flanders, France
With Jacquerie and Tyler's rise
In England, where a callow king
Reneges on freeing serfs. They've some
Success at first before revenge.
Those serfs now sold their freedom drift
From tillage to new settled towns.
Then older roles are rearranged
As lords begin to rent their lands
And with their rights to labour lost,
Most former serfs have tenant farms,
So feudal lords are lords of land;
While nobles opting not to fight,
In lieu of combat, pay their king
To hire the much-feared mercenaries.

It seems now Europe can emerge
From centuries so rife with plagues
Or hungers and a hundred odd
Embattled years that yielded France.
At last a period of peace,
When after throes a Europe thrives.

The Japanese would never joust.
A samurai read poetry
They wrote and learned calligraphy
And with their lighter armour were
So much more dexterous on their mount.

Yet rather than the Roman law
Refined somewhat by Christian faith
And mixed in with Germanic style
That's inculcated in a knight,
Confucianism will inform
The samurai's morality,
His *bushidō*, a code that binds
A kind of parent piety
Which spills into respect for rank.
Unlike the lover knight they know
No chivalry or courtly care
Protecting tenderness; instead
Their women too must be as tough.
The samurai are paid in rice
And not like knights with given land.

Two feudalisms so far apart.
Two worlds where there's a warrior class
With ties which bind obedience.
The East came late and lasted long;
America will make them trade
Just as the Silken Road had rid
The Western world of vassaldom.
The Meiji era meant a change,
An opening up to other worlds
Where commerce kills off *bushidō*.

By fifteen hundred Feudalism
In most of Europe's moribund,
Except in Russia's south and core
Till Alexander Second, Tsar,
Will set by law his unfree free.
A third of Russia after three
Odd centuries were still his serfs
And might revolt. Or maybe too
Some culture shift in thought occurred.

What form or pattern can we find?
Is there some feudal common fault?
Perhaps, apart from class, all hangs
On how such fractiousness will fray

Societies and tend to call
For states that start to centralise.

In constable and county we
Echo in our words old worlds;
Still partly in our politesse
We keep a feudal etiquette.
And maybe our mentality
Bears still an era's residue:
A Japanese submissive mind,
Our Western way to see the state
In contract terms betokens still
A trace of nobles and their knights.
Our feudal history dies hard.

(iii)

O Florence, queen of city-states,
Exile Dante's home where Giotto paints,
Stretch your floruit across your years
Till Michelangelo decamps to Rome
And you will fall to despot rule.
Most Tuscan cities, bar Pisa's port,
Crown safer hills, but you lie low
Before the Arno's flow through swamps
When you have fished, fulled cloth and dyed
Or turned your mills. A lofty dome
Eight generations build above
A fetid hotchpotch of a town
Of attic rooms and chimney pots,
Blushed tiled roofs and house-like towers
Three times as deep as they are wide,
Five stories high with terraces,
Frescoed walls and tapestries.
Their busy ground-floor *botteghe*
Room carpenters and artisans.
Alberti bankers' residence
Squats in a noisome dirty zone;
Here's S. Croce, a slaughterhouse,
Wool cleansing and the smells of soap.
In streets of clothes shops, stretching sheds,

This cluttered metropolis where
Pragmatic merchants come to trade
From Catalonia and France;
Where German and Hungarian
Hired soldiers come to help defence,
And slaves escaped from the Black Sea
Hive out here in your underworld.

It's dawn and Mass and open gates.
Big bankers and cloth merchant men
And tax collectors for the pope,
The Strozzi and the Bardi stroll,
Talk dowries and their business deals
In Paris, London and Marseilles,
In Bruges and Tunis, the Levant,
Though most in Naples and the south.
The streets are filled with farmers' loads
And cargoed cloth and dyeing stuff;
The markets piled with fish and meat,
With stalls of fruit and spice and game,
As daylight thrives on haggling life
And butchers bargain while the square
Fills up with vendors and their wares;
The pocket thieves, the whores and pimps,
Move among the crowds. A smith begins
To hammer swords and shields and hooves.
Boccaccio's *Decameron*
Tells how two-thirds once died of plague,
And wars and feuds too took their toll.

Comune turned a city-state
Still holds its tensions all in place,
Between the many and the few,
The artisans and merchant prince—
Segnori oligarchs allow
The city's guilds their spokesmen roam,
Between the constant push and pull
Of family clash and what is just,
Of private feuds and public rights.
How delicate the strain between
The city and its countryside,

155

Or mixing faith and business sense,
Religion and the rational,
Forbidden usury and gain.
Funambulists, they walk the line
And neither looking left nor right
Both innovate and still conserve
What's best, nurturing their roots
And where they are, yet reaching out.

Here Cosimo Primo walking feigns
False modesty but first among
Austere Medici shows his wealth.
His Via Larga palace hosts
The German emperor and John,
Byzantine potentate, will come.
This man behind the scenes controls
The city, a banker who rewards
His friends and spites his enemies,
A realist both shrewd and tough.

Was our Renaissance born here?
Our Europe's turning back to Rome
And Greece? How come they could combine
Classical and Tuscan roots,
Throw up a Dante to describe
The cosmos in his dialect?
Here Giotto di Bondone paints
Us earthlings not Byzantine dreams
And Cosimo the patron hosts
The humanist *convegni* where
All classes gather to discuss
How disciplines cross-fertilise.
Enthusiastic classicists,
Purveyors of embroidered cloth
And painters, lawyers, bankers, monks,
All meet in the *segnoria*.
A live-and-let-live in the air,
The Inquisition's held in check;
One Bernardino, pious friar
And would-be banisher of Jews,
Will for his trouble be expelled.

This return to Greece and Rome
Feeds tolerance and truthfulness
While artists represent a world
Proportioned, and perspective now
Depicts reality they see,
While patronage will lift their work
From skill and craftsmanship to art.

Medici turn such monocrats.
Lorenzo il Magnifico
Commissions Michelangelo,
Da Vinci, Botticelli's work.
His son Piero is exiled,
Then Machiavelli writes *The Prince*
And Savonarola preaches doom.
Medici twice return to rule—
A once republic is no more.
O banished queen of city-states,
Too small a state you're swallowed up.

Evolution no straight line,
Our city-states weave in and out.
Once Athens, Carthage and in Rome;
Still Monaco and Singapore,
Ten million under New York's mayor.
Here you can walk Museum Mile,
Where bankers built their palaces—
Kahn's limestone mansion now a school,
Or Warburg's one block further north.
Is this a quasi city-state
Embedded in a larger whole?
Perhaps old boundaries are blurred
And we will learn how loyalties
May overlap and imbricate
A city-state within a state.

(iv)

Now Dante's cosmos will no longer do,
With spheres of angels and our earthly realm;
We know our globe revolves around the sun,

And have explored so many new-found lands
Where rival states compete for recent wealth.
No Charlemagne reigns over every land—
Now fractured single realms all strive to win.
How can we think of common humankind
Or see one species ordered under God,
Unless each king's God's lieutenant on earth,
A sultan who's mandated from above,
Whom no one dares to question or to doubt,
Who answers only to his listening God.

Louis Quatorze, no wonder you're sun god,
The orb all courtiers must circle round.
Inheriting grandfather Henri's zest,
Though short, your heels and *perruque* both are high;
Gourmand and huntsman, dancing libertine
Who yet can work for sixteen hours a day:
Reports, petitions heard, an audience.
Reserved, your studied courtesy distrusts;
With calculated silences, sangfroid,
Maîtrise de soi, your iron will trumps all.
But why so secretive, *mon roi soleil*?
Was it the Fronde your childhood learned to fear,
Because they back-stabbed France at war with Spain?
Suspecting every one, always involved
And proud as any pharaoh king, your name,
Prestige and glory prompt each plan you make.

Although chaos demands an absolute,
The mayhem France that Mazarin leaves you
Calls for the despot you were made to be.
This land of latent wealth so far behind
Depends on cereals and does not know
How crop rotation works and farmers here
Bend over sickles still instead of scythes.
When you in turn at eighteen take the reins
Bubonic plague still rages and is spread
By swarms of vermin, beggars, peddlers, troops,
As war and famine stalk the countryside.
The currency more stable than in Spain,
Yet weights and value vary still by whim

And unlike Holland there's no central bank
Or stock exchange resembling Amsterdam.
French peasants must be Jacks of every trade:
They farm, keep inns, grow vines, they spin and weave,
They're poachers, smugglers, market gardeners
Who're taxed by locals, seigneurs, church and king.
Most urban workers permanently in debt
Hive out in squalid huts as best they can.
The governance of France in disarray,
Rebellions and unrest keep breaking out;
Outside the Île-de-France and Picardy,
Champagne and Loire no single law
Applies, and in Provence the king is count,
In Brittany his title only duke.
All over there are *parlements* who must
Approve or disapprove what kings require.
Unrule at home, abroad at least still peace.

A hands-on king, Louis, you will dismiss
Your counsellors, no minister is prime;
Le Telier, Lionne and Jean-Baptiste
Colbert suffice. Informed of everything—
Your subjects' place is all obedience;
State reasons can eclipse all other laws.
Each *coup de maître* humbles and cuts down
The *cour des aides* and muzzles *parlements*;
The clergy's wings are clipped, the bourgeois curbed.
Though architecture sets the royal stage,
All arts and science too are brought to heel;
Academies reel in the fancy-free
And your unerring taste loves Molière,
Racine, Lully. A once-nomadic court
Will settle for Versailles where nobles come,
A Shogunate all gathered by demand,
Who'll pay to tend to your royal bed and board.
At court adultery becomes the rage,
You, Louis, change your mistresses at whim.

Through legal loopholes in Nantes' edict,
The Huguenots are harassed long before
Its revocation. And all illicit press,

All journals and all ballad songs are banned.
Colbert of plain and merchant stock, once picked
By Mazarin, dislikes disorder so
Both he and you dream up Augustan Rome.
One France, one king, one law, all Catholics.
Militias quell revolt. In the Auvergne,
In Poitou, Berry, Bordeaux and Brittany
Disturbances are crushed and rebels hanged.

But you still need to strut a larger stage.
Determined you'll be Europe's number one,
You wage dynastic wars to widen France,
To gain for her the natural frontiers,
To be the Catholic king through and through;
Against the Dutch, against the Augsburg League,
Or steering who'll ascend the throne of Spain.
No king will ever reign as long as you—
In fifty-five grand years our Europe shifts.
At first obsessed with Spain and covetous
Of Hapsburg emperors you underrate
The English and the Dutch. What drove your youth
Of glory or your unprovoked midlife
Belligerence, your late defensive years?
O yes, Frederick, the Danes' and Norway's king,
Or Prussia's Friedrich Wilhelm rule their roost
But such sangfroid, such cold and royal control,
You remain *Louis le Grand*, *le Roi Soleil*,
And absolutist monarch *par excellence*.

A greater France more centralised and taxed
Your legacy, and yet so out of touch.
As Mazarin's apprentice you were reared
In court intrigues and glory dreams of power,
Dynastic rows, successions and frontiers—
Ideals for you cabals to be suppressed.
You're unaware the world will soon desire
An age of reason, science, liberty.
As spendthrift nobles party at Versailles,
Still to your depths a dedicated king,
Who building France neglects its colonies
And never for a moment thinks that plagues

And poverty, despite the reign of sun,
Will come to topple the next king but one.

(v)

Here we see a subtle shift:
Monarchs, though they're absolute,
Now no longer playing God's
Lieutenant, become instead,
As Prussia's Frederick Second said,
Just first servant of the state.
Older thought's inadequate
For this age of kings or queens—
Frederick, Carlos, Catherine—
Steeped in the Enlightenment,
In John Locke and Newton's globe.
Science and new worlds explored
Fed by classic literature
Yield to rationality;
Black belief in innate sin
Turns to trust our human minds.
Though Descartes along with Hobbes,
Machiavelli, all believe
Sovereignty rests with the state,
Society requires one voice,
One absolute authority
Who'll preserve us from all hell.

Who is this prince his father caned,
Secret lover of what's French,
Poet-lutist who won't hunt,
On the sly still reading books,
Planning with his friend to flee?
Caught, imprisoned, made to watch
As his friend is put to death,
Friedrich haunts his father's mind,
Playing up French dandyism,
Taunting his dyspeptic rage.
His father hated all things French,
Kidnapped giants for grenadiers
Whom his general taught to march.

Schooled by one French Huguenot
Friedrich learns forbidden things;
Falling for Voltaire with whom—
Although Voltaire laughs up his sleeve—
He remains in lifelong touch;
Friedrich shares his deist views.

Then his father dies. No oil,
No anointment ceremony,
There's no coronation rite.
In one week he parks his queen
In her palace in Berlin,
Then sends for his male friends to come
And leaves for his new Sans Souci.
All torture is abolished now,
Every faith allowed—he'll build
In Berlin for Catholics
Their cathedral and at once
Opens the academy that shut;
Censorship of books is banned,
Freedom of expression prized;
Shortages of food call for
Lavish unlocked granaries;
Friedrich comes into his own.

Author of *Anti-Machiavel*,
Young rebuttal of *The Prince*:
Statecraft is much more than guile;
Subjects' welfare is what counts.
One who could not wear his spurs,
Fearing he might hurt his horse,
Turns this king who starts to eye
Silesia and Saxony,
Who'll become best general
Of his century and place
Each enemy where best suits him,
Where attack is best defence.
War by war, by skill or luck,
Fritz outsmarts the emperor,
Makes his Prussia merged and strong.
After many wars with one-

Ninth of Prussia's people dead,
Friedrich welcomes immigrants
Till one in six are foreign born;
Still all love *Der Alte Fritz*.

Tax reformed à la France,
Crop rotation introduced,
Livestock breeding he'll refine;
Bent on industry: silk trade,
Cotton, linen all silk succeed;
In Silesia mines are worked,
Prussia's western marshes drained.
Concerned with schools he'll embrace
Jesuits who're banned elsewhere.

Forty-four ripe years he reigns,
Lutist who still loves to play,
Practising four times a day,
Challenger of J. S. Bach
Who'll extemporise for him.
But his dyspeptic genes now mean
Slowly Friedrich's growing ill,
With the loss of teeth he must
Discontinue playing his flute,
So he'll rise at five, not four.

Hail these absolutists still
Whose achievements we admire,
Even if we know events
Partly forced their royal hand;
Wars of dynasties demand
Fuller coffers than before;
Such needs will drive efficiency.
Realms tend to centralise
And make one tax, one law and yet
Monarchs only could unite
The disparate, the privileged who
Take their stand against all change;
This in turn makes bureaucrats
Who obey their monarch's will
And outsmart the nobles' wiles.
Feudal privilege dies hard.

Growing in benevolence,
They gainsay God's own given right,
Undermine all monarchies.
Once they'd organised the state,
Codified the laws and steered
Towards regal stewardship
Or Rousseau's agreed contract,
Might they slowly cede their power,
Fold dynastic tents before
Primogeniture throws up
One indecisive Bourbon king?
History's coulisses groan,
In the wings a change of scene.
Enter Madam Guillotine.

Canto 2
Rights and Territory

(i)

Europe's stage is set for change.
England's monarch's wings now clipped,
Let us hear Voltaire declare:
Men are free who want to be.
Speak John Locke of property,
Bills of rights are in the air;
Yet, old Europe, you're upstaged.
Patriots in colonies
Overtaxed and undervoiced
Call for life and liberty,
Freedom and democracy.

Plato's ghost is horrified:
Rule by people means the mob
Governing by whim, not skill.
Aristotle's ghost rejoice:
Monarchs we well know can turn
Into tyrants, good or bad;
Aristocracies become
Rule by rich or by too few.

Even as full democrats,
Those accepting Plato's doubts,
Know they need a trained elite—
Not with Plato's perfect grasp—
More a practical know-how,
Wisdom of maturity;
A mix of skill and people power
Best guides a balanced polity.

I, Thomas Jefferson, whose life and dreams
Envisage all that is democracy,
Will steer and trim to veer between extremes,
To tame and clip and keep our fledgling free.
Enlightenment has shaped my own world view:
Too long the kings and priests would ride roughshod.
Too many saddled by the privileged few;
The laws of nature and of nature's God
Entitle all to life and liberty.
For John Locke's "property" instead I write
"Pursuit of happiness." At thirty-three
I draft America's God-given right.
Determined fist well hid in velvet glove,
I am both tending hawk and soothing dove.

I know how England had restored a king
And fear our monarchists might follow suit;
Our Tories suck the homeland's teething ring,
But time will see democracy take root.
World history leaves monarchies behind
And reason's revolution sets us free;
I frame a public to my frame of mind
As much in action as in theory.
I dare more than the Federalists I'd charge
And do so much I dreaded they would do;
The presidential powers I too enlarge
And take those rights I thought just states were due.
The art of power bends all I theorise;
Democracy is always compromise.

Although some craved an aristocracy—
I'll live to see Napoleon in France—

We test a first large-scale democracy
And show the world this rational advance.
A revolutionary I did disdain
A party system and believed in time
That reason would ensure a higher plane
Where all our common sense at last would rhyme.
For all I try to shape the world I see,
Perhaps dispute creates a thought refined;
And even when my critics upbraid me,
My thin skin learns it can't afford to mind.
Unless God send his angels down to reign,
Let people rule the stumbling and mundane.

Now though some others come to free each slave,
Virginian planter of my time I know
Our races' guilty mix and so behave
As owners do and keep the status quo.
I see the people can't be everyone.
The Indians we will in time efface;
We'll free the slaves but in the longer run
Can white and black still share one living place?
Four times I tried to curb black slavery
And had to see such moves were premature;
Slave votes count three-fifths of one that's free—
A pragmatist can never be too pure.
Democracy must walk so thin a line;
Ideals with what's possible combine.

I follow science still of every kind,
Philosophy, good wine, things with French flair,
Inventions, Monticello I designed.
My love of life was never doctrinaire.
And though I'd thought through every change I find,
Democracy demands clear messages
To gloss complexities for heart and mind—
And yet not think in terms of "them" and "us."
I would not let a rebel carry on—
New laws gainsaid my declaration's words;
I send my envoy to Napoleon,

> *Approved by Congress retrospectively.*
> *A vision I pursued more than a creed;*
> *Democracy needs leaders who can lead.*

"Tired, your poor, your huddled mass,
Homeless, tempest-tost to me"—
Liberty's high torch lights all.
Polities are aggregates
Made of many different kinds
And majorities are tyrants too
If we play the numbers game.
Tocqueville praised diversity,
Sound enriched by dissonance,
Harmony not unison.

Back in London's parliament
Tory polemicists predict
Such a nation must collapse,
Given all restraints and checks,
So much power divided up.
In republics there's no one
Source of sovereignty. And yet
Federations too have power;
States are strong when roots are deep,
Bedded in community,
And America now shows
Popular consent needs good
Institutions to prevail;
Sound allegiance to new laws
Can restrain majorities.
Though some darker waters wait,
Storms to ride and somehow yet
Thin aristocratic roots
May allow such fresh attempts
To design a polity
Fare better in new worlds.
In old Europe feudal spoors
Urge more violent shifts of scene.
History rumbles a coulisse.

(ii)

Ancient Egypt, Greece and Rome all knew
How unexpectedly regimes can fall;
Forced by masses who, when mobilised
By some visions of a more just world,
Overthrow establishments to found
Institutions of their own. And yet
Few foresee the moment when what seethes
Overspills in violence. Alone
Downtrodden rarely claim their rights,
Needy on their own can seldom rise—
Only when elites and the oppressed
Under fiscal strain combine to make
In their anger common cause or share
Tenets of an ideology,
Only then do revolutions fire.

Robespierre, how do we think of you:
Cold fanatic, rigid in your dream,
First modern tyrant many imitate,
Visionary and martyr who led France,
Circumventing all the counter-coups
Keeping the republic on its course?
Were the terror, all the mass arrests
Revolution's price France paid to save
Democratic dreams of full-blown liberty?

> *Once an idol, now I am vilified.*
> *Like my fellow Jacobins I tried*
> *Somehow to make sense of such turmoil.*
> *In our revolution's aftermath.*

> *Yes, my mother died, my father fled,*
> *Yet aunts and mother's parents nurtured me.*
> *Study as a schoolboy was my god:*
> *Latin, Greek and French and most of all*
> *Aristotle's* Ethics. *Pride and jealousy,*
> *Greed, licentiousness oppose what's wise,*
> *Justice, temperance, things well understood.*
> *The sun makes light and virtue happiness.*
> *The Abbé Hérivaux, who taught me, chose*

My oration for the king and queen
Passing back from Reims both newly crowned.
It turned wet; the couple in their coach
Listened, left me standing in the rain.

After student days I went back home
Made my name in Arras where I'd lived.
I recalled those simmering Paris years,
Capital of commerce and of law,
Of professionals and artisans,
Workers, beggars, prostitutes, cafés
Rich with agitated talk, debates
Thrashing out if power should now entail
Church or secular authority.
I might have stayed there as a leading light,
Diligent, successful as I was
Bubbling up with wit and energy,
Grating colleagues with my sympathy
For outsiders, criminals, the child
Disinherited because it's born
On the sheets' wrong side—like I myself
Once nearly was, as all of Arras knows.
But elected locally I'm then
One of eight sent to the Third Estate
To Versailles and Paris for three years.

When the National Assembly shut
I'm chaired in triumph through the streets.
Long speeches, yes, but always I'd persist,
Would not compromise to limit rights.
Revolution is a turning round.
What then, is blood just spilt so pure?—
Deputy Barnave had asked of Foulon's death.
Although I know what revolutions cost
I demand reforms to save such blood.
Why should votes depend on property?
Unjust seigneurial dues we wiped,
Hunting rights for all I advocate;
Let there be elections in the church;
And even if church land becomes the state's
Why not give each priest a decent pay?

Like Rousseau, I long for virtue's rule.
Paris crowds all cheer me as I pass,
Know I am the Revolution's voice.

I oppose all foreign wars. We must
Order and secure our nation first.
Although a full republic is the goal
And, of course, most still distrust the king,
Who would want a Cromwell in his place?
But in the end it was the people's will
So Louis too must feed the guillotine.
On return to Arras I thought I'd stay.
As there was no tribunal post
Paris beckoned and I came to her.
I had to side with sans-culottes although
I abhor all deaths. I want reforms—
Blood will drown our revolution yet.
But la patrie in danger we ensure
Neither countermovements from within
Nor too indulgent attitudes can win.
Although I did defend my friend Danton
In the end he too I'll sacrifice.
Madam Guillotine is hard at work,
Averaging her thirty-eight a day.

I believe in virtue—most are good;
Still it must take so much time for them
To transcend corruptions of the past.
Even if I know what's best, I wait.
Although just thirty-six I'm overwrought;
Errors made allow soured enemies
Jealous of my life gang up on me.
Fickle Paris crowds await my head.

Liberal and democratic thought
Born at such a bloody human cost
Spreads both slowly and unevenly.
The sans-culottes' blind binaries
Could not compromise. In freedom's name
They stage their trials to purge suspects,
Scorn a people's church without their leave.
Yet for all that failed, they first proclaimed:

Men are born, as always they remain,
Free and equal in the rights all have,
Outlawing slavery and freeing blacks,
Treating faith minorities as citizens.

France, your revolution still awakes
Dreams of bloodshed change in dreams to come.
Could the push and pull of polity
Slowly have achieved organic shifts?
Ruptures lose the best that growth can keep.
Had all this to happen violently?

(iii)

Kith and kinship shift to tribal bonds;
Cultural inheritance must pass.
Drawing lines between an "us" and "them,"
We assert our ownership of lands,
Creating myths to give us reasons why
We belong and call one country ours.
Yet beyond such birthrights faiths still claim
Humankind transcends all lines we draw,
As our science and our commerce cross
Borders we too deftly idolise.
Did the world explorers opened up
Sanction variation and new greed?
Images of humankind as one
Slowly melt into new nation-states:
England, the United States and France,
Where a revolution overthrew
Unacceptable regimes to start
Nations who now share one law and lore,
Fusing territories in one name,
Finding or creating common ground
To suppress enough of local pride
And in spite of difference fly one flag.

What of Germany so splintered still?
Feudal states and minor monarchies
Freeze Westphalia's brokered peace until
One ambitious Prussian gathers them.

No romantic Garibaldi or
Grassroots claiming here Paine's rights of man—
Bismarck rules by iron and by blood.

Spleen and anger drove him all his life.
Did his icy mother make him so,
Or a too weak father that he hates?
Thirty-eight strong years his will holds sway,
Though childhood's same triangle traps his mind:
Cold-veined queen whose mild king's will he bends—
As long as Wilhelm backs him he will rule.

He's a restless *Junker* Prussian squire
Steeped in Burke's belief in land and soil.
Europe's Jewry with their bull and bear
Turn their lives into commodities.
Prussia must take over Germany.
Nation, yes, but no democracy.
Semi-absolute the king lets him
Hold his power to hold the status quo,
Boasting how he knows he beat them all.

> *Chess my image; I could think ahead*
> *Working combinations as I keep*
> *Options open, moving as needs be.*
> *Others have their loyalties. I've none.*
> *All that suits my purposes I do.*
> *Pietists who launched me I discard.*
> *Jew boy Lasker and his liberals*
> *I abhor and yet to outsmart them*
> *I embrace the socialist Lassalle—*
> *Although he's of the tribe he serves me well.*
> *Catholics I loathe but treat with them;*
> *I inveigle popes to cause a split*
> *When their votes are crucial to my cause.*
> *Outflanking socialists I introduce*
> *Welfare, care for old or sick or maimed.*
> *Universal suffrage I will spring*
> *To acquire the votes I need but then*
> *I had hoped to end that right again.*
> *Goodness that I do, I do for power.*

All mistakes he must at once deny,
Lie or weave but never take the blame.
He charms, cajoles, he browbeats and he plots,
He huffs and puffs and threatens to resign,
Wreaks revenge on all who stymie him.
Thwarted he'll fall ill at once and moan.
Every friend he ever had he'll lose;
Even his son Herbert's love he'll crush—
Too involved with enemies of his.

> *Fichte dreamt of Germans as one land.*
> *Choose* Kleindeutsch, *leave Austria aside.*
> *Playing foreign chess boards I keep cool,*
> *Using fear to make all serve my ends.*

To unite three dozen states he sparks
Three false wars and spills the blood of pawns;
Moltke and *Die Kriegsakademie,*
Railways and swift telegraphs the key;
Holstein and Schleswig from the Danish war
Fought with Austria whom he turns on.

> *Seven weeks and I defeated them—*
> *France and Russia were well mollified.*
> *Wilhelm's cousin chosen king of Spain*
> *Means that France feels threatened; I contrive*
> *War to stir all states of Germany*
> *And claim Alsace Lorraine as ours.*
> *Prussians dominate but we are one.*

Once hated Bismarck he will now become—
Though he'd barely served in the reserve—
Helmeted, severe cuirassier,
Icon of all-powerful Germany.

> *How I play the diplomatic game,*
> *Watching for this Germany of mine!*
> *All Europe holds its breath from threat to threat;*
> *Balances of fear ally and re-ally,*
> *Keep the peace until I fall from grace.*
> *Wilhelm and his son have died and I,*
> *Fired by Kaiser Friedrich, stew in ire.*

Still quick-witted I ply my bitter tongue,
Vent my rage on all who thwarted me.
I send my king still semi-absolute
Swaying towards a troubled century.

Would a slow confederation come?
Did it take a despot's heavy fist?
Iron wills invite a counterwill
Or create a spirit far too numbed
To allow a country to unite,
Choosing to combine in trust not fear,
Growing like Swiss cantons that retain
Local pride, a sense of sovereignty,
A people ruled too long by one man's will
Lose unused desires to rule themselves.
The light is bright where we must choose;
Cozier inside the despot's womb.
Bismarck's legacy a woeful myth
Of innately genius statesmen who
Mastermind and shape a nation's will.
While *der Kanzler* played his clever chess
Germany's economy has boomed:
Mines, mills, railways, telephones;
Thriving, wealthy, well surplussed in trade,
Matchless itching Prussian war machine;
And all still governed by its Junker squires,
Swaggering and still desirous of
Lebensraum where might is always right,
Grudging both modernity and Jews,
Spreading hate among the bourgeoisie.
Europe's locked in grids of nationhood.
Germany begins its slide to hell.

(iv)

Histories of top and underdog—
Why this human need to dominate?
Call it by whatever name we will:
Empire, colony, protectorate,
Rome or Turk, or Spain's conquistador.
Must we rule what we don't understand—

Driven by a dread of difference,
Fear of all we name barbarians,
Strangers in their speech and in their gods?
Maybe to dispel our fear we demonise
Others, sure that we are worthier
And as such are bound to conquer them.
Yet our civilising missions merge
With rapacity to justify
Plundering resources we desire.
Europe's nation-states now vie for power,
Scrambling colonies in Africa.

All now see the conquering hero come,
One cold determined Cecil Rhodes
Whose boyhood motto is "to do or die,"
Sickly parson's son who for his health
Is despatched to southern Africa
Where his elder brother Herbert digs
Diamond claims before he'll turn to gold.
Darwin had put paid to God, though he'd
Give a deity a sporting chance;
Yet his nature still demanded dreams
To instil some meaning in his life.
Kipling asks "If you can trust yourself,"
Elgar's *Land of Hope and Glory* calls.
Empires need their heroes and Rhodes knows
Anglo-Saxons are the only race
Who'll civilise the world. To spread their power
Serves this earth of ours as best we can.
Rhodes desires to paint the world map red.

> *Call me ruthless if you will, I serve*
> *Empire. Among the fights and feuds of digs*
> *I amass a fortune merging claims.*
> *Natives steal—we strip them when we search—*
> *Though they swallow diamonds we will purge*
> *Random workers whom we quarantine,*
> *Padlocking them in mittens to be sure.*
> *My De Beers becomes the diamond king;*
> *Money is the key to power I want*
> *For my dreams and straddle Africa.*

Loner, buttoned-up misogynist,
Awkward when just wishing friends good night—
Feelings Cecil pours into his dreams.
Each return to Britain leaves him bored
But in the Cape again he's thinking big;
People must fit into larger plans,
He only sees the woods and not the trees.

> Fair or foul, two things I want to merge:
> Diamond trade, South Africa itself.
> Life for me is brief; I dream up trains
> Running right from Cairo to the Cape.
> Portugal is pressing from the east,
> Germans from the west, but red must spread
> North to annex Matabeleland.
> Lobengula, warrior king, we'll lure
> To concede his country's mining rights.
> I persuade and play each party off;
> London grants charters, though we cheat
> Overstating what both granted us—
> Empire and commercial interest meld.
> Matabeleland we now invade.

Volunteers stake out the stolen land—
Dispossessed the Ndebele told
Not to trespass on what's white man's soil.
Rhodes doles out rich land to favoured youths.
Lobengula's herds are spoils of war;
Boundaries vague, all livestock loot,
Cattle hustlers raid Ndebele *kraals*.
Shona from Shonaland join in
Robbing back what Ndebele robbed.
Priests stir up their people to rebel;
At secluded farms or trading stores
Sudden massacres of whites occur.
Rhodes obsessed now wants to teach
Natives to behave, tells his officers
"Show no mercy, just kill all you can."
Ndebele flee to hide in caves.
Lobengula either killed himself
Or submitted to a broken heart.

When the Shona too start to rebel,
Fearing the political fallout,
Rhodes persuades this people to make peace,
Promising new native settlements.
Matabeleland, Mashonaland
Merge in one new country painted red,
Named Rhodesia after Cecil Rhodes.

> *Heart attacks I suffered all my life.*
> *Faithful to my childhood motto I*
> *Did before I died and used my wealth*
> *To extend Victoria's domains,*
> *Drive her empire north through Africa.*
> *Bury me on top of Matopos,*
> *No date or detail on my tomb's brass plate.*
> *Rhodesia is forever etched in red.*

Immense and brooding spirit, Kipling writes.
Empires and their colonies will fade;
Over fifty years by blood or peace,
One by one each country claims its myth,
As Zimbabwe ousts the name of Rhodes.
Nothing ever is as it once was;
Psyches scarred will never fully heal
Or ever compensate by looking back,
Wondering how it should or might have been
If the greed of empire and of power
Hadn't maimed a people's slower growth,
Conjuring some older golden dreams
Once upon a time before conquest.
Now is now and new hybridities
Mix and match beyond old boundaries,
Glorying in a living mongrelhood.

(v)

Surely all can share creation's goods—
But beaten down how could the beaten think?
Still in pits and sweating cotton mills,
Dockyards, print shops, toxic factories,
Dreams of better worlds keep bubbling up.

Secret mangered scriptures of the poor
Cry among the one-room cottagers:
Craving still Christ's sermon on the mount.
Who's the prophet who will stand alone?

James Keir Hardie, once a baker's boy,
Whom his pious praying boss had fired
Turns unheard and empty-handed home.
Miner, messenger, trade unionist,
Lifelong player playing against the odds
Siding with outsiders like his Christ
Mocked, reviled for being far ahead:
Asking for an eight-hour working day,
Houses built for workers' families,
Voting rights for adults everywhere,
Pay for members of the parliament
So the trodden down can also stand.

> *Although I started work when I was eight,*
> *I learn to read and teach myself*
> *Robbie Burns' songs I love to sing,*
> *Shorthand too I master, schooled at night.*
> *Carlyle shows how futile war can be,*
> *How somehow hero figures must emerge*
> *Who'll transform society. I read*
> *John Stuart Mill, John Ruskin, Henry George.*
> *Marx I study, know his Eleanor,*
> *Though she and Engels disapprove of me,*
> *Sneering at my lack of theory.*
> *Life has turned me socialist and all*
> *Poverty and hardship move my heart.*
> *Most of all my mother shaped my thought—*
> *Faces of thrifty wives who toil*
> *Dawn to dusk for those they love acquire*
> *Dignity that's sweet beyond belief.*

Temperance movements educated him
Teaching him to speak, campaign, debate.
There, though atheist by birth, he turns
Christian and demands now women's rights.

Soon New Unionism engages him.
Far too long trade unionists consort
With their bosses and forget their own.
Keir supports the suffragettes and twice
He'll oppose our wars where young and poor
Always pay with lives they never live.

> Though my wife and children almost starve,
> Time and time again I will refuse
> Blandishments, safe seats or bribes.
> Once an MP I must stand alone
> Badgering a government in vain,
> Yet I help to raise a consciousness
> Of so much that in good time prevails.
> Socialism's not arithmetic
> Or just an economic system shift—
> It's our highest inspiration's goal,
> Fraternity we'll build on justice won.

Yet so many whited sepulchres!
Noted for his gifts to charities
Rutherglen's Lord Overtoun, a strong
Advocate of keeping Sabbath days,
Supporter of all Christian mission work,
Makes the workers in his factories
Toil twelve hours a day without food breaks
Seven days a week and docks the wage
Even of his Sunday absentees—
Again a dainty-eating praying boss,
Many kneel before the bad thief's cross.

> As most through schooling learn to read,
> Let me be an agitator whose
> Words may help to educate the mass,
> Six thousand miles I clock one year by rail
> Stirring discontent at so much wrong.
> Touring India I turned my mind
> To the ways an empire undermines
> Cultures we exploited from sheer greed.
> So begins a process that two wars
> Later will unredden our world map.

Change comes slowly yet it comes.
Fabians' well-meaning middle class
Shun extremes the Marxists all embrace.
Always wary lest the Liberals steal
Labour's clothes, outlefting their reforms,
Keir defends his party pointing out
Liberals were still a moneyed class.
Flexible he fights the Marxists who
Wanted only socialists and takes in
Middle-classers willing to muck in.
Trade unionists who join need not subscribe
To full-blooded socialism, instead
Better swell the ranks and when in power
Right in stages all the wrongs of years.
Strategist extraordinary Keir,
Bit by bit by party politics
Brings the mother of all parliaments
Slowly to embrace a fairer deal.

Could the greater world now follow suit?
Dreams of heaven justifying hell,
Now the bloodiest of centuries
When each ism will shortcut history,
Sacrificing lives for what's to come
Offered on the altar of such dreams
Turning into nightmares of brute power.
Fear ideas that outreach the heart,
Chilled compassion of the ideologue.
What purports to pity broken lives
Often hides a know-all arrogance
That wants to own the future and the past,
So refuses starting from the now.
Greedy for the perfect all create
Hells of blood and soil and golden age.

Canto 3
Power

Every growth demands a patient mind.
Systems at their edges sometimes fray
When preparing for another stage,
Loosening up to gain complexity.
Instability can indicate
Readiness to change, and sometimes then
Cores can complicate a leap to growth.

Shaped by mother Russia of extremes
Where ukase still rules and serfs obey,
Large as life a boisterous anarchist
Bent on wiping out each government,
Here's Bakunin battering the world.
All creation is a tearing down
To rebuild anew from bottom up.
Though beginning as an officer
In artillery, Bakunin turns
Europe's grand ideologue who will,
Wearied of his struggle to destroy,
Die in Switzerland at sixty-two.

Easy to explain by this or that:
Coldness in his mother, rambunctious genes
Or real grieving for the plight of serfs
Fused with fashion's thoughts of change and need;
Hegel's thesis and antithesis
Melding in a synthesis, yet this
Asks for patience that Bakunin lacks;
For him it's all or nothing now.

> When a duty and a freedom clash,
> Freedom is the only choice to make;
> Our existence is as much about
> Struggle and conflict as harmony.
> How ironic that while still a youth
> I'd once branded General Lafayette
> As a spirit of destruction who

> Stirred up revolutions both in France
> And America, though now I pledge
> All my life to overthrowing power.
> Trust the eternal spirit which destroys,
> Turn all the crosses into revolt's swords.
> Passion for destruction will create
> All we cannot plan or even guess.

Brussels, so fleeing on to France,
Paris Révolution de Février,
Köthen, Poznan, Dresden, onto Chemnitz
Then arrested, sent to face the Tsar.
Death repealed, instead Siberia.
Later an escape: Japan, New York,
Sailing back to London to recharge.

> Saint-Simon I despise and Robert Owen—
> Doctrinaire, they'd soon impose their will.
> I'd abolish states and parliaments,
> I've no belief in constitutions, laws,
> Give me spirit and vitality,
> Lawless worlds where everyone is free.
> Marx in love with theory supports
> Much that I'd obliterate because,
> Sure in time the system will implode,
> He can wait and watch it self-destruct.
> I have no taste for dogged theory
> And desire the thrill of barricades.
> Even in the face of failure I
> Love a people in defiant mood
> When resplendent stars of their revolts
> Rise to heavens from an ocean's blood,
> Lodestars for a free humanity.

Clearly given such a privileged youth,
Is Bakunin preaching from above?
Trusting people's instinct for revolt
He refuses any perfect scheme.
Maybe some communes might even form,
Then confederations of communes
Schooling everyone from every class
Dreaming up collective government.

Surely God's the ultimate top-down.
Let us shed divine morality
Based on two immoral principles:
Yielding too much to authority
And contempt for our humanity.
All religion's fog we must dispel.
Jews produce a Marx but on the whole
They exploit the labour not their own.
Class divisions hang on ownership;
Slaves are those who don't possess their work.

Some ideologues with age lose touch.
Russia's younger underground called Hell
Live ascetic lives as they espouse
Terrorism and Karakozov who
Tries to kill Russia's tsar is hanged.
Though Bakunin owns that such is risk,
Still his instincts cannot throw a stone.

Never best and brightest ruling us—
It's the mediocre push themselves,
A minority controlling all.
Fit to choose, then why not rule yourself?
Though I'm a Russian nobleman's offspring,
I became a revolutionary,
Happiest when at the barricades.
Life's not shaped or fixed by consciousness,
Consciousness itself determines life.

Too many sailors and the ship ascends
Mountain tops. With no one at the helm
How could the freest ship hold course;
Every ship is steered if it's to sail,
Skippers know the loneliness of care
But Bakunin shirked his tiller turn—
Always in a netherworld that chides,
Like Turgenev's Rudin wandering on,
Floating in a permanent teenage.

Yet Bakunin never could learn how
Top-down and bottom-up can both combine.
Always freedom from and never for,

Irresponsibility can lead
Many hothead Karakozovs along
Primrose paths of arrogance to hell.

(ii)

Hell keeps spiralling deep and down—
What was always here becomes more so.
Jugashvilli when still young had shown
Boyhood signs that Stalin will fulfil:
Diligent at school but on the street
Jealous of the leader of his gang.
Although his pious mother coddles him
Pockmarked son and dreamed-of priest,
Shy and volatile resentful boy,
Beaten by his father randomly,
Georgian bandits he'd seen hanged imprint
Violence so deeply on his mind.
First a seminarian rebels,
Georgian poet patriot who'll turn
Marxist diehard under Lenin's spell.
In and out of jail he'll organise;
Fellow prisoners see a misanthrope,
Loner with a strange and nasty streak.

> I could never be a Menchevik;
> Lenin knew we need dictatorship.
> Bolshevists are realists and keep
> Tight control and secrets underground.
> Do not blame my cobbler father for
> Anger he instilled in me. I knew
> Factories and understood his rage.
> As a boy when dancing lekuri
> I had dead legged all who outdanced me.
> Violence remains the tool I'll use—
> Might for me will be the only right.
> Disciplined and doctrinaire in all,
> Power we Bolsheviks must centralise.
>
> Our October revolution steals
> Any middle ground with liberals,

Toppling every compromise for good;
Communists become the ruling few.
Poor inherit ruthlessly the earth,
Millions dying for the age to come.
State and party fuse now into one
To achieve a higher human plane.

Joseph Stalin now whom Lenin names
Commissar for nationalities
Soon declares all people free to thrive
Till beyond control he'll rein them in.
Still outsider insecure, he'll prove
More imperial than any tsar.
Politburo members vie for power;
Lenin, Trotsky, Stalin, Bubnov, all
Jockeying to rule the Soviet roost.
Kamenev, Zinoviev gang up—
They and Stalin now the three who wait
To become the party's number one
Soon after Lenin is embalmed.

Threats were everywhere about. We fight
Off white armies to maintain our state
And I held my front against the fiercest odds,
Sacrificed my soldiers for the cause—
Men don't count on altars of success.
Menaced by Western Europe's power,
Lenin made his peace with Germany;
In the east Japan is eyeing us.
Yes, in time we'll communise the world;
Now we are a sign of what's to come.
Nations on our fringe still jeopardise
Strict control; reactionaries too
Wait to undermine the state we build.
Politburo members underrate
My ambition. Though no orator,
Machiavelli's Prince I have absorbed
And Ivan the Terrible's my saint.
Party secretary, I acquire
Power as in the long grass I'll await
Sweet revenge on all who once mocked me.

The kulaks whom Lenin early on had called
Vampires, plunderers and profiteers,
Stalin names a liquidated class.
Millions shot or sent to labour camps
Clear the way for new collective farms.
Heavy industry and overnight,
Whatever means so long as it's attained;
Russia's empire struts a modern stage.

> *No, we do not ape the Western world.*
> *Modernity for us will have no waste,*
> *Communism usurps a Christian past—*
> *Why should people need an opiate?*
> *Let humanity evolve to reach*
> *Further phases of development—*
> *Food and shelter, school and work for all.*
> *Art and science we must carefully watch,*
> *Intellectuals should toe the line.*
> *If I sense I've somehow gone too far,*
> *All who did my bidding I'll have shot.*
> *Cost what it may cost I must succeed.*

World War Two and though he'd signed a pact
To maintain his peace with Germany,
Herr Hitler's Barbarossa breaks his word.
Nazis sweep through Russia and now seem
Ready to wipe out the Soviet world.
The Esperanto Stalin once embraced,
The rootlessness of communism submits
To profounder loves of blood and soil.
Only mother Russia's cry inspires
Soviets to hold world-conquering führer back.
Five months at Stalingrad, the namesake place,
Bombardments and fighting street by street,
Blood-most battle of our history,
Till outflanked the hungry Germans yield.
Lenin dreamed a root-free communism—
Cynic Stalin's Georgian instinct knew
Deeper than abstractions of our class,
Love of habitat can swell our veins.
Turning point. Slowly now let Zhukov

Drive through Eastern Europe to redeem
Countries from the Axis powers to reach
Berlin in advance of U.S. troops,
Nail all Eastern states as satellites.
Zhukov's feted then obscured and half
The returning soldiers jailed or shot—
Stalin fears that having been abroad
They'd contaminate the Soviet state.

Generalissimus's cold war starts.
Coexistence, A-bombs on both sides,
Though both parties fell one side must win.
Back the Iron Curtain show trials rage,
Purges of landlords and businessmen;
Mandelstam and Babel Gulaged north,
Kamenev, Zinoviev both shot,
Trotsky axed to death in Mexico.

> *Apparatchiks I reward but high*
> *Office holders I will hire then fire.*
> *Toying with their jealousies I sow*
> *Rivalries so am arbiter for them.*
> *I imprison loved ones on a whim*
> *Keeping all around me on their toes,*
> *Building up my pets to throw them down.*
> *Flux and vagueness feed the fear I need.*
> *No one grasps the levers of my power.*

Russia's fabric torn beyond what mends,
Even when he makes his half-retreats
Downward spirals inward and around,
Sink and sink and double on themselves.
Lonely emperor befriending cooks,
Even joking with his bodyguards,
Seeks out boyhood pals to sing church hymns.
Both wives dead. The second shot herself.
One son's dead, the other drinks through life
And, Svetlana, his one daughter's life's a mess.
Seminarian become so doctrinaire
Stalin's father bullies all his life,
Reaching out beyond the tsar's empire.

Fearing to disturb the sleeping giant
Guards find him dying, stricken and alone.

Buffer states outdated by missiles;
Boundaries don't respect the broadcast wave,
Western clothes and music still seep in.
Mindless of the blood and bone it cost,
Stalin's shut-up system somehow leaks.
Though his Russia's now a superpower,
Left alone, unable to adapt,
Apathy and dissidence abound.
Hell's a closing-off of otherness.

(iii)

Time and time again some innate urge
Flutters in the veins of history:
Hallowed soil and sacred memories,
Battle heroes, names our hearts revere,
Lives sacrificed and woven into ours,
Wrongs once done that bind us still as one,
Comforts of belonging we assume
Suddenly defined against all those
Who in their differences menace us,
Feelings more in blood than in our brain
Of boundedness that stir us to ward off
Nervous threats of strangers' otherness,
Flags and anthems of ourselves alone
Drumming every age and dreaming youth.

> *Heil! my German youth who represent—*
> *Each of you who's standing here today—*
> *What is happening throughout our Germany.*
> *You absorb the fatherland's desires*
> *And through you we are ein Reich, ein Volk.*
> *Never soft but hard you'll steel yourselves,*
> *Never fall apart. For peace but strong,*
> *Trained, obedient to self-sacrifice.*
> *Flesh of flesh and blood of our own blood,*
> *Germany won't pass but living on,*
> *The flag we tore from nothing you must hold,*
> *Meine deutsche Jugend, in your fists. . . .*

Heil der Führer! Moody as a boy,
Father-troubled he would row at school,
Ill at ease with all authority,
Would-be monk, then watercolourist.
Viennese bohemian he'll sponge
Pan-Germanic fears the mayor had fanned—
Jews from Eastern Europe crowding in
Might dilute the purer German blood.

World War One and on the Western Front
Hitler's Iron Cross for bravery;
Stabbed in their still-undefeated back
By submissive Marxists who sell out,
Loving war he's angry when it ends.
Austrian outsider he'll bestride
Lost and broken Germany's revenge.
Hitler flounders into politics.

> *I have come up from the German folk.*
> *Slowly over fifteen years both I*
> *And my movement made our fateful way.*
> *No one sets me up above* das Volk.
> *From the people I have grown and I*
> *Have remained with them and to them yet*
> *I'll return. Since I aspire to know*
> *Not one single statesman in the world*
> *Could have had a greater right than I*
> *To declare he represents* das Volk.

Every meeting now a liturgy
Where *der Führer* and the mass perform.
Crowds cheer loudly and salute *Sieg heil!*
Secret fears and hates he names for them,
Sees their need and sense of history,
And picks scapegoats to unify their minds.
Rules of law and principles are sham,
Mere form and dull consistency;
No scruples now or any moral code,
Knowing with the heart can sanction all.
Erlebnis is what counts, heroic will,
Any sacrifice life needs you make.

Master races boast vitality,
Courage and decisiveness prevail.
When Hitler and his crowds agree,
Fate and history salute the Reich.

German soil was well prepared for this.
Nature the Romantics so revered,
Raw in tooth and claw it will in turn
Always have its way—the fittest thrive;
Societies reflect all nature's force.

> Just as individuals are steered
> By the laws of sickness and of health,
> Nations, races, cultures, continents
> Follow rules of strength and malady;
> States must be an artificial means
> To an end and nations are that end.
> Wagner music spellbinds me when young—
> I absorb the world of Schopenhauer
> And know of Nietzsche's will to power.

Nature's force the party supplements,
Bullying opponents into line.
Terror reigns. An editor's arrest,
Blooded spectacles sent to his wife.
Searches door-to-door, resisters seized.
Fearing all who'd threaten Hitler's power,
Long-knives butcher SA's Röhm.
Purges, sudden round-ups, weedings out—
Wear swastika pins or else beware.
Rumours, hearsay of a nearby camp.
Neighbours now denounce from fear or greed;
Trust unhinged, the gates of Hell swing wide.

> Squeamish, I avoid most violence.
> Once I order death that is enough.
> I'm immortal and invincible—
> Stauffenberg's explosion misses me.
> His slow hanging I had filmed to watch
> Time and time again my sweet revenge.
> Bonhoeffer was hanged at Flossenbürg,

> *Some I'd strung by thin piano wire*
> *To delay a while their writhing deaths.*

Germany's enlightenment absorbed
What was once a tight community;
Europe's Jews are here so woven in.
Tolerance subsumes the immigrants
Who enrich the culture they adopt
In their long one-sided love affair.
When the Reich stirs hate to round them up
Only myths can lump the Bolsheviks
With scheming world financiers,
Fiats and laws alone can sieve them out.

> *I am certain now the Jews regret*
> *Not allowing me to paint for life!*
> *Every power needs real enemies.*
> *If we're superior it follows then*
> *Gypsies, Slavs, but most of all the Jews*
> *Taint our own authentic blood and seed.*
> *Feelings lead to riots but no more;*
> *Rational approaches best ensure*
> *Full elimination of all Jews*
> *Who through history have waged a war*
> *On our race with plagues and syphilis;*
> *Even will to power they would restrain—*
> *Conscience is a thing thought up by Jews.*

Killing off congenital disease
Aktion T4 was just a trial run.
Europe's foremost nation turns blind eyes
As good administrators start to plan
Yellow stars and chambered Zyklon B,
Timetabled trains with cattle cars for Jews.
Dachau, Flossenbürg or Buchenwald
All within the inner Reich's earshot—
Surely every German must have known?

Ruthless and both total commissars
Stalin and *der Führer* almost match,
Both dictators driven by their will,
Would-be artists, priests that might have been.

Yet for all its travesties at least
Communism began in sacred dreams
Rooted in beliefs that under God
All are equal in their dignity.
Fascists want no truck with equity,
Autarky best meets a nation's needs.
Once Il Duce's fan *der Führer* will
Soon outgrow his master in his hates.
Poland was expansion, France revenge;
Denmark, Norway, all Low Countries form
Bases for attack and Mussolini forced
Yugoslavia and Greece but then
Foolish Barbarossa's overstretch
Bares *der Führer*'s own destructive urge
To eliminate six million Jews.

Easy now to tell the way things went.
Yet, what if the will to power had won—
Blitz bombers might have taken Britain out,
Russia might have failed at Stalingrad,
The Manhattan Project lost the A-bomb race—
Knife-edge world of many might-have-beens
Can hear the fascist jackboots marching on.

Blood and soil outweigh all human love.
Götterdämmerung demands downfall.
First how many millions die before
Covering traces of the chambered camps
Germany concedes, as Hitler still
Bunkered in his own delusion's power
Shoots himself before the Russians come.

Fascists leave a nothingness behind.
Hell must be a bitter emptiness.

(iv)

Yes, democracy, but even so
Sometimes we elect an autocrat
Who, exploiting dreads and prejudice,
Seems to read the fears of everyone
And pledge returns to pasts that never were.

Queen of confrontation enter here,
Forthright Grantham grocer's girl,
Edgy loner anxious to succeed,
School miss always first to question guests,
Disciplined, determined and cocksure.
"Snobby Roberts" as she's called in class
Only socialised with those well off.
Bossy with her seamstress mother's voice,
Elocution leaves her sounding posh.
Heartened by a self-taught father who'd
Worked his way to buy two grocers' shops
And yet had always held his purse strings tight,
She'll gain her Oxford place in chemistry.

> Student years are lonely, insecure.
> If I'd been to Cheltenham, maybe
> Titled mothers might approve of me.
> Going down I have to look for work,
> Bide my time to be a candidate.
> Politics is everything to me.
> Though I have my suitors, in the end
> Denis Thatcher would accompany me.

Some who shin the tall and greasy pole
Carry in their bones a sympathy,
Want to spare all comers such a climb;
Others vaunt their courage and condemn
Weakness they had fought to overcome,
See all frailness as a threat to power.

> I have grit and drive in this male world.
> I have to charm, to bully and browbeat,
> Stand and stand again to garner votes.
> Mother of my twins I study law,
> Travel countrywide to make my mark.
> I get nothing on a plate and know
> Everything demands get up and go—
> All should stand like me on their own feet.

Icy and competitive she riles
Her contemporaries, can't care less.
Shrill M.P. so full of certitude,

She disputes and argues on her feet;
Elder Tories notice her aplomb.
Ravenous for power she'll sacrifice
Family or friends. Ambition drives
Bright but shallow minds as though
Power itself must wait to find its cause.

First Macmillan's pension's minister,
Then supporting Heath she will become
Education secretary who'll
Irk co-ministers and irritate
Bureaucrats she'll hector and abuse,
Trying to restore old grammar schools.
Shamed for stopping milk allowances,
She recovers boosting nursery care
Or by mustering extra teachers in.
Public bête noire or heroine—
Thatcher has become a household name.

> Student unions' funds I would have cut—
> Leftist protests put an end to that;
> I'd have backed a miners' three-day week.
> Still I toe the line, a European
> I declare that France is no less French,
> Holland no less Dutch and we have much
> To contribute. Though to the end I praise
> Heath, I think he'd always compromise.
> Britain's winter strikes leave him undone.

Late candidate, once secret agent Neave
Steers her in as leader after Heath.
Demagogue who'll read the middle class,
Lone and friendless she begins to trust
Younger image-makers for advice.
Grantham turns to grandeur and to pride;
Thatcher will become a Thatcherite.

> Eager now before all history's bar,
> I am prompted by Keith Joseph's words
> To rethink all in Milton Friedman's mode.
> I become a monetarist who'll break
> Union power, refuse all Brussels rule.

> *I will harass, cajole, berate, persuade*
> *All and sundry till I get my way.*

Needs of course demand new ways but yet
Time and circumstance bring out in her
Sides that are so narrow, shrill and smug.
Closefisted daughter of her father's shop
Half-awake at night when Germans bombed
She can really only ever trust
Those with English as their mother tongue.
Uncle Sam is fine but not the Hun.

Faltering start but once in No. 10
For eleven years she'll domineer.
Thatcher's cure-all lets the market rule.
Free-for-all, deregulate finance,
Privatise all state-owned companies;
Step by step destroy the unions' power.
All in freedom's name she will curtail
Fellowship that can liaise between
Individual and state affairs.
Self-help the word and unemployment soars.
So unpopular it takes the Falklands War
To retain her hold on Downing Street.

> *I'll be pleasant if I get my way.*
> *All settlements are only wooliness.*
> *Never trust a burglar once he steals.*
> *Absolutely no! The fleet sails on.*
> *I am not for turning. No means no.*

Britain hadn't tended to the signs—
It's war that never should begin.
Margaret is playing Churchill's ghost,
Swept back into power on jingo waves.

Steel employees' strike is met head on.
British Airways and Rolls-Royce sold off.
Scargill's hasty miners' strike then plays
Into her hands and sees their union crushed.
Thatcher has become a way of life—
Morals now the ledger's bottom line.

Reagan too sees eye-to-eye and so
Thatcherism will spread across the world.

> Society is individual
> Men and women and their families,
> Private property and personal choice—
> Each must take responsibility.
> Economics are of course the way
> We can strive to change the human soul.

Listening less and less to her colleagues,
All who disagree she'll brand as wets.
She demands, insults, interrogates.
Rancour in her third-term cabinet grows.
Shuffling her frontbenchers once again,
Thatcher's ousted for the heir she chose.

Lifelong bearer of each bitter grudge,
Baroness of anger in the Lords
Plots to undermine and seek revenge,
Loathes the heir she finds she didn't know.
Forgiveness she admits is not for her.

Though she rages still her mark remains—
Many souls absorb the change she wrought.
Lost the value now we know the price
Instead the disciplines of marketplace.
Contracts yes, but little covenant
Where relationships lay down the law.
Greed and gluttony trust Adam's hand,
If all bonds are broken by distrust.
Society's love-ravelled fabric torn,
Self-interest is a lonely underworld.

(v)

We are meaning seekers who desire
Broader narratives where we can find
How our earthly sojourn somehow counts.
In a time we name eternity
We weave the fabric we are woven in,
Tell our sacred stories to retrace

Threads of memory which we hallow still
By adapting what was once to now,
Blessing life's own open-endedness.
Some responding to a fear or need
Cling to older certainties, insist
Once is now the same once and for all.
To improvise implies too great a risk,
Better so by far to tie things down;
God becomes their well-tamed golden calf.
Corruption of what's best is always worst.

What is it that so closes down a mind?
Once Bin Laden was a pious boy.
Did his father's death when nine leave him
Prey to father figures through his life?
Could a billionaire who'd built great mosques
And had fathered fifty-four in all
Really lavish time on one young son
By an unimportant lower wife?
Though he's rich Osama chose to shun
Playboy lives his brothers had espoused.
Shy and six foot tall he will maintain
Just four wives the Prophet had prescribed—
No divorce to get around the law.

> Any Muslim of my time must face
> This dilemma: how we modernise,
> Make our own of all technology,
> Yet not lose our Arab sense of self,
> Fuse what's Arab and American.
> Boarding school in Lebanon apart,
> I am educated here at home
> And am bright enough at school but still
> Lack the drive to finish my degree.
>
> First a teacher, come from Syria,
> Proves to me how we must now return
> To the ways we Muslims knew as ours,
> Merge religion with our politics.
> I refuse to watch all films and shun
> Music—both are haram (even though

I indulge my children's youthful tastes).
I have read Sayyid Qtub's Milestone
And already grown my full-length beard.
I become a zealous Islamist.

There're two father figures yet to come.
Azzam, global father of jihad
Urges him to help to fund the war
Which Afghans now wage against the odds
To evict the Soviets. Once there,
He assembles his own Arab squad
To combat the godless Communists.
Arab confidence is low. Defeat
In the Six-Day War had humbled them.
Sympathy among inhabitants
Plus guerilla-friendly territory
And resources sent through Pakistan
From the Saudis and from Uncle Sam
Finally defeat the Soviets.
Here's his chance to play at holy war;
But unskilled his squad's effect is slight,
Yet enough to launch Bin Laden's myth.
In Afghanistan in turn he'll meet
Fatal father figure number four:
Ayman al-Zawahiri, who divides
All the world in two: the infidels
And Islam as both are locked in war,
Mujahidin hate Crusaders, Jews.
Our whole region mimics Palestine—
Zionist America desires
Greater Israel in the Middle East.
Oneness, prayer with fasting, haji, alms
Pillar our Islam but now a sixth—
God is punishing our straying ways,
So jihad's a sacred duty too.

We have learned how in Afghanistan
Superpowers were brittler than we thought;
Like the U.S. leaving Vietnam
Beaten Soviets depart Kabul.
Look at how the mighty Satan quit

Bullying Somalia and fled.
Civil war for four years then before

Newly installed Taliban take power,
When Afghans face their puritan regime
Under Omar's strict Sharia law—
Women wearing burqas, men their beards.
Back at home Bin Laden's squad becomes
What in time will be al-Qaeda's men.
Growing messianic now he's sure
Allah's calling him for his jihad
To rid the Arab lands of infidel.
Slowly now Bin Laden will believe
His compatriot the Saudi king,
Like Egypt's rulers, is the foe within.
So apostate Muslims must be fought.
Arab streets believe his growing myth—
Hero to his own, a dread elsewhere.
As al-Qaeda grows and spreads its cells
Worldwide. Tens of thousands pass through camps
Trained as terrorists, a networked threat
Linking up across the Internet,
Both trained and local volunteers,
Extremists ready to attack
All apostate Muslim countries backed
By the U.S. and its allied states.

When Hussein invades Kuwait I would
Raise an army that could drive him out,
But instead my king took U.S. aid.
I removed my household to Sudan.
Zawahiri's al-Jihad now joins
With al-Qaeda. Democracy
Sins by giving people rights instead
Of allowing Allah's rule and so
Civilians who have voted we can kill.
Let deception too become a tool—
Furthering the cause we too must lie.
In Sudan I ran my business, am
Popular until I'm pressured out
Hightailing it back to Afghanistan.

Watching towers in Lebanon that fell
I dreamed up my vengeance in New York.

U.S. embassies are now fair game.
Suddenly four hijacked planes attack,
Levelling New York's two symbolic towers
Twins of trade, a city's beating heart—
9/11 when three thousand die.
Terror in Bali and in Istanbul,
Bombs exploded on a Madrid train,
Then a blast in London's underground.
Now Bin Laden's riding high and hopes
To involve the U.S. in a war,
Lead them to another Vietnam,
Wear them down within Afghanistan.

Three American regimes will try
To kill him or to capture him alive.
Just a decade after the Twin Towers
U.S. Seals will shoot him in his lair.

How is it that a pious Muslim boy
Step by step can come to contradict
Years of mores when jihad had meant
Struggling in defence or even more
Striving with oneself so not to sin?
Fundamentalists of every faith
Own the God they say they kill to serve.
Corruption of what's best is always worst.
Angel Lucifer once fell to hell.

Canto 4
Breaking Ground

(i)

Eight years of age and all agog I watch
Union guards march through Augusta's streets
The Confederation's president—
War has stained my boyhood's memory.

Small and frail and hypersensitive
Son (and grandson) of a minister,
Whose assemblies welcomed blacks to pray
From their balconies but not the nave,
Tommy Woodrow Wilson, southerner
Scarred by civil war his childhood saw,
Makes up constitutions for dream worlds
Childhood reveries in him demand.

> *Slow to read I learned to learn by heart;*
> *Shaping sentences I will become*
> *Orator extraordinaire who'll mix*
> *Rhetoric with reason fired by zeal.*
> *Mesmerised by Gladstone who like me*
> *Came from Scottish Presbyterians*
> *To become the statesman of all time.*

Princeton student, star at history
He absorbs John Bright and Edmund Burke—
Politics require morality,
People need economies that work.
Anglophile young Wilson is convinced
English government is surely best.
Friendships bloom, this ardent student thrives:
Sport, debates, societies he'll found
Whose constitutions he designs with care.

After college he's some years at sea.
Let a decade pass: two graduate schools,
Then one brief and boring law career.
Fervent suitor showering billets-doux
He has married Ellen, wife and muse,
Bearer of the daughters he'll adore.
Finally he's settling back to teach
At his alma mater Princeton, which
Now still maintains a kind of country club,
Playground for the Gilded Age's sons.

> *I still miss my heart's own first desire.*
> *Where is the statesman who I once would be?*
> *Yet I'll be content if I inspire*
> *Youth to learn to read the past into*

How in turn we live our present lives.
History is not remembering
All that happened, rather it's to find
Where we might be headed here and now.

Wilson throws himself into his work;
Book by book his reputation grows;
Lecture theatres fill to hear him teach.
Soon involved with every side of life,
Coaching teams, committees, he becomes
Leader and their chosen president
Who'll in time transform this country club
So it earns its academic spurs.
Twenty years and twenty books that delve
Parliamentary systems to replace
Congress, histories and types of states
Till New Jersey's party bosses choose
Wilson as their puppet governor.

Nations need enlightened men to take
Charge not of our fortunes but our lives—
We should live by poems not by prose.
All these years I have prepared myself
To accomplish real tasks and change,
Take the flutter from my restless soul.
Once elected I'm no party pawn;
I strive to make this state a better place.
I reform child labour laws, curtail
Women's weekly hours, reorganise
Boards, appoint the first Supreme Court Jew.

Fifty-three years old this pedagogue
Plunges into public life and thrives.
Soon he's talked of as a candidate—
Two years later and he's president.
Promises fulfilled now law by law:
Tariffs giving way to income tax,
Stronger antitrust and federal laws
To ensure free enterprise for all,
Not allow the few to own all wealth;
Federal reserves fix interest rates.

Wilson gives his secretaries their heads.
Racists in his cabinet on their own
Segregate departments' staff by skin—
How could white women have a black as boss?
Wilson's southern soul capitulates;
On his watch the Jim Crow laws expand.

Eighteen months as president his wife,
Ellen, dies and zombielike he works
Till his second love again pursued
Ardently as thirty years ago—
Edith Galt will never leave his side.

> *History turns geopolitics.*
> *World War One and first I stand aside*
> *Dealing most with neighbour Mexico.*
> *I believe the days of conquest gone;*
> *Though great powers once ate up small states,*
> *Nations can no longer war alone,*
> *Strife disrupts world equilibrium.*
> *We've become one nation's neighbourhood—*
> *Smaller nations share all rights with great.*
> *Armaments must be controlled by states.*
> *We must have some league of nations to*
> *Guarantee the boundaries of each.*
> *France and Britain plead with us to join;*
> *I hold fast to our neutrality—*
> *Childhood showed me war and aftermath,*
> *It's as much a shame to rush as shirk.*
> *Better yet to broker peace abroad.*
> *German U-boats sink our U.S. ships.*
> *Though I'm re-elected president*
> *Owing to my stance against the war,*
> *I'll admit the German submarines*
> *Leave no choice and so we must declare*
> *War against autocracy for good.*

In this war where all romance has choked,
War of shrapnel, trench foot, shell shock, gas,
Where some eighteen million worldwide die,
U.S. soldiers tip a balanced scale.

While decisive and adroit as chief
Thoughts of doughboys' deaths still haunt his mind
As he allows his cabinet free rein
Curbing speech, repressing dissidents.
Other powers expect their post-war spoils.
Still belief in Providence drives dreams,
New world orders, covenantal peace.
Childhood's love of constitutions drafts
Fourteen points to found a nations' league.

Never did a man so look the part:
Elegant profile and courtly mien,
Cultured, well read and above reproach,
All the world applauds this president
Sailing east to broker post-war peace.
Paris's world conference awaits.
Kaiser Wilhelm has had to abdicate;
Three more empires too are lost:
Hapsburgs, Ottoman and Romanov.
Never did the world expect so much.

> Clemenceau, our host, just wants revenge
> Petulant Orlando huffs and puffs
> And Lloyd George is oily as an eel.
> Since I know the U.S. saved the day
> I persuade the Powers to take my points.
> Mandates we rename the colonies
> Germany has lost and though they claim
> Otherwise, still not a lot has changed.
> I demand and Clemenceau agrees
> Then rows back to where our talk began.
> Secret treaties made throughout the war
> Mean that three of four of us are now in hock.
> Yet the world is hungry for just peace.

This devout and hopeful man still trusts;
Patiently the president persuades.
Freedom of the sea not yet secured,
Many borders drawn against the grain;
Yet in much his fourteen points prevail,
Covenants are open, in the light:

Belgium and Alsace-Loraine restored,
Poland recognised, the Hapsburg realm
Turned discrete and independent states.
Wilson hopes the League of Nations can
Solve all else and hold the hope of peace.
Praise this man who dreams before his time.

Opposition has been brewed at home.
Teddy Roosevelt and Cabot Lodge
Balk at what the Congress didn't choose.
Wilson tries a whistle-stop to win.
Broken by a stroke when halfway through,
Point-blank refusing any compromise,
Congress won't approve his nations' league.

Would a stronger League of Nations save
World War Two? Should he have compromised?

Is it illness that his Edith hides?
Or some tragic flaw that blinded him?
Maybe it's the visionary's curse—
To maintain a dream so prescient
Means keeping it so pure it fails,
Never strikes its roots in common clay.
Loneliness of seeing things alone
May create a kind of stubborn pride
Which persuades the lone prophetic heart
That a glance of heaven is his own,
Lets a dream fall short of paradise.

(ii)

Eleanor steps on the stage.
Such a happy child—I love
Everyone and everyone loves me—
Daughter of New York's elite,
Roosevelts and Halls both swells.
Mother, brother, father die
All within a two-year span.
Orphaned as a twelve-year-old,
Storing up her father's love

She pulls through though unaware
Till an angry aunt reveals
How her father died of drink,
Left maid Kathy with a son.

> *Mother and grandmother were*
> *New York belles, which I am not.*
> *While a woman may be plain*
> *With both truth and loyalty*
> *Stamped upon her face she'll win.*
> *Even as a child I'd learned*
> *Joy is sorrow overcome;*
> *Yet I'm often insecure.*

Fifteen and she's sent to school:
Allenwood Academy,
Near to London's Wimbledon
Where Marie Souvestre reigns.
Praised for helping lonely girls,
Bright and so alert she's soon
Favourite pupil of them all.

> *Yes, at Allenwood I learned*
> *Independence of the mind.*
> *Back among the New York swells*
> *Once again society*
> *Guides my fate. I marry well,*
> *My fifth cousin once removed*
> *Franklin D. who will become,*
> *Like my uncle Theodore,*
> *U.S. president. At first*
> *I succumb and am all wife,*
> *Bear six children in ten years,*
> *Cling to Franklin's mother's strings*
> *Till I find out his affair*
> *With my secretary whom*
> *Franklin says he won't remeet.*
> *Partners in our politics,*
> *Closest friends who always hope*
> *Love between us may rebloom.*
> *He's too jovial for me*
> *Too flirtatious for my taste.*

> I'm too serious for him—
> Sex for me was always tough,
> Motherhood ill-suited me.

Slowly seeds her school had sown
Flourish now in Eleanor.
Breaking with her mother-in-law,
Radical new friends expand
Her attitudes. A girl who'd seen
Darkies as below the whites,
Waspishly disdained all Jews,
Finds all human beings friends,
Wants her husband to outlaw
Lynching which, for fear he'd lose
Southern votes, he will not risk.

> I'm the one who nagged at him
> Urging him to dare much more.
> Paralysed by polio,
> I exhorted him to train.
> Standing in for him I rove,
> Franklin's New Deal's eyes and ears,
> Visit poor communities
> That I try to hearten in
> Scots Run, West Virginia.
> Awkward in my motherhood,
> Public warmth's my other side.
> Bonding in our partnership
> Both become compassionate—
> Though I sometimes disagree
> In the columns which I write.
> Entering orbits of my own
> I am glad that Missy tends
> His emotional desires.
> Though no love comes right for me,
> I obsess, have crushes on
> Women and on younger men
> Who assuage my loneliness.
> No one lives at all unless
> We adapt to how life is.

Spiritual poverty
Ends in war and Eleanor
Shuns all warfare. Yet she sees
Dictatorships in Germany,
Italy, Japan are worse.
War becomes her peace crusade.

Franklin lives to see war end,
Dies before the dreams of peace,
New worlds orders he might build.
Yet avoiding Wilson's faults
He'd prepared the Congress well.
Truman asks her now to join
U.N. commissions they've proposed.
Chairing a group on human rights,
Eleanor will make her mark,
Challenging old diplomats,
Seeing through a document,
Chartering all our human rights.

> *Nazi horrors are revealed—*
> *Borders no defence from now;*
> *All humanity is one.*
> *Refugees the Russians want*
> *Homed for punishment encourage*
> *Us to state our human rights,*
> *Holding individual*
> *And community intact*
> *Surely might is never right*
> *And everyone has dignity.*
> *France and U.S. both declared*
> *Rights in revolution's heat;*
> *For the first time here on earth*
> *All sign up to human rights*
> *We believe may change the world.*

Heaven glimpsed and lost again.
No accountability
And no rule of law applies.
Soviets upbraid the West;
Joe McCarthy's time has come,

Hunting reds he's whipping up
U.S. dread of Communists.
Heartened by their human rights
Empires start their fracturing;
Britain drags its worldwide feet.
Covenants she'd thought they'd sign
Falter now, take no effect;
U.N. motions flounder in
Esperantos of thin air
As each nation cites what suits—
Thirty articles on rights,
Bit by bit but seldom whole.
International courts embrace
Vetoes from the superpowers.

Yet a standard written in
Constitutions of new lands;
Though more cherished in the breach
Glimpse of heaven woven in
As we like Eleanor still pray:

Save us from ourselves and show
Visions of a world made new.

(iii)

Strange how lives and history interweave.
Just when war-torn Europe needed him
Jean Monnet shows up to shift her course.
Brown moustache with piercing chestnut eyes,
Short and stocky Cognac's merchant's son
Moves so skillfully behind the scenes,
Schemes beyond our fractious nation-states.

> *Tired of school at sixteen I'd become*
> *Trainee in my father's firm. I'm sent*
> *For two years to serve my London time.*
> *Here I learn how businesses team up—*
> *More it seems than I have seen in France.*
> *I market Cognac around Canada,*
> *Moving on to comb the U.S.A.*
> *Where I love their fierce get-up-and-go;*

Egypt, Russia, Scandinavia,
Spreading father's cognac I become
Travelling citizen of all the world.

Twenty-eight advising Clemenceau
How both France and England should liaise,
Pool resources for their worldwide war,
Not compete for wheat and other goods.
Post-war League of Nations officer,
He resolves Silesian disputes,
Mends the Austrian economy
Till he leaves frustrated by the League's
Lack of power to implement its plans,
Homes to save his family's company.

Millions made and millions lost again
Years an international banker when
My beloved Sylvia and I first meet.
Partner in a New York firm I worked
Sorting Chiang Kai-shek's finances out.
Networking still across the globe it seems
I prepare for all I'll still achieve.
Fifty years' experience I gather up
When our world again erupts in war.

I approach this as a businessman:
France and England surely must combine
Form an Anglo-French conseil suprême.
Winning over Churchill I am sent
To persuade the U.S. to provide
Aircraft which the Allies sorely lack.
Roosevelt's home isolationists
Disapprove but soon in Canada
Factories begin to make the planes.
Back in France I mediate between
Charles de Gaulle and General Giraud,
Steer the National Committee for
Liberation, unify my France
To continue war and lay the ground
So when war ends we'll have democracy.
Even now I sound out Charles de Gaulle,

Urge a post-war economic blend,
Binding France with some new Germany.

Sixty million dead across the globe;
Bloodiest war in all of history,
Five long years of loss and squandered youth—
Touch and go on every battlefront;
Slowly now the Allies turn the tide,
When the U.S. joins in on their side.
Aircraft factories were in full swing.
Did Monnet's request for planes and aid
Shorten our world war by several months?

Post-war France's leaders all agree
Drastic economic shifts could make
Plundered France a country great again.
Jean Monnet already has a plan
Giving grounds for U.S. funds to flow;
Setting up commissions to direct
Quick recovery. Bypassing all
Government red tape, a Soviet-style
Commissar's determined to succeed.
Eastern Europe now is Communist,
Western Europe must recover fast—
Truman signs the Marshall Plan for aid.

I believe my mission's to unite
Europe so our nations will not war,
Slowly all our states must integrate,
Bound by trust that we negotiate.
Coal and steel provided German power—
France now needs the Saar if it's to grow.
The Korean War begins and so
Truman wants a stronger Germany
Fearing it might turn a Soviet pawn.
Walking in the Alps I think this through:
Why can't France and Germany both share
Coal and steel production and allow
People in the Saar decide by vote
Whether to belong to France or not.

Schuman, France's Foreign Minister,
Guides my sharing scheme through parliament;
Adenauer's Germany concurs,
Faces down the coal and steel cartels.
Though de Gaulle as well as Communists
In the Soviet Union and in France
Balk at yielding any sovereignty
And in Britain Eden too says "no,"
Benelux and Italy all join
Europe's Coal and Steel Community.
Managed by a High Authority
With a Council of Six Ministers.
I too found the European Court,
An assembly formed from member states.
In my mind this is just one first seed,
European Union's embryo.

Though Monnet will push for further schemes:
His plans for European defence
And his Euratom de Gaulle will sink.
Jean Monnet's influence starts to wane.
Still unhampered by all loss of face,
Egoless and driven by his dream,
Jean will found his Action Committee
For United States of Europe and persist
Widening contacts, linking ministers,
Bonding Europe and the U.S.A.,
Urging his Atlantic Partnership.

I am proud my blueprint will become
What at Rome is named the EEC.
Though by now at only sixty-nine
I no longer walk power's corridors,
I am telephoning friends with my advice.
Turning minds beyond the nation-state,
All my years I yearn for Europe's peace.

Hard to understand how this can be,
How Monnet, one unmandated man
Changed the mindset history held in place.
Cognac man in love with English suits

Who to relax pulled on red woolen socks,
Trusted messenger of presidents
Cultivating powerful friends he makes,
Pushes Europe past its shibboleths.

Shaped by what a salesman learns of bonds—
Charming, cunning, fiery when opposed,
This pragmatic visionary whose
Spirit's never dampened by events,
Scores by dint of personality,
By persuasiveness, connections made.
Strict, obsessive as an ideologue,
Plaguing his officials late at night,
He will drop a friend who disagrees.

Europe's greatest strategist of peace,
Gifted and constrained by his background,
Conjures up a common marketplace
To create a cogent superpower
Where finance and labour freely flow,
Mirroring it's smaller nationhoods.
Must our peace now merge all difference?
Reader of newspapers but no books,
Jean Monnet the ideologist
Misses out on deeper bonds and ties,
Ligatures of tongues, a sense of place
Coloured by a common narrative
History houses near our human core.
Union somehow yet remains unreal;
Orders issued, Brussels' one-fits-all,
Starred blue flag so dutifully raised,
Still not fluttering in our chambered hearts.
Heaven is no timeless superstate.

(iv)

As the Qing regime is overthrown
Deng turns six and diligent at school
Starts to learn to read Confucian texts.
Though his father dreamt a learned clerk,

Fifteen and tired of middle school he leaves,
Travels on a study scheme to France,
Works in factories in Montargis.
Shocked at how his homeland lags behind
He's determined to effect a change;
And yet appalled how factory hands must slave
He knows free markets' sweated darker side.
First he talks of finding some third way,
Cross between the West and Communism;
Then with other student émigrés
Turns Communist, abandons studying
To advance the revolution's cause.

> While in Paris we're so eagerly
> Plotting making China Communist.
> I encounter Zhou Enlai who'll teach
> Both precision and delight in work.
> Undramatic, I am most at home
> Drafting documents, a back-room boy
> Combing minutes and minutiae.
> In stepped increments I slowly earn
> My authority and leverage.
> Though I often love to joke and laugh,
> Inexorably, I climb the ranks—
> Power is hiding in the finer points.

Singled out now Deng is Moscow-bound,
Learning as the Soviets have learned
How in time it's best to implement
Marx and Lenin's ideology.
Home again in China he enlists,
Tries in vain to heal the rift between
Communists and Nationalists but finds
He has to flee to where in turn he'll meet
Mao Zedong, a sidelined Communist,
Soon behind an uprising that fails;
On the run in Shanghai once again
Deng climbs up the party's echelons.
Here in Shanghai his first comrade wife
Married him but in her childbirth died.
Harried in the city Mao will back

Farming proletariats and so
Spurning Moscow's plans instead he founds
Jiangxi soviet which will thrive until
Mao is forced to flee by Chiang Kai-shek.
Too associated with Mao's thought.
Out of favour Deng now too is shunned—
Jin Weijing, his second wife, leaves him.

> *Backing Mao, I'm on the year's Long March—*
> *Breaking through a Nationalists' long siege*
> *Mao's one hundred thousand tramping north*
> *Where nine thousand only will survive.*
>
> *Japanese armed forces then invade;*
> *We defend the northern ground we gained.*
> *Liu Bocheng commands; political*
> *Commissar I fight the war with him.*
> *Visiting Yan'an where Mao is based*
> *I'm married in a cave to Zhuo Lin.*

Once Japan is beaten by the bomb,
Bitter civil war resumes until
Mao proclaims the People's Republic.
Still the south-west's under Chiang Kai-shek.
Deng is sent to liberate the zone.
Mayor of Chongqing day by day he learns
Pragmatic politics that shape his thought.

> *Back in Beijing I start to climb again*
> *Slowly up the greasy rungs to power.*
> *All looks well until my patron Mao*
> *Wants his hundred flowers of thought to bloom,*
> *But afraid too many disagree*
> *Mao cracks down and purges dissidents;*
> *All proclaimed as rightist sent to camps.*
> *Keeping out of trouble's way I do*
> *All I can behind the scenes instead,*
> *Saving those I can as best I can.*

Bent on his collective-farming scheme
Mao begins his Great Leap Forward plan;
Private farms are banned and then are merged

In collectives. The economy now shrinks—
Tens of millions killed or starved to death.
Peng who'd marched a year with Mao Zedong
Dares to fault his ideology,
Spends long years consigned to outer dark.

Slowly Liu and Deng will concentrate
On restoring the economy,
Quietly leaving Mao Zedong aside.
Piqued, the chairman moves to take revenge.
To regain prestige his failures lost,
Launched in May of 1966
His Red Guards will rove the state to purge
Bourgeois remnants, intellectuals,
Any threat to dogma as laid down,
As "revisionists" both Liu and Deng
Banished from the hub of Beijing power.
Ancient monuments are torn down,
Relics and religious sites ransacked,
Faction struggles boil across the land,
Torture, jailings, seizures, harassment,
Populations forcibly displaced,
Chairman Mao and his red book become
Hallowed signs of revolution's cult,
China falls in deeper poverty.

> I'd been ostracised before but cope,
> Though my eldest son was paralysed
> Jumping from a window when pursued.
> With my wife Zhang Xiyuan I survive
> Working in a rural factory,
> Reading much, renewing myself until
> Zhou Enlai, persuading Chairman Mao,
> Brings me back to Beijing's government
> Where again I slowly regain power.
> Fighting off Mao's wife's own gang of four,
> I begin with Zhou to take the reins.

Humble, balanced, tenacious and astute,
No one tells him what he wants to hear;
Faulting nothing that the chairman did,

Never basing judgements on revenge,
Cloaking all in Mao's philosophy,
But preferring Khrushchev's new approach.
Pragmatic, not utopian reforms:
Agriculture first, then industry,
Strong defences and technology.

Zhou Enlai is dead and so is Mao,
Hua Guopfeng his designated heir—
Deng's solo ruler now in all but name,
Motivating folk to make things work.

> *I announce renewal's Beijing Spring.*
> *Knowing what I lack I seek advice.*
> *Freer now for businessmen with flair,*
> *Opening up I bring expatriates home.*
> *Rong Desheng, non-communist, returns*
> *Starting Chinese International Trust*
> *And Investment Corporation which*
> *Boosts the whole economy's advance.*
> *Hua I will sideline then remove.*
> *Some support whatever Mao had said,*
> *Whatever Mao had done. Instead, I say*
> *Search the facts for truths that you can test.*
> *Known abroad as "leader paramount,"*
> *I'm in Malaysia, Thailand, Singapore,*
> *Even in Japan and U.S A.*

> *Socialist free markets my ideal,*
> *Well-ruled Singapore my paragon.*
> *Shanghai blooms and economic zones—*
> *We have dragged folk out of poverty.*
> *Xi Jinping is chairman, I retire,*
> *Though at eighty-eight I will return*
> *Touring through the south so I ensure*
> *China's boom will not now be reversed.*

Deng's acumen glanced the kingdom's light
Yet never seems to want democracy.
Even though all talk of class is gone,
He went with the anti-rightist moves,

Didn't help the Tiananmen protest.
Was he prisoner of his youthful drill,
Faithful to his years of Moscow's skill,
Locked still in a limbo of control?

> Speaking out like Peng I know I'd too
> Be in the cold. I'd seen such lack and want.
> All too many grind their lives away,
> Eking an existence, scraping by.
> Shelve democracy. We'll keep control
> To attend the hungry needs of all.
> Though my eye falls short of paradise,
> I will see my people yet well fed.

(v)

Europe's final empires now will fall.
Gorbachev treads history's boards on cue.
Born near Stavropol in Russia's south,
Bred a Communist he'll rise in turn
Through the local ranks. Then patronised
By elite red-tapists summering there,
He'll become the party's Kremlin tsar.
Trained in law, a shrewd politico
Outmanoeuvring foes, at fifty-four
He'll begin to change the map we'd known
And despite himself collapse his world.

> Young advisers with new liberal views
> Glad that I was not too old to hear
> Shaped my vision for our Soviet realm.
> Glasnost, our new openness will mean
> We can learn and spread the skills we lack.
> Artists all must speak without restraint—
> What Khrushchev had begun and Brezhnev stopped
> I'll continue to advance. We want
> To allow our Soviet state to thrive.
> Perestroika is our second word—
> Overhauling the economy,
> Giving new and freer markets rein.

Tragic Gorbachev who cannot see
How, for all his courage in this change,
Perestroika and glasnost undo
This one-party union he still wants.
Once the market frees there's no control—
Business sharks crave fortunes and before
Older structures are regeared or changed
Oligarchs, all manner of tycoons
Crack the economic whip instead.
Glasnost is the genie he has let
Out of history's bottle. Openness
Undermines this last imperium.

> *More, I want the party to elect*
> *Candidates they choose. One party, yes,*
> *But a Soviet democracy.*
> *In addition we must think anew*
> *Our relation to the outer world.*
> *With Raisa I will travel out,*
> *Take the planet's media by storm.*
>
> *Often in the past our empire split,*
> *Europhiles and Slavophiles diverged;*
> *I will look at once both west and east.*
> *Europeans share one house with us—*
> *China and Japan know we belong*
> *In the Orient. Politicos*
> *Face whichever way we need to face.*
>
> *Why prolong cold wars that no one wins?*
> *Reagan, U.S. president, and I*
> *Meet three times. As best I can I try*
> *Banning nukes of every kind but fail,*
> *Though at least we lessen what we hold.*
> *Bush and I in turn too meet and talk;*
> *Cuba and Afghanistan agreed,*
> *We discuss the fractious Middle East.*
> *I propose we two together should*
> *Settle world affairs, but Bush demurs.*
>
> *My Raisa loves to fashion-shop.*
> *Wearing my designer suit and watch,*

I can charm the worldwide cameras.
Popular abroad but back at home
Perestroika falters and I'm caught
In between reformers and diehards.

Many say they knew the end was near.
Retrospective pundits claim they saw
Signs of classic overreach. In truth,
Most forecast a bitter slow decline.
Though both Budapest and Prague had seen
How a rising and a spring were crushed
Proving Communism ruled the roost,
Now their national desires outweigh
Ideologies. Yet no one knows
When brave Czechs, East Germans take to streets,
Demonstrating thousands who demand
Freedom from oppressive state regimes,
That Red Army tanks will not roll in.
Quickly in some Soviet satellites
Party bosses sensing how the wind
Blows, turn into ardent patriots.

Tallinn on through Riga, Vilnius,
Some two million form a human chain.
Kremlin masters threaten Baltic States,
Still there is no will to follow through.
Ousted from Afghanistan and bled
Dry financing states as satellites,
Soviets now lack the will to act.
Half a year and Lithuania
Blazons independence. Gorbachev
Sends red troops, then silently withdraws.
Georgia and Moldova too depart.
Hungary turns a multiparty state.
Václav Havel has been sent to jail.
Solidarnošč galvanises Poles,
East Germans shout, "Wir wollen raus!"
Years of shoot to kill come to an end.
Bringing down the death-strip Berlin Wall.
By and large old empires end in pain.

Hard-fought revolutions bleed them down.
Gorbachev's beloved union falls
Less by force than domino effect.

> *Seeing chain reactions I let go;*
> *Molotov and Ribbentrop pact states*
> *One by one declare autonomy.*
> *I believe they will return in time—*
> *We'll attract them still as satellites.*
> *I detest parades of sovereignties,*
> *I'd impose by force all-union laws.*
> *Bonding with hardliners I attempt*
> *Stopping Yeltsin's protests in the street.*
> *Slavs will balk at shooting other Slavs;*
> *So I waver and withdraw the troops.*
>
> *I propose a novel treaty now,*
> *Binding up the union which remains*
> *In eight of nine republics most will vote*
> *To remain in federation, share*
> *Foreign policies and president.*
> *Calls I make to Yeltsin have been tapped—*
> *KGB chief Kryuchkov hears his job's*
> *On the line and plots his August coup.*
> *I'm arrested when on holiday.*
> *Strangely, it is Yeltsin who stands fast*
> *And in days the putschists lose their nerve.*

Yeltsin clearly gains the upper hand.
U.S. Bush who'd backed up Gorbachev,
So the Soviet Union would survive,
Starts to see the writing on the wall,
Shifts and leans instead to Yeltsin's side
Who by now is Russia's president.
Slowly Yeltsin will appropriate
Gorbachev's remaining Kremlin role.
Russia which holds sway with oil and gas
Will not fund a Soviet president.
Gorbachev ghost-leads an empire lost.

> *By the millions party members leave.*
> *Is my only power base breaking up?*

Our new treaty must be made to work,
Russia and Ukraine belong as one—
Even Yeltsin could agree to this.
All depends on how the Ukraine votes.
Though I play the ethnic card and warn
Russians in the Ukraine will then face
Hardship under any new regime,
Still the Ukraine chose autonomy.
At Belavezha and when my back is turned
Yeltsin gathered with the presidents
Of the Ukraine and of Belarus
Founds what they now name the C.I.S.—
Commonwealth of Independent States.
Nine more republics soon are joining too.
Where then has my Soviet Union fled?

Hero in the West, a has-been face
Staring at a past that slips away.
If he only could have compromised
Chosen federation he'd have saved
Something of the union he so prized.
Komsomol had entered his young soul.
Though he had allowed for candidates,
All remained within one-party mode.
If he could have left the stage on time,
Exited before he's pushed aside . . .
We can only pity Gorbachev,
Visionary who opened up a door
Leading further than his eye could dream.

Canto 5
A Beckoned Dream

(i)

We're in the upper house for saints
Where a chosen five must represent
Hallowed politicians who across
Time endure and by their lives uphold
All who struggle still to steer

Our imperfect ship in changing seas.

Politicians always will fall short
However much we strive because we know
People whom we serve will disagree.
Once we don't dictate we must accept
State and rule of law where there is both
Accountability and drive to find
How to reach the good life for us all,
Or at least an aggregate of wants.
We accept that heaven slips from sight
Yet we are, we hope, the signs that point
Towards a paradise of politics.

Let us name our saint politicos:

William Ewart Gladstone, who advanced
Britain's slow democracy, prepared
Half-unwittingly an empire's end.

> Dare I ask if you all journeyed too?
> Speaking for myself I know I did.
> Though prime minister you see I lead
> First the Tories, then the Liberals—
> After all I spanned a century.
> Once high Tory under Robert Peel
> I believed that church and state are one,
> I become a Liberal who tries
> Slowly to remove the barriers
> Of both class and creed that still curbed growth.
> Church of Ireland's disestablishment
> I achieved, though many disapproved;
> I introduced the secret ballot box.
> So although Home Rule for Ireland failed
> I prepared an empire's unseen end;
> Even if I'm of my times I guide
> People towards another century
> Following the paths I pioneered.

Spectacled, mustached and slight of frame
After him Mahatma Gandhi comes,
Who resists, unravels Britain's Raj.

> *Once I was that hapless shy young boy*
> *Haunted by a fear of thieves and ghosts,*
> *Scared of dark I'd need a lamp to sleep.*
> *I recall those London days I strove to learn*
> *Foxtrots and French and speaking properly,*
> *Tied my necktie, wore top hats of silk*
> *Walked with my own silver-handled cane.*
> *Yet I journey to my ashram, sit*
> *In my dhoti, tell how we remake*
> *Inner selves so we can change the world.*
> *Only when I'd journeyed far enough,*
> *Reached the point of fearlessness,*
> *Could the Indian people follow me.*

Now Dag Hammarskjöld, a lonesome Swede,
Slate-eyed, blond-haired global diplomat,
United Nations' guiding star of peace.

> *I can add my voice to both of you.*
> *Hammarskjölds down through the years had been*
> *Civil servants and good soldiers too;*
> *Father was a while prime minister—*
> *Mother's crowd were mainly clergymen.*
> *Did I journey less than all of you?*
> *Yet I had to fight off arrogance*
> *Learning from each side that service is*
> *My deliberate dying to myself*
> *While unflinchingly still holding to*
> *What I am convinced is just and right.*

Watch Mandela's widening his smile,
Beamed to reconcile South Africa.

> *Certainly I journeyed as you did.*
> *Leaving clan and tribe behind I forged*
> *Visions of a country that could room*
> *Black and white with justice and in peace.*
> *Some would flush the Europeans out—*
> *Most followed on my pilgrimage.*

Guesting from the lower living house,
President Mary McAleese arrives,

Builder of beam bridges thrown between
Ghosts of Europe's once religious wars.

> Born in Belfast I remember how
> Threatened and forced out by Loyalists
> We had fled our home for safety.
> I suppose I might have nurtured hate
> But I learned we blossom best in love;
> Its absence shrivels us till we grow hard.
> All my presidency I would try
> To alleviate distress and heal
> Dead hatreds with the oils of hope
> Asking all to journey as I have.

Gladstone once convinced that he was right
Gambling his career he would persuade
Others to convert to what is just.
Gandhi said he shrunk his self to nil
Only to in turn evolve the power
To achieve his satyagraha which
Earned the independence he strove for.
Through his life Dag Hammarskjöld endured
Loneliness while always occupied
Trying to steer a neutral course to peace.
Twenty-seven of his ninety-five
Nelson spent in locked up in jails and yet
Twice he still refused to leave unless
Granted full democracy for all.
Mary's vision feeds the lame or hurt,
Building bridges over bitterness,
Healing wounds of broken histories.

What is the cost? We hear Mandela's cry:
Yes, to father a nation yet to lose
His own children's laughter. Did Hammarskjöld
Pay with his life as Gandhi did?
It's a far, far better thing I do. . . .

At the core their service is their gift
This is what we mean by politics—
Tending polities beyond the self,
Struggling to find how a people thrive.

Power for only power is emptiness,
Demagogues or glorious egoists,
Jugglers of ideas who know best,
Rigging all the thimbles to succeed.

We serve and in our service coax
Polities to share a beckoned dream.

(ii)

Some might say we lack a theory—
Surely we should have a scheme of things,
A new framework or approach that's key
To explaining past mistakes we made,
Tenets that should lead to solving all.

But Dag Hammarskjöld's high forehead frowns
And recalls a painful episode:

> I still see Khrushchev lambasting me
> When he wanted his triumvirate
> In my secretary U.N. post:
> One for Soviets, one for Western powers,
> One to hold the balance in between
> Tightrope-walking ideologies.
> Civil servant for humanity
> I held my ground just solving day by day
> Troubles as they fell. There is no key
> And no quick fix or golden age,
> We can only start where things are now.

Here Mandela in his bright blue shirt
Puckers up his smile as he replies:

> Hammarskjöld is right. South Africa
> Never could return to where it was.
> History holds so much that should not be.
> Yet for all unfairness in the past,
> What's the point explaining our mistakes,
> Harping back to what we cannot change.
> Truth and reconciliation count,
> Help to heal the traumas we have known;

> Yet I'm sure that in the end it's true
> Politics begins from where we are.

Gladstone now and Mary McAleese
Nod and so the conversation flows:

> To be sure, there is no perfect state.
> In the nineteenth century I led
> Britain towards its new democracy,
> Fought conservatism's status quo,
> Ideology of frozen now.
> Reading scripture every day I saw
> In my leadership a pillared cloud
> Floating just enough ahead to guide,
> Resting while my people rested, then
> Travelling to enticing honeyed lands—

> Picking up on what Mandela said,
> South Africa, of course, was colonised;
> Yet we cannot now turn back the clock,
> Go on blaming unforgiving pasts.
> Look at how in Belfast our two tribes,
> Amplified by nationhoods that vie,
> Echo Europe's once religious wars.
> Every future begs to start from now,
> Dogma-free to reconcile both sides,
> Break recycled bloody tit-for-tats;
> Then recognising how we disagree,
> Rise above the perfect win or lose.

Cynicism and doubt will wither us;
There's no blueprint but beginning here,
No simple template can be put to use.
Still there is one constant theme on which
We can improvise, a leitmotif:
Our nagging deep desire for equity.
Again our starting point must always be
Not the perfect system but instead
How our justice now is best advanced.

Three of our five saints have trained in law;
Hammarskjöld had read economy,
Gladstone was at first a classicist.

Yes, a classicist. Whatever else
I'd no overall design and justice came
Piecemeal. Rebel Poerio's chains
Shocked me—so once home from Italy
I began to plead his cause and when
Russell tried to curb the Catholic Church,
Though no Roman, my defence upheld
Our religious liberty; I tried to stop
Civil service that's based on patronage.
Women of the night I sought to help
Thrilled me as I worked to save their souls.
Slowly, lack of justice niggled me,
I would follow my expanding heart.—

I'm sure that Gandhi just like me
Praises Gladstone, lauds how he progressed;
He had a choice and chose against the grain.
Indians and we South Africans
Knew we had no real alternative;
Justice drove us into politics.
We wanted no revenge on colonists,
Neither were we zealous patriots.—

Indians might well have kept the Raj
Till I discerned the road to justice was
Independence from an unfair rule.—

Though we know that rule of law maintains
Democratic states we also know
Justice with compassion is our goal,
Otherwise the balanced scales will rule
Pound for pound and neither cup dare dip.
Though hard cases may not make good law,
Fellow feeling evens up the cups.

Year by year as Ireland's president
I addressed our country's most estranged.
Often inequalities can lurk
Under our society's veneer;
Dulled by greed or grudge we can exclude
Those forgotten sidelined by despair:
Lonely adolescent gay young men,

> *Aged or broken homeless down-and-outs.*
> *Though compassion may begin at home*
> *We cannot now pretend we do not see*
> *Bloodstained streets of Palestine*
> *Or Honduras' bare and bleak hillsides;*
> *Kenya's slums seek solidarity.*

Such unbalance dulls the marketplace,
Lack of justice harms both rich and poor.
Why now talk of either left or right?
Both extremes imply ideologues—
In our lives we both conserve and change.
We need compassion and wise enterprise.
How can we measure lines of poverty,
Counting means or incomes in hard cash?
Need is stunted opportunity,
An education lack of funds denies,
Openings shut off by circumstance,
Joys of talents never quite revealed.
Seeking still to grant an equal chance
We adapt too evenhanded rules;
Law's a theme on which we improvise;
Justice must remain a kind of jazz.

(iii)

Why our longing for old certainties,
Borders drawn without ambivalence,
Boundaries that never overlap?
What if, confusing our identities,
History's beckoning more ways than one?
Conflicts asking us where we belong
Pressure us to choose the flag to fly,
So we compensate for our disquiet
Clinging all too zealously to one.
Might we be at once both this and that?

> *International servant and a Swede*
> *I at once could walk the global stage*
> *And be proud I was a Hammarskjöld.*
> *Nations grasped how in a shrinking world*

We depend on one another now.
All the same those times the going's rough
Many countries fearing to take risks
Suddenly withdraw behind frontiers,
Beating their own drums, protect their own.
Only knowing how we're interlinked
May allow us break with binaries.

Gandhi smiles his moustache smile,
Bowing, signalling how he agrees:

Deep in our subcontinent's mind map
There's a vision of life's unity
That resurfaces through centuries,
Glories in our innate human good,
Mutual dependence's axiom.
I devoted all my sway to hold
India as one, the way the Raj had kept,
Hindis and Muslims and Sikhs in peace.
Even when Swaraj was split in two—
India and Pakistan—I'd fast
To curtail religious violence.
In the end a Hindi extremist
Seeing me as weak would kill me off.

Though induced by two world wars,
Strength in union Aesop's fable knew
Humans always understood. And yet
More than simple union we can learn
How identities may implicate
One another, each embedded in
Greater wholes which means we needn't choose.
Every sense of self can fit within
Bigger regions where we too belong.

Dare I say I was before my time?
Just the way I saw us all inside
Europe's own enveloping domain,
Prime minister I argued for Home Rule
Picturing our Ireland still
Snug inside an empire's wrap-around.
History decided otherwise.

Does that sound too much like Russian dolls,
Too encompassing or too cocooned?
Let us say a variegated leaf
With its coloured zones and overlaps.
When diversity delights our eye.
Sameness yields to imbricated hues.
Yet for variance to captivate
We imagine worlds beyond our own,
Stand in awe of other modes of life,
So becoming less and more ourselves.

> *With my Belfast background I'm aware*
> *How identity and creeds entwine.*
> *Religions our Enlightenment thought dead*
> *Still enrich the ordinariness of lives.*
> *Though across the world extremists plot*
> *Bomb attacks and terror in faith's name,*
> *We must learn to want diversity,*
> *Confident that all can show respect*
> *With no need to find one common ground.*

No one has monopolies on truth.
Rather, like a prism's dispersed side
Rainbowed truth allows us variants
Of another side's pure gathered light.
Each tradition draws on its own hues
To extend a hospitality,
As host to host they all in turn unfold
Millennia of riches in their thought;
Sharing they then better understand
Other texts and practice and their own.
Hosts, of course, may often disagree,
Seeing eye-to-eye discuss in peace.

> *Peace I'm sure was foremost for us five.*
> *The United Nations tries to end all war.*
> *In the long term peace is more than just*
> *Absences of strife—it is a confidence,*
> *Maturity beyond perfection's shine;*
> *Our greatest prayer's for peace not victory.*

In the shorter-term discussions I,
Giving full attention, hoped I'd sense
Ample decency to start our talks;
Broadening their agreements on both sides
By and large I found I brokered peace.
Conflicts where a war kept breaking out
We dispatched peacekeeping troops to hold
Combatants apart. We would resist
Taking either side but flying in
To negotiate Katanga's fate
Something downed my plane and took my life.

We revere too much a land's frontiers.
Now I wonder if there is a time
Force should halt a genocide,
Overstep a country's boundaries
To prevent internal butcheries;
After all, humanity's our home.—

Though assassinated by my own
I must still believe no matter what
Mutual humanity brings peace.
I reject all violence and I won
Independence for my India.
Satyagraha is never an approach,
It's a way of thinking and of life . . .

I disagree. In South Africa
No one heard our freedom's cry or cared.
I supported harming property.
You, Mahatma, knew behind the Raj
A faraway democracy might hear.
Martin Luther King too knew for all
The discriminations and the hate
Somewhere in the psychic hinterland
Roosevelt's four freedoms might still sound.
Even though we needed violence
We, unlike your India, held whole,
Welcoming our prism's dispersed hues.

Maybe we no longer need to choose
Absolutely either this or that,

We can be both proud of who we are
And affirm the other we might be,
Fly whatever flags we need to fly.
Rather than our fixed identities,
Daring acts imagine something more,
Sanction our traversing now with ease
Spectrums of our variegated selves.
Heaven loves our rainbow humankind.

We aspire to porous boundaries
So allow identities to flow,
Learning difference has dignity,
How to be at one and disagree.
We discern in time how best to act.
Who are we to judge in absolutes?
Living politics is on the fly.

(iv)

All too easily we can forget
Contours of a face we do not see,
So the other side too soon may seem
Figures on a distant landscape's edge
Megaphoning messages to us.
We respond in soundbites that are aimed
More to please our own than meet halfway,
Trapping us in attitudes we've struck,
Media will gladly amplify.

> Those eight years I served at the U.N.
> I was master of the media game.
> Answering in hints and metaphors
> I would play my cards close to my chest—
> Every word a hostage to our fate.
>
> Flying to Beijing I met with Zhou
> And spoke in private meetings one-to-one.
> Though we had disputed all the facts
> Zhou agreed in order to relax
> Tension in the world he'd think about
> Freeing U.S. airmen held as spies

> When we sent our buffer troops to keep
> Peace along the Suez once again
> Man-to-man with Nasser we agreed
> Terms that settled things and stopped a war.

Eye-to-eye by nature we desire
To achieve some kind of compromise;
Shuttling talks between conflicting sides,
Diplomacy's the art of face-to-face.

> Sure the whites were looking for an out,
> Taken from my cell by private car
> I would meet with Coetsee in his home
> And was struck by how he heeded me.
> Futures turned on us: one black, one white;
> Years' misunderstanding and campaigns
> Coming down to how two men could talk.

Gaze-to-gaze in our humanity
Enmity can thaw. Was Levinas
Right? The other says don't murder me.
Still there is authority that counts,
Eminence, an aura some exude—
Not just from the offices we invest
With prestige but also what derives
From a lifetime of integrity.
German mystic Meister Eckhart thought
Best think less of what we ought to do,
Thinking more of what we ought to be.

> In my ashram I had always tried
> To experiment with how to live,
> Shaping habits made my life my art,
> Politics begins within our souls.
> Slowly we can learn to work in signs.
> Charkhas and salt marches undermined
> Britain's vice-like grip on India.
> Symbols sway and change a mind and heart.—

> Gandhi is right. Our tokens can compel.
> Every office has authority
> And embodying it I did my best

To encourage and uplift the weak,
Giving our outsiders all a voice.
Calling Unionists to celebrate
In our presidential residence
July Twelfth when William crossed the Boyne,
We embraced our variegated past.
Though I knew I'd shock my Belfast friends
Turning ingrained habits upside down,
Only such a sign could reassure
That we can accept our history.

Yet integrity comes at a price.
Leaders know it's lonely at the top.
Confidants advise, but in the end
No one can take charge or bear the brunt.
Sometimes we have to risk it all alone,
Going out on daring lonesome limbs.

Eighty-four and still prime minister,
Maybe I mistook the house's mood—
Many I'd promoted welshed on me.
Should I've pushed my second Home Rule bill?
Speaking for three hours I did implore
Parliament . . . but failed by thirty votes,
Damaging my party when I left.
Still I know my honour was at stake.—

All my twenty-seven years in jail
I beat off the hound of loneliness.
But to meet with Coetsee on my own,
Knowing if I asked the ANC
They'd refuse, required my leader's nerve.
Come what might, I knew I had to dare.

Politicians need broad shoulders when
Vilified unjustly or they err.
Good achieved too often is ignored;
Politics must be its own reward.

Most of us by times have been reviled.
Friends to many, intimate with none,
All my life I suffered loneliness.

Just as Gladstone kept a diary,
Writing his account of time for God,
All throughout my busy life I wrote
Markings on the journey of my soul.
And although I had my interests,
Day and night I worked to keep world peace
Even-handedly as best I could.
To be sure it hurt when hardened Soviets
Charged me with a bias for the West.
Even that I learned to tolerate—
Worse was being a prophet in my land—
Herbert Tingsten, Swedish journalist,
Through my U.N. years upbraided me;
This I found the toughest to endure.

Bringing our integrity to bear,
Neck stuck out, a head put on the block,
Venturing all, we either win or lose.
Generous signals given, risks we take
Wagering conversations face-to-face,
Lonely daring of all leadership,
Crucible that shapes our statesman saints.

(v)

We desire to helm the ship of state,
Changing course as best our talents can.
Sailors know a sudden tiller shift
Pushed or pulled too far slows down the craft;
Better let the rudder slowly turn.
Steering is a calm and patient skill.

Even when world peace might hinge on me
And I worked around the clock to deal
With the U.N. Council's shifting moods,
I became aware that all work done
With anxiety about results
Is inferior to work in calm
Self-surrender. Patience can succeed
Where anxiety and haste fall short.—

Clearly I'm at one with you on this.
Even while salt-marching I retained
My detachment—neither apathy
Nor indifference but more a trust.
Why so worry whether the results
Follow your desire? Enough that your
Motives still are pure, your means correct,
Things work out. I leave it up to Him.—

Steerman, too precipitate in acts . . .
Tennyson, my friend, had read me well.
I'm the real offender here. You see,
Once I'd change my mind, I couldn't grasp
Why all others didn't share my views,
Shed their Tory stance and see the light.
I'd ebullience, fierce stamina—
Felling trees I'd try to work it off—
Still I know I was a strong-arm chief,
Caring more for aims than for my votes
Till at last I started waiting for
Healthy slow fermenting of all minds.

Patience is a generosity
To forgive all mutual defects
Both among ourselves and then outside.
Histories traumatise us leaving scars
Only we can mend by letting go.
No, it's not that we forget how we
Understand the past, more that we learn
How to recollect things differently.

Forgiveness can begin in one man's heart
And so persuade communities to change.
Shortly after Enniskillen's bomb
Under rubble Gordon Wilson lay
Comforting his daughter who'd soon die.
Wilson tells the newsmen how he bears
No ill will and will not bear a grudge,
Asks that no one would avenge her death.
Now instead he tries to understand
What it was that fanned the bomber's hate.

Did his courage break revenge's ring,
Pardon tip the balance towards peace?—

Does forgiveness need imagine how
Someone else's heart imagines us?
While on Robben Island warders spoke
Afrikaans and so I studied hard
To access the chambers of their mind.
Gladstone, you the European spoke
French, Italian, German, understood
"Europe's concert" as you named that realm.

What's required to open up our minds?
How's another generation trained
To evolve, to flourish skilled and wise?
Much of politics addresses how
We ensure that we can balance all
Needs of individuals to grow,
Thrive in our diverse society.
We endeavour to allow our youth
Meld both learning and well-being so
They fulfil the promise of their gifts.

I have given education thought—
It's UNESCO's brief to further this.
Newman's attitudes affected mine:
Some philosophy must shape our mind.
Given how our disciplines divide
And demands the marketplace will make,
We must see how many things at once
Still create a whole and find their place
In one universal system where
Each is valued, all is intertwined.
Education shows life's plenitude.

Earthlings we belong together now,
Serving one another's needs and gifts;
In our trust our future's one shared globe.
So prestige or standing, what's achieved
Matters little—there's no starring role.
Slung between what's past and still to come,

Bonhoeffer's earned wisdom resonates:
Let's not play heroic games instead
Only ask when all is said and done,
How another generation lives—
Answering this the thrill of politics.

> Tabloid anecdotes and stereotypes,
> Sneering soundbites, headlines simplified,
> Naysayers and doubters still abound.
> President I shone forensic light
> On outsiders many had ignored,
> Heartened them by speaking out the truth,
> Certain that painstaking can redress
> Grievances unbalancing our land.
> In the end it's only hope that's real.—
>
> Even in the freeze of our Cold War,
> I could not abandon hope's seed corn.
> I believed as servant to the globe,
> Common decency would yet prevail.
> Some who trust in love's community
> Still are willing to expose themselves,
> Risk the process of all politics.
> Though not taken in by anyone
> I still knew I could not just assume
> Everyone was double-crossing me;
> Fearing to be fooled I'd fool myself
> Sacrificing chances to bring peace.

Politics is acting out of hope.
Heaven is the joy that leaves the world
Fractions less imperfect than before.
Beckoning dreams a dream will beckon us.

4

Finding

Canto 1

A Shifting Scheme

Beloved Madam Jazz, be with us now;
We search again the unsearchable one.
Do you know the balancings of the clouds,
wondrous works of one with perfect knowledge?
O minx so far beyond our mind's embrace,
what is this room or void we sojourn in,
what moves or holds in place the earth we walk,
how old our marrow and what we're made of,
where time and space bend at once their arrow;
or even whether we can know or not
as woven in we never stand apart,
so every universe we summon up
may seem a while at least to meet our need.
Although we know that so soon with hindsight
our view too will date, seeming so inept,
yet we can only live the lives we live
travelling by repair or strange detour
to pick up older thoughts we'd set aside;
hints of lights recalled in new cul-de-sacs
seen afresh with the eyes of other times
beckon us to learn.

As the heavens are higher than the earth
so too my ways are higher than your ways.
Madam Jazz, show the wonders of your laws.
Out of colonies and scattered cities,

out of broken bones of Crete's Minoans,
Herecletean Greece now doubting its myths,
pleading such harmonies or living fire—
all things change, nothing remains at rest—
puzzles over a shifting firmament
to find in lonely Zeno's Stoic gaze
clusters of stars in an infinite void;
or with Epicurus to stare beyond
at countless worlds across infinite space,
everything a wickerwork of atoms.
Will Aristotle's scheme of two spheres
rule Europe's psyche for two thousand years?

Who then can number the clouds in wisdom
or who can stay the bottles of heaven?
Hider-go-seeker, Miss Unfathomable!

Still at home in a cosmos of their gods,
Babylonians and Egyptians watched
the entire fixed map of stars that daily
dips below our ken, a merry-go-round
of pulsing travellers; carefully marked
the strange backsliding motion of the Sun,
a fairground collector on his platform
circling dizzily around while dropping
slowly back from glittering horse to horse
to take the fare of every rider,
both turning with the stars and lapped each year.
For Greeks these charts and geometries of sky,
these spun asterisks become their cosmos
where Mother Earth is a tiny hanging globe,
concentric circles' unmoving bull's-eye
fixed in a turning shell of fastened stars,
while in between our world and whirling dome
the behind-hand Sun rides its carousel.
But still the puzzle of nagging planets,
wandering stars that like the Sun and Moon
in between the universe's two spheres
journey daily west, though their starting point
slipped east before then doubling west and back
then catching up; both Mercury and Venus

slowly shuttling across the moving Sun,
the others turned between the Sun and stars.
Aristarchus's Sun-centred murmurs
unheard in all this music of the spheres,
for centuries astronomers ponder
such loops and strayings that Ptolemy
sees as celestial wheels within wheels,
marvels of epicycles and deferents,
a logic of its own all parcelled up—
enough to hold until Copernicus,
enough to send Columbus on his way,
Aristotle's framework still holding sway.

The heavens are yours, the earth also yours,
the earth and its fullness you founded them.
O my Madam, O Never-to-Be-Caught!

The sweep of Aristotle's mind so wide,
his contours the unquestioned common sense
that if our Earth spun, a ball thrown upwards
would then be left behind before its fall;
that surely if we rotated eastward
we'd forestall motions of the easting clouds;
that the universe is filled with matter
which rubs through space driving all by friction
round a symmetry of concentric shells
where on midpoint Earth everything changes—
birth and death, generation and decay,
sublunary region of humans—
while in heavenward perfection's ether
a majesty orbits above the Moon,
all ageless, unchanging and impassive.
For most the enigma of the planets'
circles turned on rims of other circles
a detail either unknown or ignored,
as taken by the neatness of this room
that seemed to fit what intuition holds,
other answers merely speculations
and so like a word that at first appears
to solve a crossword clue but only holds
us back or, like a misprint that makes sense,

ages are lulled to forgo the questions
contained between the earth and firmament
in schemes that serve and put us off the scent.

Make me understand your commandments' way
and so shall I ponder your wondrous works.
Demurring Lady playing at the chase!

Already as Roman empires crumble
Augustine the Platonist belittles
Greek probings into the nature of all—
views aftercomers soon exaggerate:
already Huns arrive at Orléans
as Slavs and Bulgars contest the Danube,
as Europe grinds its five dim centuries
and so in fragments or in commentaries
shreds and tatters of Greece's thought survive
while al-Mamun dreams of Aristotle,
his Muslims fallen heirs to Greek learning,
Arabic Euclid and Ptolemy
and algebra across the Caliphate;
until a dazzled Europe retranslates
to Latin texts the scholars will dissect,
poring over Aristotle's two spheres
where Dante moved from hell to paradise.
But more Greek manuscripts now newly found
and soon in Paris Buridan will explain
impetus we'll later call momentum
and his pupil scholastic Oresme
searching for new Platonic harmonies
queries Aristotle's proofs to show how
a still or moving Earth might be a choice.
But no trailblazer—happy with his question
We still await Kopernik of Torin.
At thirty-four Canon Copernicus
believes the Earth revolves around the Sun—
but sings dumb another three dozen years—
did this travelled cleric and half-noble
hold back, tremble at his own discovery?
At last his *De revolutionibus,*
traditional in all but one Sun thought,

a pontoon thrown between old worlds and now,
sober and dedicated to his pope
advising papal calendar reform,
a book that yet decentres Mother Earth—
more a rumour than a revolution
it slowly percolates through Europe's mind.
Open Pandora's box. What will you find?

See how ships glide the sea by Allah's grace
so they may show you of his wonders.
I spin in your love's nexus, Mistress All.

An upstart astronomer tries to show
the Earth revolves but sacred scripture says
Joshua ordered the Sun to stand still
and not the Earth—Luther tells his table—
the Sun ariseth, the Sun goeth down,
Earth is stablished that it cannot be moved.
This book for cognoscenti coils its way
among astronomers, few who believe
our planet spun around the Sun but find
this fiction serves to calculate the stars.
By stealth Copernicus has taken root
when after sixty years of silence Rome
joins in to forbid this teaching of the Sun.
More than gainsaying scripture at stake here—
textures of a story tightly woven,
our place between devils and the angels,
our Earth as centre of God's universe
all threatened by such a revolution
that could unhinge the doors of our belief;
Dante's sacred cosmos called in question
by galaxies still waiting to unfold
To open vistas of some infinity;
out in the hollows of an endless space
a question rattles in an empty can:
how here could man find God or God find man?

Your majesty above the heavens praised
The moon and the stars that you have ordained.
Wild madam, do we think we have you tamed?

A few take Copernicus at his word,
enough to pass the torch from hand to hand
until it flares in Johannes Kepler,
whose troubled childhood a life's desire
to find God's harmony in his planets—
O God, I am thinking thy thoughts after thee—
an exile in Graz this maths teacher writes
to his mentor Mächlin in Tübingen:
God is glorified in astronomy.
Fervid Kepler, heir to Danish Tycho
observations, struggles to explain why
Mars's orbit doesn't fit the pattern;
and so choosing mathematics to prove
his dreams of harmony and symmetry
into another century he riddles
out how planets do not move in circles
but with the Sun as an off-centred hub,
one focus in an elliptic orbit—
they gather speed travelling near the Sun,
following just one other simple law
so space swept out in units of time
remains the same and seems to tally with
his belief in the Sun as prime mover,
a thought which though it doesn't stand through time
works to break the spell of circled orbits
and turns his mind to try an ellipse—
an errant hunch that gives a useful hint,
ladder thrown away when the climb is done.
More Copernican than Copernicus,
he mines the vein Copernik opened up
And banishing now all wheels within wheels
he ends epicycles and deferents
to grant the centred Sun its fullest play;
Aristotle's spheres no longer hold sway.

Bless and make his face to shine upon us
So that you may be known upon the earth.
O worship her, hold her a moment in thought!

Slowly now, inevitably, a new
Sun-centred common sense filters through

as Galileo, Tuscan lutist's son,
from rumours how a Dutch lens grinder
with two lenses magnified distant things
builds a telescope to scan the heavens,
astounded at how wherever he turns
his glass new stars appear: the Milky Way,
which to the naked eye was just a glow,
now an enormous shower of stars so clear
they no longer twinkle or seem so large
as Tycho said Copernicans reckoned;
now the Moon a land of pits and craters
with its shadow-measured dips and highlands,
while a perfect Sun shows its darker spots
to tell how it too turns on its axis;
and scandalous Jupiter has its moons
that orbit just as Copernicans claim
our own moon satellites this planet Earth;
with Venus waning as it draws closer,
showing it too revolves around the Sun,
matching Copernicus's scheme of things.
All of which prove nothing and yet provoke,
making what was a theory seem more real.
Already sixty-eight, Galileo,
not in learned Latin but Italian,
prints *Dialogues* and scorns Aristotle,
with his friend Pope Urban's pet arguments
echoed in words of mocked Simplicio;
but forced to recant spends his shadow years
between his patron archbishop's palace
and a villa in the hills near Florence,
where he writes *Discourses* to prove all weights
fall under constant acceleration,
something he'd discovered rolling balls down
slanted boards while singing to measure how
time squared against the distance covered
or how the greater the tilt the further
from the table the ball would hit the floor,
holding its momentum so with constant
acceleration of a fall it tracks
a parabola that yet allows us,

keeping motion and fall in counterplay,
to send into orbit a satellite—
drift and pull in mutual devotion,
a starbird held in perpetual motion.

Who stretched the line, who laid its cornerstone,
The time the morning stars sung together.
My femme fatale, she shapes another face.

Who was it then that decentred our Earth,
undoing Aristotle's two neat spheres
to send this proud planet into orbit,
another bee around the honeypot
of Sun which now, instead of Mother Earth,
will move a little while to centre stage
and play the role of universal hub?
Perhaps no one hero—more a process
that refuses any step-like progress,
a river carving out its needed course,
switching again direction where and when
landscapes alter; looping around or back,
leaving all dead waters to sleep behind
as picking up its feeders it expands,
an interaction and a filling out,
a flow transforming even as it flows.
Yet all must feed according to their gift
and times, even though we never can know
what curves the rivers we now feed desire
or how another tributary in spate
may fill that extra inch that bursts a bank.
Copernicus has taken a score years
or so to dare within learned circles
his revolutionary thought and still
never dreams he'll begin modernity
that Tycho Brahe tries so desperately
to stop, but inventing his mistaken
scheme gathered with his beady naked eye
accounts which, despite himself, lay the ground
where Kepler sweats his calculating way
to find ellipsis and so make the most
of Copernicus's thought, which in turn

Galileo's glass makes more credible,
though he can't believe in Kepler's ellipsis.
Yet none of these could ever have foreseen—
now Aristotle's sphere is obsolete—
how old currents of Greek thought resurface;
Leucippus and Democritus who'd taught
their atomists' infinite universe
containing many moving earths and suns
find their voices once again in Bruno,
who in praising God's endless creation
echoes Cusa's strange and mystic vision
a boundlessness we'll slowly learn to trust,
decentred Earth become a speck of dust.

Chased like chaff of mountains before the wind
and like the whirling dust before the storm.
O Madam, embrace me in your swirling.

Each loop and advance both interwoven
and by nature incomplete—even so
our temptation to foreclose the process
insisting on the final word, a claim
too cut and dried or else in injured pride
at how every endeavour still falls short;
we withdraw to scoff at our own mistakes,
refuse to see all truth as an event
with constant loopings and imperfections
as each claim is tested over again,
a countless series of verifactions,
a chain reaction of fresh becomings.
Our Sun no longer at the hub of all,
an age is shifting from old common sense,
a static image we so long assumed,
a steady down-to-earth portrayal of things
shatters and gives way to intangibles,
a newer abstract knowledge seeking rules
with comic sway with which we can predict
the works and motions of all creation;
different modes of thought begin to stitch
fabrics of another epoch.

As your hands have made me and fashioned me
give understanding to learn your orders.
Madam Jazz plays a new variation.
An era and a river starts to curve,
bending a little to alter its course;
but only when the slow arc of water
completes its turn does its upstream drop out
of sight and seem so strange, so different
as the new direction of this downstream
would seem against the flow for even those
who once half-wittingly began this move;
the same way a generation changing
the endings of words starts an avalanche
they never had envisaged which becomes
in hindsight shifts from Middle to Modern.
The first adherents those in the know
who'd seen the riddles these changes solve,
while others balk at what seems too at odds
with all our physical intuition,
an ad hoc move without reality
that slowly then becomes a science tool,
a thought that's leaking through a century
till astronomers worth their salt agree;
almost another hundred years before
it will infiltrate as common knowledge,
seeping down and through our understanding
as thinkers and enquirers readjust,
as all in their right mind believe it's true
and so madcap ideas of the few
turn norm—only flat-earthers' lunacy
now denies this Sun-centred galaxy.

We've knowledge only of what you've taught us
You are the All-knowing and the All-wise.
Madam, show us how. Only you know why.

Canto 2
Laws and Measures

The scheme and works of our world are shifting
in thought and practice, yet so many ends
untied, so many questions unresolved,
fretted holes in half-completed jigsaws,
ragged spaces there nagging underneath
that still beset a novel paradigm,
dogging an easy take-for-grantedness—
our newer version of how all things are;
resisting the close of explanations,
the knock-down proofs and certainties
that let another universe take hold,
lull us to think we own the laws we name,
and numb us, Madam Jazz, to think you're tamed.

Not even the weight of a speck of dust
in heavens or earth escapes his knowledge.
My Mistress Jazz, don't lullaby our pride.

Planets in our now-outdated structures—
however they were once set in motion—
stayed well within their rounded comfort zone,
the geometric sameness of an orb,
and turned and turned their eternal circles
unlike the ellipses Kepler described—
those new and strange elongated orbits
with their double focus and change of speed
that under later observation warp,
refusing elliptic exactitude,
as if to agree with Kepler and yet
to hint at something else undiscovered
which unsettles and leaves us all wondering
how this braver framework explains much more
but still can't quite tell us how a thrown ball,
in spite of our planet's endless whirling,
will fall again directly back to earth.
Kepler too had stared at some nagging gaps
he tried to close for, though he kept the Sun
as centre of his finite stellar sphere,

his core could just as well be anywhere,
so long as all revolves around a sun
as in his soon-forgotten grand design
a Neoplatonic sun's shining drive,
its *anima motrix*, set off against
magnetic force combines to nudge and hold
the swirling solar machine in motion,
which even yet for all its offbeatness
bequeaths a new mechanical image
that when refined commands two centuries
and so, although his take remains off beam,
his reflex how we'll view the grander scheme.

Even darkness is no darkness with you,
darkness and light to you are both alike.
Our Madam out of broken tunes play jazz.

Canto 3
Cage of Reason

Now following in the wash of Newton
a wide and deeper river in full spate
will flood surrounding fields it makes its own
until its sweep and reach is common sense,
the only sober-minded way to view
a world revealed through weights and measurements—
a universe mapped out by ticks and tocks
their probes and sunderings will analyse,
allowing underlying laws and shifts
turn mysteries to problems they'll explore,
unravelling things with all the self-belief
of knowing there's a certain key to find
some logic science wants to ferret out—
a knotty crossword yielded clue by clue.

So I'd gaze on you in your holy place
that I might behold your power and glory.
Bebop Madam, show one glimpse of your face!

Let Robert Boyle try out his new air pumps,
and blundering slowly towards chemistry

first Becher and then Stahl name "phlogiston"
the colourless, odourless, tasteless stuff
which parts from wood when it is turned to ash
and all that burns releases in the air;
a scheme of things which for a hundred years
holds sway until, like Aristotle's world,
its own anomalies will sow their doubt—
as when magnesium that burns gains weight,
although it should have shed its phlogiston
(something Islamic chemists once had known),
or, heating red oxide of mercury,
Priestley gathers up its gas to tell how
this is common air with less phlogiston;
but tweaking theories he carries on
while Antoine Lavoisier in Paris,
that tax-collecting eager scientist,
with often-unacknowledged hints and cues
from Priestley, Black, Cavendish and Scheele
(who still believe that air's the only gas),
can see how phlogiston no longer serves
or copes with all the temperings it needs
and dares to break with what was orthodox
to say that Priestley's gas was not pure air
but something he now labels oxygen,
just one of two main parts of atmosphere,
another element in lists that grow
where he begins to weigh and log and name—
a harmoniser, pilfering genius,
pulling threads of many minds together.
As Epicurus told Herodotus
that nothing is created from nothing,
and what disappears does not cease to be—
a thought the Persian Tusi also knew—
Lavoisier's elements merge or change
as oxygen turns iron into rust,
or inhaled breath can burn organic food,
and yet their mass will still remain the same;
so banishing the ghost of phlogiston,
he explains his law of conservation

to formulate how in a closed system,
even though it's juggled or rearranged,
no matter is created or destroyed;
his *Traité élémentaire de chimie*
laying down the names and definitions
all normalised in metric measurement,
chemistry's father tidies elements
before at fifty, pleas of science in vain,
he too bends under madam guillotine.

Be not like her who undoes the thread
She has spun after it has become strong.
Madonna Blues cries in her undersong.

The age of reason weighs the elements,
their finer measurements achieved by pans
they hang on horizontal balances,
so Proust can show two elements unite
in definite proportions, proving how,
unless combined in given sums, they'll leave
an overrun of one, and so concludes
the elements reduce to what he names
the atom nothing can divide and so
will only blend in certain ratios—
a fact John Dalton will in turn confirm
in his atomic theory, which claims
all atoms in a given element
are both identical and different
from those of every other element
and are distinguished by respective weights
with their relationships, although they can
connect with those of other elements
to form compounds whose combinations still
retain the same relation in the sum
of atoms they contain; and now along
with Guy Lussac, who knows how oxygen
links up with hydrogen in ratios
that too are fixed, John Dalton settles for
this notion of the atom which, although
it soon becomes the chemist's stock-in-trade,
the physicists still doubt what chemists weighed.

That I may see the wonders of your law . . .
Lead me in the path of your commandments.
My Lady Jazz, unclothing veil by veil.

On Jamie Watt's grandmother's kitchen hob
his seething kettle's lid begins to drive
the steaming pistons, which in turn demand
hillsides are cut away by oiled machines
to mine for coal and level railway tracks,
revealing inner scapes of earth and rock
where aeon-buried fossils redisplay
their telltale snapshots frozen into stone—
the sort which Aristotle once explained
as shells and skeletons, marine remains
preserved by shifting levels of the sea,
and some maintained were relics of the flood,
but reason's eye that turns on light and space
or probes the atoms' ratios and weight
now sleuths these relics of our hemmed-in past;
and William Smith at twenty-five begins
his Somerset Canal and has to learn
to classify the stones as porous ones
would drain canals of water they required.
As Persian Ibn Sina had observed,
or China's Sen Kuo too had clearly seen,
and Steinsen did a century before,
Smith tracks how different kinds of rocks are tiered;
so he discovers every overlay
contains a trademark fossil which can help
identify the layer—an approach
by which he shows the vertical extent
of strata, leading him to chart the land.
Though soon "the map that changed the world" is poached
and ruined Smith lands in London's debtors' jail,
although by now his method spreads to France
where Cuvier maps out geology
and also will compare anatomies
of fossils with the living and conclude
so much is now extinct there must have been
catastrophes between the changing tiers—

a thought that for a while can dominate
but Lyell, born the year that Hutton died,
revamps his fellow Scotsman's view of things
that two contending forces back and forth
deposit sediments that too in time
erode again in age-long cycles, so
both rocks and soil are washed into the sea,
compacted into bedrock and then forced
to re-emerge by some volcanic burst,
the same again until the human mind
can't grasp an age that's long enough ago
so continents have time to come and go.

Behold thou hast made my life as handbreadths
My lifetime is as nothing before you.
All down the aeons Madam riffs and jams.

The eye that sees the amber insect trapped,
congealed within the resin's long recall,
now turns to read what stories we've inscribed
in scapes and mounds and buried artefacts—
the tools and graves our forebears leave behind,
those hints and spoors of how they lived their days
that wake a curiosity in us,
well known among Muslims who first had read
Egyptian hieroglyphs, or polymaths
in China rooting out long-lost techniques.
The age of reason's eye begins to note
and sift as Johann Joachim Winkelmann
arranges Greek and Roman objets d'art
by style and age, while Thomas Jefferson,
a man before his time, who excavates
a mound of native graves and tries a wedge
to probe the tiers, and England's Robert Hoare
some generations later on records
a Wiltshire barrow delved so carefully,
and trowelling this sun-clock hill reveals
no trace of any legend's grand King Sil
interred upright astride his golden horse;
instead Europe's largest man-made mound,
a tumulus of mostly chalk and clay,

a gravel core and kerb of sarsen stones,
hill grave and hidden chamber of the dead,
whose massive season-dial still conceals
behind millennia its own intent
beyond the hoe and careful trowelled scoop;
and yet, however crude is Hoare's attempt,
we have begun the move to stratigraph
and names to classify the tiers of time,
our layered reason's gauge and paradigm.

I will remember the works of the Lord
And call to mind your wonders of old time.
My vampish Madam, hidden in your jazz.

In new domains and far-flung satellites
the burdened white man restlessly explores
exotica of fauna, plants and flowers,
geologies and maybe most of all—
in spite of such superiority—
new minds beyond the grip of what they know,
elusive thoughts, encoded sounds and tones
which somehow both intrigue and frighten them
with inner needs to know the sweet unknown
and yet the otherness which seems a plot,
a muttering of native dark unease;
but faced with everything unlike their own
a few like Persian scholar Biruni,
whose wise eleventh-century research
compared the worlds around his Middle East,
allow the mood of reason turn the light
it poured on how the Earth and stars behave
to probe the source of words we use as tools.
One Thomas Stephens missioner wrote home
to tell his brother words in India
were like the Greek and Latin learnt in school,
a fact Dutch Boxhorn later too had grasped
and Russian Lomonosov also saw;
but it's two hundred years from Stephen's note
until Sir William Jones the polyglot
colonial judge propounds a common root
for Latin, Greek and Sanskrit, which in turn

extends to Celtic and Germanic tongues,
a shared beginning Dr Thomas Young
first named the Indo-European base.
Franz Bopp expands, comparing word for word
to find out, built on what's already known
about how language change occurs and how
to use the rule-bound correspondences
he spots to reconstruct the mooted tongue
that common forebears spoke, from which
through six or so millennia have grown
the ones we speak, and showing how the words
brother, bráthair, frater, Russian *brat,*
along with Sanskrit *bhrāter,* all suggest
a source that's shared; but Franz Bopp begins
comparing how the verbs and nouns inflect
to learn what grammar's patterns underlie
six thousand years of slow divergency.
No wonder Lomonosov was amazed,
imagining such depths of time as though
behind each sound a million sighs can hide
millennia of whispers overheard—
in all our talk, geologies of word.

How small a whisper do we hear of him,
The thunder of his power who understands?
Untameable Madam, I surrender.

And still the story of what happened shapes
its trail in frozen relics, which record
how tier by tier each animal evolves,
as word derives from word in tiny steps,
or languages diverge and ramify;
and how so many species have died out
among those fossils tracing lines of growth,
a lineage of forks and climbing stems,
until details and subtleties of some
anatomies anticipate a change
within the next, so they contain the roots
of present forms of life; and now the French
Lamarck, Geoffroy and others have begun
as several Greeks and Rome's Lucretius did

to take for granted evolution's course,
when many still believed in one-by-one
creation of each species that emerged;
though change according to Geoffroy occurs
within the womb, whereas Lamarck maintains
some drive insists on more complexity,
and limbs well exercised can pass their strength
from one generation to the next to start
a template shift which then becomes innate.
In England too freethinkers have begun
like Darwin's father's father to propose
the same descent for all hot-blooded life
and speak of nature as our "earth machine";
but enter now this grandson, in whose head
the rifts and schisms of England push and pull,
this consummate Victorian who fears
he'll lose respectability, and so,
obsessive measurer and tracker-down,
his mania pursues details and still
retains a love of broader sweeps and weaves,
his path between idealists who see
so slow but great ascent to perfect man
and those hotheads for whom his theory
provides another route for underdogs—
outsiders from the swelling middle class—
to rage against the church and Oxbridge rule,
establishments who too in turn suspect
a breach of dignity and dread collapse
of all that holds society in check
and point to France's busy guillotines.
A fallen medic, would-be ordinand
impressed by Paley's clock-designer God,
Charles Darwin earns his scholar's spurs aboard
The *Beagle* sounding out an empire's shores;
though sick at first and reading Milton's tale
of paradise once lost he comes to spend
five years across three continents and sends
to London crates of specimens he finds—
the fossils, flora, fish and animals,
flycatchers, molluscs, mockingbirds and shrikes

all shipped and labelled to await the names
by which colonials possess their trove;
yet all along he ponders what he sees
as cut-throat eyes of England's Malthus Whigs
keep watching plants which struggle for their light.
And on return Charles Darwin's name is known
so Richard Owen begins to analyse
his finds, discovers most new animals
prefigured in the local fossils too
reveal descent with change that links the past
with now in geographic patterns which
confirm how all of life evolves and shifts,
Pre-Cambrian to Cambrian and on,
and brings our nature under rule of law
within this scientific scope and range—
the question now what brings about such change.

So shall I keep your word; open my eyes
That I may see the wonders of your laws.
O Mistress, how you slide from key to key.

Poor tortured Darwin's years a country squire—
afraid to lose his sense of properness
he gathers facts to back his hunch and waits
while every sideline makes a monograph
on barnacles or coral reefs, flytraps,
volcanoes, doves and even climbing plants,
and greyhound breeders, pigeon fanciers
explain how every variation can't perfect
but nurtures freaks and runts as suits itself,
all measured, watched, recorded day by day,
his mind and health observed and noted too
through constant bouts of nervous throwing up—
obsessive Darwin failing to let go
until at last, when younger Wallace too
has understood the chance of passing traits
and how what's passed can vary so in time,
those variations suited to survive
must dominate, and by this simple means
all life evolves to fit our habitat,
that pigeon-fancier who chooses best.

To pip young Wallace Darwin coming out
completes his masterwork on origins
while racked for fear his inbred family
will prove to be too weak to make the cut,
but free-trader to his bone and core
he stresses struggling for our scanty means
or sexual selection, which somehow
believer Wallace finds he must reject,
though men like Hooke and Forbes and Waterhouse
row in behind where time is on their side
and Huxley that self-made anatomist
debates the case with Bishop Wilberforce
to score against the old establishment
or flouting ape forebears in workers' halls;
while Haeckel trumpets Darwin's cause abroad
as revolutions fade and laissez-faire
prevails and still despite all sour disputes,
a Darwinism keeps striking deeper roots
and Darwin full of every contrary trait—
a dissident and scientific squire
obsessed with both detail and simple sweep,
both self-absorbed and kindliest papa
so spirit-bruised by daughter Annie's death—
becomes half-willingly revered icon
for disenchantment's energy and rage,
an emblem for a new and worldly age.

Be exalted, O Lord, in your own might;
we will make music and sing of your power.
O Madam who thrives on variation.

And all the while an age of reason brings
so many traits of nature under laws:
that energy is neither made nor lost
but only changed, a fundamental law
of conservation named beside the one
Carnot describes as entropy, the trend
of working energy to dissipate,
as of its own accord what's hot turns cold
or order dwindles to disorder's waste,
time's arrow coded in our nature's pith.

Now too the amber and the lodestone's power
and lightning's force that throws the compass off
yield up their lore to come within the law,
as years of keen experimenters trace
their lineage in names for measurements
in farads, volts, amperes, coulombs or ohms;
discoverers of how the amber's charge
shows plus or minus while the magnet's poles
point north and south and still they both agree
in how like charges and like poles repel
where those unlike like gravity attract.
A Galileo of this new domain,
sharp Faraday, great intuitionist,
by tabletop experiments can sense
that amber, magnet and the light are one,
how lines of force will crowd a magnet's fields,
whose generation or collapse can send
their rippling vibes into our endless space,
before Clerk Maxwell playing Newton's part
to Galileo brings his maths to bear
on Faraday's, Ampère's and Gauss's laws
to grasp in four equations this domain
we call electromagnetism, where
he proves how light in turn belongs here too,
although he still believes some ether bears
this stress that keeps a Newton world intact,
the vibes and fields of force pervading space—
still Faraday terrain he can't embrace.

Bless you the Lord, all you works of the Lord;
Sing his praise and exalt him forever.
My mistress trembles in her whitest noise.

In Darwin's wake a double shift of mood:
part disillusionment like those who'd thought
our earth the core of all, so too we'd seen
ourselves as God's most beautiful one-off
but find that, grown by chance and habitat,
we have no right of privileged overview
and move within the riffs of here and now,
our only patterns sensed in retrospect;

and part the time of reason's naive pride,
distrusting wefts of thought or metaphor,
believes in concrete causes and effects
to better now our lonely human lot.
Our reason's beam can turn its probe to show
a world that's not what it appears to be,
as Durkheim, follower of Comte, unearths
the unseen webs that hold our lives in play,
a resined mesh of rules we sleepwalk in,
our take-for-granted underneath we call
by other names, while those who stand outside
and seek to take the nowhere view of things
find laws beyond our wills we must obey,
until it seems this age of measurement
becomes an underworld where we're entranced—
our minds suspended in an amber gel,
we're falling under reason's thumb and spell.

For a brief moment I abandoned you,
that which they hadn't heard they shall ponder.
O Madam, Madam, you'll reimprovise.

Canto 4
Surprises

Have we the measure, scale and rule,
in limbos grinding to a routine's halt?
In physics and in chemistry it feels
as if our search is fairly well complete
but science of surprise awakes again
as Röntgen tumbles to his strange X-rays
and shows his wife her deathlike bony hand;
in Paris, twiddling with what Röntgen found,
the photographs he's setting up expose
to Becquerel spontaneous new waves,
and Thomson when deflecting cathode rays
detects electrons he concludes turn up
in any sort of matter that exists.
Now Einstein, born the year that Maxwell died,

a child the magnet's needle drew apart,
aloof, unsettling student who becomes
Bern's patent office technical expert,
young man outside the academic guild
consulting friends like Habicht, Solovine
or Michele Basso, colleague engineer,
and keeping something of his bird's-eye view,
begins to publish papers one by one
where, like a Thomas Young but in reverse,
he shows both light as particles not waves
and entropy of radiation which
behaves like gas and probabilities
imply it fits the quantum leap of Planck;
although he knows full well he can't dismiss
the waves that Maxwell knew and Hertz could prove,
but sees how light as particles can smooth
the problems left where light and matter meet,
as when on metal someone shines a lamp,
somehow a frequency of light increased
augments electrons' energy released,
a change which Maxwell's tenets can't explain;
a first foreplay to what will overthrow
the frames of time and space we think we know.

That which hadn't been told them they shall see,
That which they hadn't heard they shall ponder.
My wriggling Mistress, how you syncopate!

Where am I now and how is it I move?
In Newton's frame a clash and hidden glitch
where laws require a space that's absolute,
a place that's featureless without an end
and time that flows unwaveringly on,
so he could deal with motion or with rest
as something independent of all else,
which gave a steady base for him to start,
though Gottfried Leibniz and George Berkeley knew
as Newton too had known, a desert space
provides no clue for gauging length or pace,
a contradiction which then went to ground
as if this science burrowed in denial.

While Poincaré and Lorentz both unknown
to him still strive to hold the Maxwell world
while keeping both of Newton's absolutes,
a twenty-six-year-old Einstein steps in
to make his own the take-for-granted sense
that when two part and both are walking off
for each the other seems to shrink in size,
in mutual contracting of their bulk
as if both move in private time and space.
So now, presuming no experiments
detect an absolute for space and time,
since too no message can outpace the light
and in an empty space the speed of light
does not depend on movements of its source,
then say a spaceship flies on past an earth
and as the midpoint passes by a man
who watches from this earth, a light is flashed,
which someone on the ship will judge to reach
the equidistant stern and bow at once;
whereas the planet-bound observer now,
because the ship is moving all the while
the light is travelling, will see it reach
the nearer stern before the further bow—
for him the two arrival times don't match;
the watchers on the ship and earth contrast.
No simultaneity is absolute,
all time and space relate to something else,
which means that distance too is relative,
so speed, acceleration, energy
or force are all affected by this view;
if clocks at stern and bow are synchronised
so light between them takes the selfsame time
to travel back and forth and yet the man
on earth will see these clocks as out of sync—
or if reversed the clocks on earth are slow,
as two who part both seem to shrink, for each
the other's clock is slower than his own,
our tick and tock are gone beyond control;
at speeds near light what's certain seems to shift,
old dreams of absolutes now cut adrift.

Open my eyes, O Lord, open my eyes
that I may see the wonders of your law.
O Mistress, catching us again off beat!

Both Poincaré and Lorentz were so near
but Einstein still a patent office man,
exiled like Newton from the London plague,
details on surreptitious paper scraps
his young outsider's daring sweep and range
which grasps what others only hinted at:
how matter, energy, like time and space
prove interwoven variants of one
continuum where Maxwell's laws hold good.
And soon Minkowski tells the worlds at large
how space or time alone are doomed to fade:
reality is space and time combined,
the four-dimensioned room that we describe
is where we know our whereabouts by way
of distance from the ground and from two walls
at one exclusive moment in our time;
a point where world lines stretch and so endure,
where four still intermingle as a whole,
which two who part are slicing unlike ways
though plays of mathematics still can show
how somehow both can share what's yet the same,
the way when interlocked rectangular
triangles own the one hypotenuse,
if summed their squared two other sides will match,
like private worlds that never quite detach.

Make me know the ways of your commands,
so shall I ponder your wondrous works.
O this Madam of always even more.

But Einstein still a man of twenty-six
can show us now by calculation how
if bodies give a certain quantity
of energy, their mass diminishes
the same amount divided by the squared
velocity of light and so he makes
a single law for loss or gain of mass—

and yet it takes two years before it dawns
on Einstein's love of simple symmetry
why differentiate at all between
what's lost or gained and what's contained within:
let mass and energy be both the same,
so every feather, brick or speck of dust
becomes a cache of pent-up energy
defined by his equation which declares
that energy is mass when multiplied
by light's speed squared—amazing theory
on which this outside mind now dares rely,
a thesis no one yet can verify.

Teach me true understanding and knowledge
for I have trusted in your commandments.
Madam, I only travel in your riff.

A rising star among the physicists,
a Prague professor, Zürich, then Berlin
where Einstein with misgivings wonders if
his hen-like head can lay another thought
in years of anxious searching in the dark,
as trusting instinct he confronts alone
that strange and vexing action from afar
called gravity which Newton left unsolved
and puzzling why a falling man can feel
no gravity concludes it's relative;
imagining a lab that floats in space
accelerated upward we could tell
the rate of what behaves like gravity—
where any fall will show the same speed-up—
and so the thought occurs why not allow
inertia and gravity to merge
in Einstein's statement of equivalence;
then, following his own equation too,
for energy the mass must be the same
with gravitation or inertia.
But does electromagnetism fit?
He now takes over Maxwell's Newton role,
the part Maxwell had played for Faraday
and Newton played for Galileo once.

A light if sent as ray across the lab
accelerated upward also curves
a little downward in relation to
the lab and therefore Einstein can infer
that gravitation too must bend light rays,
so now the light slowed down by gravity
can also warp a time that atoms gauge
in frequencies of waves they've given off,
but time and space he'd proven interlock
so just as time can warp so too can space.
So little he deduces verified
that sometimes he must think he's going mad
but Einstein trusts his instincts—will find how
when light now slants in constant downward curves
free particles accelerated move
among coordinates of time and space;
if every motion should be relative
then all coordinates are on a par.
He is both sure and yet somehow confused.

You encompass me behind and before;
such knowledge is too wonderful for me.
O Mistress mine, I love your dissonance.

Beyond his repertoire he turns again
to Marcel Grossmann, student friend who'd once
arranged in Bern the patent office post,
who now by chance is master in the field
of metric tensors, mathematics' tool
to deal with more coordinates, the way
in two dimensions, given just a grid
of latitude and longitude before
and after, we can calculate the length
a ship which took the shortest course has come;
though in a fourth dimension human minds
can't conjure how it works and we must yield
to ten equations Einstein sweated out
to represent the works of gravity,
when tensors show, as Gauss and Riemann saw,
a geometric shape—the way we know
when one triangle's angles summed are more

than two right angles, something bends or bows
and gravity no longer now a force
becomes a curvature of time and space
where bodies move in orbits round a sun
because there are no straight world lines but like
free particles obeying Newton's laws
they travel here the only way they can,
describing on a sphere what corresponds
in two dimensions to a line that's straight,
a geodesic path about their sun
in whose allure we so long thought they'd spun.

The glory, splendour and the majesty,
everything in heaven and on earth yours.
Will Madam now unveil another veil?

In Riemann's four dimensions Einstein twists
the curvature of every starlight's course
in gravitation's fields of space plus time,
where bodies like a gymnast's weight distort
the surface of a space-warped trampoline—
and this it seems implies a universe
expanding and contracting, even though
his ten equations factor out this thought;
and yet how wonderful that what's abstract
can prove so sound when Arthur Eddington,
observing an eclipse in Príncipe,
reports deflections which in turn confirm
what Einstein calculates, or when the drift
in Mercury's unruly course which shifts
its orbit's perihelion conforms
to what his heady theory expects
because it's closest to the sun and moves
along the steepest gradient which curves
within the solar gravitation's field.
But rumours spread and so now heroised
he visits Britain, Japan, America;
iconic scientist, unworldly sage
or Jewish decadent in Nazi eyes
who must retreat to Belgium's Le Coq
and then to Princeton, where he spends his days

believing still in laws of paradise
where God can cast the die but not the dice.

Great the wonders you've done, O Lord my God. . . .
There is none that can be compared with you.
O Madam, still your jazz defies control.

In frenzied years before Einstein had fled,
unease at how the quantum thought conflicts
with Newton or with Maxwell's view of things
flares up when Rutherford describes the way
around an atom's core or "nucleus"
electrons spin like planets for a sun.
They should give off a photon and collapse
if Maxwell's laws still hold but Bohr now claims
electrons circle orbits which increase,
in scales of certain hops, determined spurts,
in jumps of energy called quantum leaps
when light can radiate or be absorbed;
and using Planck's known quantum rule now Bohr
can link the frequency of light to shifts
within the spun electrons' energy.
Soon Einstein shows the Maxwell analogues
in quanta when an empty atom grabs
a matching particle of light, while one
that's full emits a particle at whim,
although if one that's full attempts to snatch
a second particle, it ends with none.
But quantum thought and Maxwell still contend
and so a rash of theories ensue;
for Einstein light consists of particles,
Broglie believes they're moved along by waves
but Heisenberg with Jordan and Max Born
refine this quantum thesis which Dirac
alone at Cambridge also formulates
as then, to Schrödinger's chagrin, instead
of Broglie's mooted waves of matter which
he too by now was busy working out,
Max Born begins to speak of amplitudes—
a wave of probability that still
remains in some strange way a particle.

One day pours out its song to another,
one night unfolds knowledge to another.
Madonna poised between tonalities!

Though relativity has undercut
our science sense but deeper now the gash
of indeterminacy Heisenberg
proposes, where we find we make a choice;
electrons we observe we too will change
by quantum jolts which alter what we see;
our seeing is itself a cause of change,
between our observations we must guess
by probabilities the route of waves—
we either know the place or else the speed,
a choice Bohr follows with his coup de grâce:
though we begin and end in normal lives
while in the minute quantum wonderland
the waves and particles don't contradict,
they're one or other just as needs may be,
not this nor that but complementary.

To Allah belongs the east and the west,
He guides whom he pleases to the right path.
O Madam, how you slide from key to key.

That photons could behave like particles
when hitting atoms, yet could move in waves
as if in many places all at once—
the way an infant's face can switch so fast
between two unlike parents' looks and genes
but in the end like light it is itself—
remains for Einstein's mind a stumbling block
so he opposes it for all he's worth,
but Bohr and Bohm and Heisenberg prevail,
successes in their Copenhagen mode
predicting how our atoms must behave
anaesthetise the doubts of common sense
which means another shift in how we think,
a vision change, a world view inside out,
until like post-Copernicans who watched
how comets wandered through those heavens once

immutable, we see a subtler world
where problem-solving can begin again.
And yet as always continuity:
so much from day to day remains the same
as only near the speed of light we need
to ponder relativity as such
or in the subatomic mill to think
how particles can billow as they move
or how our prying human minds must choose
between our seeing where electrons are
or gauging their exact velocity,
foretelling things in probabilities.

Even darkness is no darkness with you . . .
darkness and light to you are both alike.
Cool lady jazz, your rhythm's still my guess.

But who then is this dapper exile there,
white-suited and fedoraed younger man
who treks each day with Einstein to and from
their Princeton institute so deep in thought—
and what can bond two humans so unlike?
There's Einstein in his braces, down-to-earth
clearheaded lover of a common sense
and twenty-seven years his senior bows
to hear the highly strung young Gödel show
his logic and the physics once begun
and now the mathematics, where before
he'd reached the age of twenty-four he'd proved
his theorem of incompleteness which
declares in any formal system fit
for number theory there must exist
a formula we can't prove right or wrong—
and even more, consistency remains
unprovable within the system's frame;
a maths man who, inside the citadel
with all the rigours of his manic trade
unveiling what his trade can really do
in technical and a priori proofs,
unlocks a Trojan horse of paradox,
the self-referring riddle Greeks had known:

if we declare "this very sentence false"
whichever way we turn we contradict—
for if it's true, the sentence then is false
but if it's false, our sentence must be true—
a crux he's woven through his theorem
to show that even mathematics too
must beg the questions which it claims are true.

Great is the Lord and highly to be praised;
His greatness is beyond all searching out.
O Madam, in you we're extempore.

Do they fill out each other's might-have-been:
Einstein the physicist that Gödel dreamt of
and Gödel the maths man Einstein left behind?
They share a German-speaking world they fled
and each has done his ripest work while young
but more than this, for both the meaning counts:
for Gödel there's nothing due to accident,
for Einstein God is always immanent,
and seeking minds have left these men misfits;
for both the relative and incomplete
no softening to a vague subjective view
but proof of some great truth beyond themselves,
the sacred Euclid book of Einstein's youth,
the far out yonder found in certain laws.
But discontented with what merely works
these Platonists are walking side by side,
two purgatorial disciples who
can hear the chant beyond the wall of fire
yet somehow never manage to pass through
to where a stubborn independent streak,
which in their bloom could serve them both so well,
might come to terms with something less precise,
relearning childlike plays of paradise
where gambling God can throw a lover's dice.

In the tender compassion of our God
the dawn from on high shall break upon us.
Madam Jazz, you play me ad libitum.

Canto 5
All Dance

Is knowing there are things we'll never know
another kind of freedom which admits
that, part of all that is, we too belong;
for since the view from nowhere is not ours,
in ceding such control do we embrace
the always more in what we still must probe
by test or theory as best combined
to find our ways of knowing all we can?
No longer Atlas bearing up the world
or Laplace with such iron in his soul,
perhaps in rigour now a sense of play,
abundance in abundance we unfold
in symmetries which in their downrightness
just seem to be the way they had to be—
so simple that it's difficult to find
the right equation for such symmetry,
for lovely parities of left and right
like this and that each side an equals sign—
although we always know how systems leak,
how thoughts detour and loop as we advance,
as poets still believe they'll catch the wind
so too a dream of final theories,
a deep desire for supersymmetries
to close the gaps in life's invariance
that drives our search to understand still more,
to knock again on God's all-knowing door.

You encompass me behind and before . . .
Such knowledge is too wonderful for me.
Madam, the tune I catch I lose again.

We know inside the atom's airy room
electrons swirl in tendencies to be
held in by nuclei as small as specks
of dust within St Peter's skyline dome
and how, as spun propellers show a disc,
excited massless particles can whirl
six hundred miles a second to appear

as solid as the things we know we feel,
and yet they don't rotate as planets do
but somewhere in the orbits they describe
they turn in such a way their ends can meet,
contouring certain well-defined designs
of standing waves as strings on plucked guitars
or billowed air inside a flute when blown;
so shapes and space between the orbitals
remain alike for every atom which
contains the same electron count and since
the orbit, energy and speed and spin
are designated quantum numbers too,
the interplay of solids, liquids, gas
reveal their bonds between the elements;
the physicists can leave electrons be
and concentrate on nuclei which hold
the tiny hearts within the atom's whole,
the plus-charged cores which pull their minus moons
in rooms one hundred thousand times their size,
and yet so dense they own the bulk of mass
within the atom's largely empty space
and close as if our bodies were compressed
until they'd neatly fit on heads of pins.
At first colliding atoms Rutherford
discovers protons in the nuclei
which match the negative electrons' count
and leave the atoms with a zero charge,
but then Chadwick, his protégé, reveals
the chargeless neutrons, which when they're confined
with protons race around the nuclei
at up to forty thousand miles or so
a second while held by forces they name "strong,"
which only work when close together, though
too near they drive each other far apart—
the yes and no which keeps this dance in play.
But here we reach the 1930s start,
when all of chemistry seems well explained;
at last we have the smallest building blocks,
the bits of atoms Greeks first thought made up
our world of matter, all now cut and dry,

and nothing new we must identify.

Let us know, let us press to know the Lord,
his appearing is as sure as the dawn.
Madam, where you end you re-begin.

Those Greeks within our minds still seek what's fixed,
imagining how to break the pieces down
until we reach the fundamental bits;
but as we learn how best to track their path
still more new particles appear and so
as these move nearly at the speed of light
both quantum thoughts and relativity
combine in ways that force us to admit
that things will not reduce to basic stuff—
all matter in the end is energy;
we only trace in its dynamic forms
the endless process of this energy
that sometimes can reveal itself as mass.
Dirac has shown in theory the way
sufficient energy can well call forth
electrons' antiparticles—the same
in mass but with their polar charge reversed—
and soon experiments will prove that all
known particles can have these counterparts,
such pairs that energy sometimes creates,
sometimes draws back into itself again.
In huge accelerators we collide
the nucleons that near the speed of light
so particles emerge and die away
within a second's millionth part and leave
in spirals, line and curlicues the tracks
magnetic fields induce to find a trace
that's larger than the particles themselves;
and even when we smash them into bits
kinetic energy we use instead
of breaking down the parts can just create
more particles the same as those we've crashed.
In subatomic worlds what we called force,
the power that now attracts and now repels,
consists of swaps and sudden interchange

among these particles which whizz and glance,
our static thoughts still learning how to dance.

I count them, they're more in number than sand
And at the end I'm still in your presence.
Mischievous strategy, O Madam Jazz.

For all the patterns in the ceaseless dance,
the constant come and go of energy,
there's order here as matter still consists
of protons, neutrons and electrons which
can radiate a photon too at will—
and three of these are stable while the fourth,
the neutrons, by themselves sometimes can turn
to proton with electrons now to boot,
and what the German Pauli first proposed
but afterwards Enrico Fermi named
"neutrinos," which though hard to find have mass
that's miniscule but do not have a charge.
In cyclotrons' accelerated slams
collided nucleons can now reveal
unstable particles are forced to leave
a trace their finders name now one by one,
a growing list of subatomic sorts:
the lightweight leptons like the electrons,
unstable muons and later tauons too
that turn into electrons in a trice;
the mostly heavy hadrons which are classed
as mesons and the weighty baryons.
So let the dancers in the dance unfold
in litanies of subtype mesons named
"pions," "kaons," "etas," "Ks" and "Ds" and "Bs,"
and newer alphabets of baryons
beside the protons and the neutrons show
the lambda, sigma, chi, cascade and omega.
But subtler still the way these dancers spin
in ratchet quantum twists which, turning twice,
will then come back to how they started out—
where we rotating once have then returned.
Yet numbers of returnings also count:

if odd called "bosons," even "fermions"—
the ones as Pauli shows are not allowed
to let the same kind share a quantum state,
where bosons have a freer hand to play.
Such odd and even numbered elegance
within the moves and weavings of one dance.

For you, Lord, have made me glad by your acts;
I sing aloud at the works of your hands.
Demurring Lady playing at the chase.

But seeing how the hadrons multiply,
are they themselves composed of other parts?
George Zweig suggests four "aces" might explain
The complex make-up of the nucleons;
Then Murray Gell-Mann names a triplet scheme
and so the "quarks" we never isolate,
as they're too tightly bound to show their face,
which still map out for us in theory
how hadrons must behave within this dance.
At first there's three: the "up" and "down" and "strange,"
but then the fourth called "charm" Glashow predicts,
which twelve years later Lederman observes,
a fifth named "beauty" or the "bottom" quark,
which after eighteen years will get its match—
the "truth" or "top" quark heavy counterpart,
which leaves, like leptons, six, all fermions;
yet since these quarks have each three kinds of charge—
someone at whim dubs red and green and blue—
we end up with our eighteen quarks in all;
the heavy baryons contain three quarks,
in mesons there's a quark and antiquark,
small points observed in scattered electrons
shot through a particle or in the jets
from hadrons which decay when they collide.
Are these the fundamental particles
or maybe quarks in turn have structures too
below where we as yet can find a trace,
a seething dance beyond our mind's embrace?

The glory of God shall be revealed
and all people shall see it together.
I spin in your nexus, O Mistress All.

And still the dream to make four forces one:
the long-range gravity which builds with mass
but hardly counts in subatomic worlds;
the charged electric and magnetic force,
long-ranged but positive and negative
can cancel one another out and cease
yet, hugely stronger than our gravity,
it plays a greater role on minute scales;
the other two are both subnuclear:
the strong and short-ranged one all hadrons feel,
both stronger than electromagnetism
and complex too as quarks are triple-charged;
the weak and even shorter-ranged which shifts
the kind of quark or lepton and explains
the way neutrons decay and so become
a proton and electron and as well
a swift neutrino antiparticle.
All four it's now believed use "messengers,"
those particles which carry force or field:
the photons in electromagnetism
where gravity may use a graviton;
eight gluons mediate the force called "strong"
and Weinberg's z's and w's the "weak."
First Faraday and Maxwell fused in one
the old electric and magnetic force
which Einstein tried to join with gravity
which Kaluza in turn had also sought,
but Sheldon Glashow spots the common core
electromagnetism and weak force
can share, then Steven Weinberg finds a way,
as Abdus Salam also did, to let
the messengers acquire their hefty mass
(whereas electrons have no mass at all)
by setting the great boson Higgs predicts
beside electromagnetism's fields,
so leaving their gauge symmetries intact,

they meld two forces neatly into one
now called electroweak, explaining much
where older weak force theory had failed,
inspiring more to find a way to fuse
all four—and swathes of theories predict
they'll heal the gap between the quantum realm
and bigger worlds where gravity still reigns.
Some trust in supersymmetries, while more
in Kaluza's dimensions—now at ten:
our three plus time and six curled up inside
a string within a particle which then
vibrates in certain modes to generate
all particles and forces that we know.
Yet now to prove these things we need
accelerators with such energies
imagined in creation's starting trice,
so physicists gaze heavenwards and hope
colliding atoms in our milky ways
send hints or proofs among their cosmic rays.

Then return thy gaze, again and again,
the gaze comes back to the dazzled, weary.
My femme fatale now shapes another face.

Although a few had long expected more,
our Milky Way was all when Hubble gazed
at spiral nebulae that lay beyond
the bright and clustered cities of the night,
and measuring the light which they emit
he sees how furthest stars give furthest light
and shift across the spectrum's frequencies
like falling tones of sirens when they've passed,
which tells us how the galaxies recede
and how our universe expands—the space
between the galaxies still growing so
the distant ones move quicker than those near,
as when a pebble drops into a pond
remoter waves spread faster than the core
or dots on a balloon we're blowing up
where furthest dots part swifter than those close,
which fits with Einstein's relativity

except for the one fudge he'd introduced
to keep the stable picture then in vogue
and later calls his lifetime's biggest gaffe,
though Friedman soon restores his first impulse.
It seems there was just one great bursting out,
exploding at the same rate everywhere
and filling all of space right from the start
as every particle of matter parts,
our universe kept blowing out and on,
so galaxies recede from us at speeds
proportional to distance—and from here
this means we have no privileged view or place
within the cosmic flow of galaxies
as every pair of clusters parts alike;
although some years friends Bondi, Gold and Hoyle
proposed their steady state where at the edge
galactic matter disappears while near
the centre more develops and so forth—
though entropy might end that endless ring,
predicted cosmic microwaves when found
put paid to steady states and so confirm
a first big bang which even still expands
across some fifteen billion years to now;
and yet Fred Hoyle shows us how carbon forms
by triple-alpha process, which in turn
can in the long term lead to life on earth.
But does our cosmos just expand for ever,
though entropy once more might answer no,
perhaps it bubbles in a greater pot
or sphere-like both unbounded and finite
could it then pulse between big bang and crunch?
If gravity creates black holes that suck
in all beyond the point of no return,
where each known law no longer can apply,
these too remind us where our knowledge falls
as out of reach as just before the burst.
Has entropy a low so it ascends
so as we have beginnings, have we ends?

The heavens declare the glory of God,
and the firmament shows his handiwork.
Madam's tunes die in metamorphosis.

We'd thought the cosmos turned itself on us
and now by radio astronomy
we count in millions swirling galaxies
and in one spur of one galactic arm
within one galaxy our Earth is spun;
revolving still its anticlockwise tours
each quarter of a thousand million years
our Sun rotates within that Milky Way
with its few hundred billion stars in train,
which each in turn gyrates in its own way.
Compacter than its paired Andromeda,
yet twenty thousand light years side to side,
with two Magellanic Clouds as satellites,
our native flattened disc-like galaxy
throughout the twenty turns the Sun has made
has rearranged the skies above our head,
refiguring the stars once formed from scuds
of molecules and dust which photons stir
to where self-gravitation can condense
them into globules Bok at Harvard names,
which when collapsing finally are stars.
These spend a lifetime fusing hydrogen
to helium while blowing stellar winds
until, their fuel spent, they start to cool
and make red giants whose hearts compress to fuse
a helium, which when consumed creates
a hub of oxygen and carbon, while
the larger stars now shell by shell can fuse
to neon and to silicon up to
the final iron phase before breakdown.
Then average stars must shed their outer layers,
their residue becoming dwarfs named white
at first, though over time they fade to black;
whereas in larger stars which can't support
their mass, the core succumbs to electrons
undoing protons in reverse decay

so they turn supernovae, bursting forth
to leave behind a broiling neutron star;
while those with mass five times our sun depart,
as past event horizons they withdraw
and sucked inside themselves they seem to end
in closed black holes we still don't comprehend.

What's man that you should be mindful of him,
the son of man that you should seek him out?
My Minx, you're still beyond my mind's embrace.

It seems it all began with one outburst
but yet a gravity so finely gauged
has kept expansion just the way it is;
for if that blowing out had even been
a hundred thousand million millionth part
slowed down, our universe would recollapse;
a fraction quicker and no Earth could form;
if comets hadn't brought our building blocks—
their carbon, water and some nitrogen—
so one great soup could cook just how it did,
if asteroids had missed and didn't kill,
our world would then unfold another tale.
Are we the twig on this one lucky tree,
the children of a chance that's dumb and blind?
Did something rig the thimbles, stack the deck?
Or is there still some richer interplay
between what's chance and what's necessity
narrowing in the seas of what might be
as probabilities allow unknowns
or how in chaos islands can attract?
So even in our evolution too
those parallels where traits or growth converge
as lives that seek safe havens where they'll thrive,
distinctive lineages again evolve
adaptings which will fit as needs may be
marsupials and sabre-toothed cats,
the lizard and the sandfish common eye,
the star-nosed mole so near the point of sight,
an attine ant, a social wasp and bee,
the fungal colonies grown underground,

those bonobos so busy making tools—
and if we hadn't walked from Africa
then somewhere soon our like would sally forth.
In fits and starts we push an unlocked door,
a lover's dice half-loaded but no more.

Bless you the Lord, all you works of the Lord,
sing his praise and exalt him forever.
Madam, you give the notes; we find a tune.

Lamarck and Darwin didn't understand
what Mendel with his garden peas revealed:
the traits which we inherit are discreet;
what we name genes were known as chromosomes
composed of protein and of DNA
but it is 1953 before
James Watson and co-worker Frances Crick
with Franklin's X-ray crystallography
unravel how our DNA makes up
two strands that turn a double-corkscrew shape
with inward molecules like careful steps
on some long winding sideless stairs.
So now we read our genome book of life
in twenty-three such chromosomes which fit
the several thousand genes which we receive,
consisting of the exons that make sense
(divided by the introns' nonsense stuff)
and they in turn contain the codons which
are triplets of an A, C, G or T,
four nucleobases spelling out our life—
a recipe that's stored within one cell,
whose chromosomes would stretch to some six feet,
inscribed in chains of sugar and phosphate,
these bases now the treads that climb the stairs
where As with Ts and Gs with Cs combine
so strands that complement, then replicate,
returning sequences which started out.
The same base-pairing way a gene's transcribed
to RNA with Us instead of Ts,
which edits out the random intron mess
and with the help of ribosomes translates

each codon to a corresponding chain,
a score amino acids form that then folds up
in various shapes now called a protein which
can switch a body's genes both on and off.
But RNA, the messenger, translates
from sixty-four compounds down to a score
and in the overlaps mistakes occur
from one life to the next—our genes mutate
to let the course of evolution run.
So now when male and female genes combine
four billion years of learning cumulate,
the genomes playing messages by rote
as genes we get create for us a brain
designed to shift to fit our habitat:
synapses change in shaping memories,
our nurture and our nature interlocked,
behaviour and our genes a feedback ring
both unpredictable yet not unfixed,
a theme of variations unforeseen,
the loving freedom of the in-between.

Great are the wonders you have done, O Lord;
my God, how great are your designs for us.
A battered tune, my Mistress, you renew.

Again the strange enfoldment of a world
our loops and detours keep on opening out
as we, undoing dreams of strict control,
begin to learn to live in paradise
disclosed in patterns always on the move,
where everything combines with something else—
the image of the whole in every part
as structures yield to processes instead—
and we are players in the interplay,
enmeshed within a nettedness of things,
where more and more and more now still invites
a love whose freedom keeps its knife-edge keen
between what is and what might not have been.

Be exalted, O Lord, in your own might;
We will make music and sing of your power.
Madam, I am your tune until the end.

5

Meaning

Canto 1
Word and Mind

(i)

You angel of the burning bush, inspire
me now as I once more begin, and fan
in me again a falling tongue of fire

to find somehow the words as best I can
to trace, if not explain, the ways we came
across our centuries from where the clan

or tribe together merge to share the same
impulse, propitiating gods by rite—
invoke the spirits we both praise and blame

for gifts or ills they slow or expedite,
appease by sacrifice or charm and prayer
those powers nearby but always out of sight.

So much is numinous and everywhere,
force field of shadows either bad or good,
the sacred wells and long-assuaged forebear,

the holy mountain climbed, the hallowed wood,
the two-edged gods which we must pacify
to flourish in a cosmos understood

as endless cycles where we're born and die,
a chain of rebirths we're embedded in
until that age when some beliefs defy

the timeless gyre, allow a world begin
from out of nothing, spoken once alive,
a genesis outside both tribe and kin;

and though we still do all we can to thrive,
depending on some overriding scheme,
a God beyond ourselves we trust to drive

a cosmos where within a blessed regime
we shape what flourishing for us may mean
and children banished from the garden dream,

in spite of Eden's long-since-fallen gene
entrusted here to better what's below,
we now allow for all that's still unseen

while crying out against each status quo
in God's subversive drama of exile
and exodus. *O let my people go*,

let homesick Moses rescued from the Nile
by Pharaoh's own, obeying God's command
to turn the Red Sea into land a while,

as Hebrews cross before the rod and hand,
and drown the horsemen following this guide
who'll never even reach the promised land—

who though he'd eaten manna and had eyed
the face of God most living must not see;
the milk and honey taste is still denied.

Two-edged as Noah's flood, the parted sea
for some the saving water but for more
releasing precreation anarchy,

like Babel's doubleness we've seen before,
a ziggurat of pride that can become
Jacob's ladder reaching heaven's door.

Such textures spun from one millennium
into the next in midrash and belief,
a code and nettedness of idiom

we weave in which each Middle East motif
explores a god of process and repair
in histories of ordeal and relief

those following the foolish cross then share,
and which the Prophet's angel too had known,
so all we Abrahamic heirs can dare

allow our God a purpose not our own
and here outside a timeless roundelay
we dance within our fragile ecozone

where in and outness both are held in play.

(ii)

As any change takes centuries, so too
this move allowing God unknown designs
a slack and stumbling shift that slowly grew

and while an older way of thought declines,
in unreflecting minds the two now mix
taboos and blessings, fairy forts and shrines,

the banshee with the sacred oil or pyx,
a midnight rosary and rowdy wake,
our dead cajoled by goods or crucifix.

In overlapping faiths no sudden break;
unconsciously our bets are hedged in case
we make mistakes we can't afford to make

and so the ordinary commonplace
conflates the favour coaxed with prayers of praise
as Shintō and the Buddha share one space.

Our cloistered monks withdraw to spend their days
at peace in work and prayerful flourishings,
a world where other-worldly thought outweighs

the fuss and mess of mundane happenings—
our hopes and falls, our rows or family slights,
the helter-skelter of such daily things

we meld with carnival, with fairs and fights,
with relic, pilgrimage and Virgin prayer,
where time both flows and warps in feasts and rites;

so laity and monks are each a layer
in earthly faith with thoughtful overlays
and come-day, go-day working laissez-faire

until the drift to towns and urban ways
or in the wake of plagues some psychic urge
or scandal set reformers' hearts ablaze.

Again and again the same desire to merge
our two-tiered Christendom in one,
so we conform to higher things and purge

all heathen traces that real faith should shun,
as friars grey and black and white begin
to ratchet up our fears for what we've done

and thoughts of wounded Christ now underpin
new fears of death and bodies we forsake
as sins of sex become the utmost sin,

which once had been the human bonds we break,
our sundered loves; and now too long before
the great doomsday we die alone to take

whatever punishment that lies in store,
a private judgement for our solo span,
with purgatory to settle up the score.

And then a Council of the Lateran
demands confessions must be made by all,
a new crusade and inner clean-up plan;

but some protesters setting out their stall
presage a reformation in their flight
from signs as both Hussites and Lollards call

for change and many pious souls take fright
at hosts some rakish priest could consecrate—
the singer of their song not living right.

This seething undertow must somehow wait
until new doctrines undergird complaints,
encourage then to split and separate,

this need to tame the mass, impose constraints,
this rife desire some old reforming itch
to turn the faithful into living saints,

this dream that all should live at fever pitch.
Such bids to close the gap by fears and dread
begin a process where our ties unhitch;

the ante raised turns out a watershed:
before a people judged by what they'd done
but personal rapport now counts instead,

Our dealings with our God more one by one.

(iii)

In broadest strokes and sweep so far so good.
But now, my burning angel, you well know,
although the scene is set and understood,

unless my words turn flesh, unless I throw
this epic to the winds so phantoms speak,
become your earthly impresario,

unless . . . is there a hint of something sleek
between the bowl haircut and doubling chin,
a trace of light across his high-boned cheek,

as out of Cranach's portrait painted in
the year he and Katharina wed
he steps and asks, "But where should I begin?

"I'm not your guiding Virgil but instead
let me explain my views on grace and sin
before your other guests take up the thread.

"Whatever else my heart is genuine.
O no! Hans Luther didn't spare the rod—
a trading Europe needs its discipline.

"Perhaps my father's strictures tinge my God;
I'm not the lawyer he wanted me to be,
my vow as monk he always found too odd.

"No matter what my one anxiety
  that nothing I can do will be enough;
  for all my fasts and prayers the same old me

"with scruples and a sense of God's rebuff,
  but Prior Staupitz' protégé I'm soon
  Herr Doktor Luther, who now knows his stuff.

"At Wittenberg by thirty I have hewn
  new doctrines which will open up a sluice;
  I turn from Aristotle (Greek buffoon!),

"Aquinas, people playing fast and loose
  who think that thought explains His sacred mind—
  we have in Scripture all we need deduce.

"In Psalms and Romans too again I find
  Therein the righteousness of God revealed;
  as sinners, pardon for our humankind

"depends on grace; who God decides is healed
  and all our own exertions wasted sweat.
  By faith and faith alone our fates are sealed.

"Far better than indulgence your regret!
  Augustine, teacher of grace, knew few were saved.
  Forgiveness is our Saviour's prepaid debt.

"But Tetzel's scaled indulgence was depraved—
  his bishop sharing half and half with Rome.
  If they'd repent, admit how they'd behaved

"extorting funds to build St. Peter's dome,
  while asking I recant to save my soul.
  My church that once had known the catacomb?

"Then everything spins out of my control.
  At first appellant, soon a heretic,
  reformer handed out a rebel's role.

"A spark in tinder, all my rhetoric
  sets old Italian phobias alight,
  our bias turns so anti-Catholic.

"In Regensburg some thought we'd reunite;
  at Trent popes stole our Reformation clothes
  But I see how with ghostly second sight

"I let my bêtes noires become my foes,
  despised all Jews and Turks, but wasn't stern
  enough on Hesse when the chance arose.

"And yet I learned in James what deeds can earn—
  My hymns and Bible set our German tone.
  But one thing more before I must return:

"Remember, friend, how easily sparks are blown;
  The air we share can fan an unseen flame.
  Here I stand. But no one stands alone.

"I climb again into my Cranach frame."

(iv)

I walk among my guests and silhouettes,
  a chosen few whose work and one-time fame
  have tied our drifting history's tangled nets,

and watch how Luther freezes in his frame
  with so much now unleashed beyond his ken,
  so much let loose he knows he'll never tame;

Samaritan and Jew at odds again,
  a dream mired down in bitter rivalries
  of Europe's nations' painful mise en scène.

But who's that profile beginning to unfreeze,
  his tautened face an unplayed talking drum,
  that right eye cool with deep intensities?

"My forefinger pointing and my thumb
  already drumming home my argument . . .
  take care if you're to be my medium

"that you explain exactly what I meant.
  For me as well no rescue without grace;
  I go with Luther as far as Luther went.

"But I am coming from another place;
    abyss and maze my images of awe—
    my mother's early death has left its trace.

"First student for the priesthood, then of law,
    I know my Latin, Hebrew and my Greek;
    a humanist with all these doubts that gnaw.

"No monk, in hour-long sermons week by week
    I preach the heart, yet reason has its place
    to keep in check my own hot-tempered streak.

"You see it in my tight-skinned angled face—
    and Calvin's Latin for 'bald-headed one,'
    though with my cap no knowing if that's the case—

"how something in my nature had to shun
    what seemed those sacraments legerdemain,
    believe that nothing done or left undone

"will change what God chose once to foreordain;
    all-knowing and almighty, He must know
    straight off just who is Abel and who Cain.

"All's predestined, nothing touch and go,
    before the world began He chose our fate;
    the way we live the only hint He'll show

"if we're the chosen or the reprobate;
    all hangs on motives and our inner zone,
    how we elect decide to navigate

"between ungodly going it alone
    and that temptation we may feel to fall
    into our sins' despairing monotone,

"refusing so God's gift which could forestall
    His saving grace or even show a sign
    we're not among those few he chose to call

"and sins will lead to chaos, mar design.
    Each should have a seemly trade: we need
    no blessed hobos stepping out the line;

"the few must show the only way and lead.
 Servetus I had testified against,
 condemned his dangerous mistaken creed.

"Though Titian caught the way my cheeks have tensed
 with age, yet still my spirit folds back in
 to where my unknown profilist has sensed,

"despite my eye and tightly drawn in skin,
 the way my thumb and index always warn
 my hearers not to lose their discipline,

"forget that sinners all we still are torn
 between our choosing and the devil's cup
 and mustn't slide into complacent scorn;

"our every ladle short we daren't sup
 with demons; covenanted now we wait
 between His pointing finger and thumbs-up

"that inner zone we chosen navigate."

(v)

But Europe soon turns inward on itself
in wrangles mixed with new religious hate,
outdoing older Ghibeline and Guelf

and shaping now the future nation-state.
A broad-brushed portrait starts to stir and peer.
Is that a Stoic air? At any rate,

another Franz Hals knowing cavalier,
his large white collar lighting up his eyes,
but left side on, without a hat or leer,

instead a lived-in look which, zigzag-wise
between Renaissance and enlightenment,
allows both sweep and detail compromise.

"O yes, Franz's brush has caught the lineament
 of that Cartesian doubt named after me;
 perhaps reserve is in my temperament

"since *Maman* died and from my infancy
  my *grand-mère* and my nurse in turn have sown
  a love of reason and a gaiety

"before the Jesuits make me their own
  with classics, science, maths for us *bonhommes*
  and Aristotle still the cornerstone.

"I keep such sources to a minimum
  As lying late in bed I think from scratch
  And therefore am: *cogito ergo sum.*

"I only want that knowledge life can match.
  First law, then where the world's own book has led;
  I travel, mix among all ranks, and catch

"As catch can do. With Beeckman I too spread
  my scientific wings. My proofs, though done
  for geometry, use algebra instead.

"Yet from my teens our Europe's wars begun,
  at home some years a bon vivant in France,
  before the fall of La Rochelle I run

"to Holland as I daren't take the chance—
  opposing Aristotle I might burn!
  By background I'd an open-minded stance.

"From Rosicrucians, though I've much to learn,
  I flee their magic choosing Bacon's way
  and all beyond our reason's doubt I spurn;

"what's not self-evident per se
  I leave or break things into smaller bits
  and so deduce what keeps the whole in play.

"No vacuums now, each corpuscle transmits
  all force, our universe one great machine
  where every single part precisely fits.

"God has no ends and doesn't intervene;
  as wax that melts stays whole within the mind,
  so too, although our God remains unseen,

"if I conceive of Him as good and kind
  who therefore couldn't lie, He must exist,
  though we must shape the world as we're inclined.

"But both philosopher and scientist
  dividing now our mind and flesh like that,
  or is there still some wholeness I have missed?

"Before you judge me, this one caveat:
  remember well the times I'm living in,
  uncertain world of warring tit for tat,

"an endless strife where neither side can win.
  No wonder I retreat from bodies, then,
  and choose the mind beyond this bone and skin.

"As I wish well so many other men,
  forgive mistakes I did or didn't make
  now I take up my painted stance again."

As Europe falls to peace, so much at stake
  our need for certainty, and fixed frontiers
  turns inwards in Descartes' far-reaching wake;

a whole world view already shifting gears.

Canto 2
Binding and Freeing

(i)

The dust of thirty years begins to clear
and, now we curb such wars and fervency,
the aims of God can seem to disappear

as we pull back and learn a dignity
where reason must control all wild desire;
detachment, stoic "what must be, will be,"

noblesse oblige of *gentilhomme* and squire,
the *vous* for *tu*, the "you" for what was "thou,"
a distancing we know we must acquire.

"A gentleman should rise above a row.
 In all my work I sought a golden mean
 and so God-given reason must allow

"our human will to find a space between
 the papist hocus-pocus laissez-faire
 and the fanatic rage for sweeping clean. . . ."

Is this John Locke with long and steely hair
swept back and face that narrows to his chin?
It's strange as I was waiting for Voltaire!

"I'll be brief! I know I'm butting in—
Westminster and my Oxford taught me grace—
a once-blank mind has learned such discipline.

"Friend of Boyle and Hooke, I too keep pace
with science. How is human knowledge gained?
Descartes's all mind—but me, I rather place

"my trust in what experience ingrained,
for we're our own aware reflective mind;
embodied self that we have shaped and stained

"and each of us has willingly assigned
our rights to states to take us in their care
but only laws for all our good should bind. . . ."

A red lining caught by Largillière
with rouged cheeks and knotted white cravat
in place, the sudden eruption of Voltaire:

"O no, Monsieur John Locke, don't give me that!
You and rights of revolution though
you've shares in slaves despite your caveat.

"Forgive my interruption as I know
I'm barely ten when you had passed away;
I too am in this story's ebb and flow.

"Then Jesuits before my father got his way,
I started law but life became my pen.
Two thousand booklets with one thing to say

"and said in my famed *phrase voltairienne*:
my *sans diversité*, no liberty.
Eleven months in the Bastille and then

"exile in England where I at last felt free
and learned from you, John Locke, though my Marquise
and I interrogate the deity.

"Our God has no such church tomfooleries.
Yet more than books, my Jean Calas campaign
prepares the way for revolutionaries."

"But your Candide, Voltaire, remembers Cain;
you see in Hobbes the Pangloss I see too.
And did I set your deist line in train?

"I hadn't seen the plot as I now do
or how such shifts of heart and mind accrued;
perhaps there'll always be the things we rue."

A host, I'm busy working to include
my guests who come from these communities
of thought that talk across our drifts of mood

and, brokering between the centuries
in conversations, try to understand
how tone and mode can change by slow degrees

to move in stranger ways than ever planned,
how time ahead has depths we never plumb;
for unseen worlds we write our ampersand.

A thought we think can shape so much to come.

(ii)

Ideas which begin among the few
can filter out until one probing thought
becomes the take-for-granted point of view,

and slowly modes of living long inwrought
give way as mind and practice interflow
through years of argument intense and fraught.

Voltaire and Locke depart as two more show:

it's Hume, so plump there in his finery,
along with dark-eyed, hurt Jean-Jacques Rousseau.

"Rousseau was born just one year after me;
I sheltered him in Scotland for a while,
and yet such strange excitability. . . ."

"But Hume, I was by nature volatile;
in bearing me my mother died, so guilt
and being loved I'll never reconcile."

"You're crying over milk you hadn't spilt—
I was myself blackballed by academe.
My life's philosophy I slowly built

"on shunning faith and rationalism's dream;
our minds impressed, ideas just combined
imprints, like variations on a theme—

"our psyche less some godly mini-mind,
more process of related entities,
impressions we've transposed or intertwined.

"For me, it's science. My *British History*'s
six volumes show in style as best I can
detachment, cool-eyed clarity and ease.

"Morality's no godlike given plan
and from what *is* we can't derive what *ought*
to be; our morals all are made by man

"and yet my most unreasonable thought,
that there may be a life still after this,
which I confide to Boswell who had sought

"me out as I approached that great abyss.
Yet you Rousseau still wanted to believe,
a deist in the last analysis."

"You're right, perhaps I am naive—
at times I even dreamed I'd be a priest.
A Scot, you'd know the Switzerland I'd leave;

"becoming Catholic in France at least
my mother-figure, dear Françoise-Louise,
persuaded me my guilt could be released

"by sacraments of pardon. But Genevese
at heart, I reconvert on my return
and all my life I'm driven by unease.

"Deep down I know we're good and only learn
what's evil; culture causes our decline.
To teach each child to reason's our concern

"so it retains a nature that's benign.
I fought with Diderot, that atheist;
Emile, my novel's priest explains my line:

"No scriptures or dark sins; there must exist
a first kick-starter for the great machine.
They turned on me and my protagonist!

"On my abandoned son I will come clean,
but there's no way I'd know how I'll become
beloved of wielders of the guillotine

"or how my well-meant deist minimum
will later be the Revolution's creed
and beat a reign of terror's tight-skinned drum."

Our sacred world is starting to recede,
a god of mystery so long avowed
mechanic now we soon won't even need.

Will we no longer see the pillared cloud?

(iii)

"I'm Kant. (You'll know me by my high-browed face.)
A saddle maker's son and pietist,
slow starter, I am cutting to the chase.

"A man of routine, would-be synthesist,
it's you, kind Hume, who woke me from my sleep—
mine now the Enlightenment's last twist.

"Ten years alone and I'm still digging deep
to find how faith in sense and logic meet,
some room where God can fit our reason's leap.

"Our causes and effects not quite complete—
though that is how the mind grasps all it can.
Yet He remains beyond this balance sheet.

"My sweep too broad, my God a narrowed span—
and yet my work ensures that after me
no flash or fiat from the Vatican,

"no usefulness or stale authority
will dodge strict thought and judgement's touch-and-go,
critiqued by each and argued publicly.

"That our own Mother Earth's rotations slow
because their rubbing tides can cause delay
I was the first to calculate; I know

"the spinning disc we call the Milky Way
must turn among so many million more;
yet nothing will compare or can convey

"my awe at what I hadn't seen before:
we humans store a moral sense within,
a cache our senses never can explore,

"and know what we should do and what is sin,
although too easily we can believe
that we're inspired by guess and bulletin.

"Yet now I see the legacy I leave
and deeper than both Hume and you, Rousseau,
for all that I meant well I find I grieve.

"My proof of God will deal a final blow:
the internal possibilities of things
presume some greater impresario

"who must have tuned our finer inner strings.
What seemed to solve the crux of modern man
will turn the inward screw which only brings

"all mystery within our human span.
But Luther wanted faith? Such irony.
Belief now measured out by gauge and plan.

"Each afternoon I walk at half past three
and wonder secretly if we resent
our lonely corner in one galaxy?

"And must it always be that we well-meant
like Shakespeare's lilies fester worse than weeds,
believing most we cause most detriment?

"I see so clearly where my ethics lead;
between our mind and our humanity
a slippage where a God can now recede.

"Always too dutiful, somehow unfree,
I keep on missing out on Cana's feast,
the pietist inside takes hold of me.

"And yet if even at the very least
I push beyond an utter worldliness,
and try to curb the raw-boned godless beast . . ."

My guests from the Enlightenment regress.
In all their intellectual hauteur
I sense a loss of lightness and finesse.

Too much head, a lack of cri de coeur,
their scientific torch has shone too bright
to catch the finer grain of shade or blur.

So much that's this and that and yet not quite,
a world of subtleties in hint and sign
now lost in our too downright black and white.

But where's the dream that crosses reason's line
and duty's heavy-footed push and shove,
the rash Samaritan pouring out his wine

who oils and binds our bitter wounds with love?

(iv)

While Europe's thinkers slowly reason out
belief in God and weave their filigree
of subtle arguments for faith or doubt,

again the joiner's son from Galilee
awakes an oil and wine Samaritan
to ride across our reason's century

and ask, if we believe, how then we can
half-heartedly before the crowing cock
so fail to watch the broken Son of Man.

Unbarbered hair, a narrow plaited stock,
a simple collared preaching troubadour
with raised palm to quiet his spellbound flock:

"I know the Judge is standing at the door,
the guilt, the power, the pain He will redeem;
so full of light, rejoice for evermore!

"And I, John Wesley, bring the joiner's dream
to London, Bristol, York, Newcastle, Wales
as I embrace the cross's rough-grained beam,

"the crown that's made of crucifixion nails,
God's frail and erring children lost and lone,
All inmates of our hospitals and jails.

"O Lord, your broken ones I make my own;
in nobodies caught in the web and mesh
of want or sin, I bless the good seed sown.

"Deep down I love soft cushions and the flesh;
confusing each romance with pastoral care,
although I make the same mistakes afresh

"I'm glad that during youth's first love affair
I took my stance on fate and I refuse
predestination's doom as too unfair.

"Though some are chosen, others too can choose
and so I horse through hail or wind or snow
to save another soul and spread God's news.

"I ride a quarter million miles or so
and forty thousand times at least I preach
to warm those hearts and leave God's afterglow.

"The Church of England I still love and teach
the souls I save will come to undermine;
the walls which I defend I also breach.

"I always know I have to cross the line
 to tend the underdog, the waif and stray,
 to oil their wounds and pour the sacred wine

"until they grow in grace which may outweigh
 the darkest burden of the apple sin,
 perfection we so often may betray.

"But sing *where shall my wand'ring soul begin*
 or how *with thee I shall forever dwell.*
 My brother Charles's hymns still underpin

"a perfect fellowship I preach. Now tell
 at eighty-seven hymns before I leave,
 my parting words 'I'll praise. I'll praise. Farewell.'"

Severe mother's son who must achieve
 so grace and works can somehow countervail,
 a heart where faith and doubts may interweave.

Now for a while allow the pulse prevail.
 Will we with time discover we must find
 how both our cries and logics can dovetail

and will we learn to match the heart and mind
 to know so much and still not lose the zest
 in worlds of thought and spirit countersigned?

This chrism for broken, balm for dispossessed,
 as Europe's cool domains of thought still shrink
 inward to the self. O preaching guest!

A light shines barely through my bushel's chink.

(v)

New inwardness forgets a world beyond
 and now a claim that all our mysteries
 reflect our own desires and correspond

to endless dreams we name as deities.
 A heavy bearded visage starts to stir,
 another guest beginning to unfreeze

the angled head and air of vague hauteur
he's folding in his arms, the deep sunk eyes . . .
it's Ludwig Feuerbach, philosopher.

"A student, I was soon to realise
we carry every moral law within,
but unlike Kant I cannot compromise

"our reason's gift to find some origin
in what our own desires and dreams create,
in webs of gods our human minds can spin.

"Such idolising traits which are innate
maintain belief in sacrament and writ
which, knowing better, we've put out of date.

"A would-be priest, I found I didn't fit—
my only law is love of man for man;
religion is whatever's infinite

"within our human consciousness that can
command infinitude and so we find
our gods within the mind's own timeless span. . . ."

Here enter David Strauss, his head inclined,
a clean-shaved chin just touching off his chest,
a face that's serious but not unkind.

"Of course I'm interrupting now your guest,
but, Feuerbach, I know your overview
and those projections of the self you stressed,

"yet I, a would-be clergyman like you,
react much more against the god in Christ;
I sift and strain his history's residue

"and miracle by miracle I spliced
the rational and wonderstruck to show
how it was more the power of myth enticed

"belief, and echoing motifs they know
from older Jewish writs they fabricate
an unintended mythic counterglow.

"On text and detail I now concentrate.
My *Life of Jesus* still will guarantee
for years to come my thoughts must carry weight."

And as these guests withdraw they both agree,
whatever else they've done, they'll leave their trace,
a shadow thrown across a century,

a mode young intellectuals embrace;
a keen George Eliot translates them both
and soon such thoughts become a commonplace.

How curious that we, who once were loath
to let the heavens have their own sweet will
and only prayed for sun and crops and growth,

appeasing deities for needs until
like Job we love our God without such gain
no matter what befalls us—good or ill,

look earthward now and walk the ways of Cain;
our wants again the only will we know
but this time in a world that turns profane,

a new and lonelier scenario
which grows more self-contained and secular,
no god above or any pit below.

And we whose dust and bone fell from a star
now strut along a haughty precipice,
so confident in all we humans are.

Does no one see the homeless self's abyss?

Canto 3
Laying Bare

(i)

So down the pit within the hollowed mind,
down dim and buffered shafts of self we fall
to corridors and chambers we have mined

to room our lonely psyche's free-for-all,
  as dreaming dreams of power and headstrong gain
  our dark we try with darkness to forestall.

Friedrich Nietzsche sneering in disdain
  arrives to scorn all guests who've come before
  and lacked the will to kill and rule like Cain.

"The way French nobles yielded I despise;
  democracy is when the strong take fright,
  a rabble rule the well bred must deplore,

"a gutter reign by vote and plebiscite—
  I'd rather open all the doors of hell!—
  for only fools don't know that might is right.

"The shame of how at Jena Prussia fell
  and Germans buckled under Bonaparte;
  the world belongs to those who can compel

"the weaker to obey. Let no upstart
  dare even speak of what is bad or good,
  our lives are swayed by will and power, not heart.

"And even as a child I'd understood
  that pity is a form of cowardice;
  my father dead, I'm choked by womanhood.

"Let Kant project his god because he's nice
  just like my mother, sister and my aunts.
  I loathe the thought of selfless sacrifice

"and fear a suffocating care that grants
  the nurture we require while under guise
  of kindness kills the inner Corybants.

"Compassion is a word which I despise,
  morality a show I've long seen through
  and gone beyond the weakling's compromise

"we too imbibed from Christian and the Jew—
  both slaves that turn the tables on their boss
  so power and strength and will become taboo,

"the self-indulgent suffering on a cross;
  instead of all that's vital now the meek
  keep making such a virtue out of loss.

"And we beyond morality must wreak
  our will; what's pitiless and masculine
  will overwhelm the foolish, maimed or weak.

"I have the secret which will underpin
  all living. Darwin doesn't know what thrives;
  it's not survival but the will to win

"more power, the Übermensch who always strives
  in all his nature's power and might to flee
  the endless pointless shuffle of our lives.

"I can't endure the thought of deity—
  and if there was to be a god I know
  I couldn't bear that god would not be me."

This nightmare will an impresario
  of zealots who, like Zarathustra, boast
  to justify a culture's overthrow;

more than your neighbour, love a future ghost.
  In Stoeving's oils his would-be tyrant's stare
  withdraws, demented now and self-engrossed.

Despite his detached mind's strange solitaire,
  for all mad Nietzsche's overreaching claim,
  his genius shows how humans overbear;

within his hell we're purging flame by flame
  the hidden powers so easy to ignore,
  each secret dominance in love's sweet name.

Such gloom may open yet its veins of ore.

(ii)

"But Nietzsche, wait! Let's talk before you go!
  I undermine the tyrants you admire
  but we both share the god we'll overthrow."

307

Guest Freud, rotund in burgher-like attire,
contained but curious, cigar in hand,
conquistador of dreams and sly desire . . .

"Too late. Dementia. I understand.
In time I might have eased your angst and read
the midrash of your nightly hinterland.

"I name the symbols our desires have fed
the brain, which daylight minds won't let run free,
explain dark signs that slumber in the head,

"which slips of tongue and jokes and reverie
reveal: each silent shame and secret lust,
our carnal drive, the id that's master key

"to conflicts we repress because we must
obey unconscious patriarchs within.
I never cure. I only readjust,

"attune desire and inner sense of sin
to find a poise, a hovering between
our id and superego's discipline.

"In dreamy science listening we can glean
what to revise. *Der Kleine Hans* I free
from transferred fears and godlike intervene

"to see why horses cause anxiety;
unravelling signs, from hidden dread I wean
this boy whose father trots his fantasy.

"I'm petit bourgeois and no libertine,
yet by my couch I live my passion's lives;
an archaeologist I dig unseen

"below the surface where the ego strives
to stop its own libido holding sway
in patients I find caught between two drives.

"Through drink or love affairs or falling prey
to gods or zealots who refather us,
a man can hold a childhood guilt at bay—

"the mother-loving killer Oedipus
 I disclose and somehow bring to light
 a burden which then seems less onerous.

"My drug is work. Every thought I write
 and measure every day by what I've done
 to show my father what I'm worth each night.

"And yet I have what in the longer run
 Assures a man: my mother trusted me.
 Mein goldne Siggi! O my darling son!

"Disciple Jung, that mystic broken free;
 my youngest daughter, Anna, will become
 my star of hope, my nurse and prodigy.

"Addicted to cigars I now succumb
 to cancer of the jaw and yet, in spite
 of Eros, drives to death will overcome.

"An unbeliever still a Moses heir,
 I know his god who's always out of sight
 but Christians of all sorts regress with their

"new earthly god, their selfless do-good knight.
 My subtler faith psychoanalysis
 can bring the suzerain within to light."

And drifting back to memory's chrysalis,
 himself a patriarch who's now resigned
 to travel inward, choosing his abyss.

Is innocence forever undermined
 as neither stoical nor too naive
 again in Sheol we now leave behind

a father-figure god who grants relief,
 and we like Job relearn how we must gaze
 at glory that's beyond our joy or grief?

All latent symbols, we must reappraise
 our myth both in the past and fancy-free;
 such signs and hints so often point both ways.

Still Freud pervades our whole psychology
as mistrust asks what lies behind desire;
our own subconscious under scrutiny,

we walk on cinders of suspicion's fire.

(iii)

Exuding surety that's scruple-proof,
Earl Bertrand in his three-piece suit of tweed
Appears, aristocratic and aloof. . . .

"The right to rule was in my seed and breed—
the love of power is still so strong in me—
and though my soon-dead parents both agreed

"their two sons would be raised religion-free,
for grandma Russell it's cold baths and prayer.
In mathematics I find certainty

"as youthful loneliness roves near despair.
My intellect fights every inch of ground:
a *primus motor*, Kant, then nothing there.

"Wesley, Scott and Coleridge are unsound
with treacly talk of how life interlocks;
Berkeley, Locke and Hume are more profound.

"Let's break things down into their building blocks!
All maths is logic I have shown in signs,
though even there I find a paradox

"I solve in ways that lead to Wittgenstein's
philosophy of language that's unclear.
But anyhow Kurt Gödel undermines

"a logic I was sure could undergird
my world. But every system incomplete,
my search must fail; all certainty's absurd.

"Sometimes an ecstasy of sex could cheat
my cloistered mind. But six or seven years
with wives and then I know I must retreat,

"my motherless desire still in arrears.
All those entanglements and yet I find
I never move outside my mind's frontiers.

"But there is restfulness, something refined
in Lady Ottoline or my Colette;
in their aristocratic turn of mind

"my sense of coming home each time we met.
For years with Ottoline I correspond.
At first her strange and mystic faith upset

"my intellect; again I grow beyond
such homelike comforts of a creed. I can't
now pray or lean on God. I won't be conned.

"Belief is harmful and irrelevant.
What strength I need I know I'll find within;
much nobler, sterner, brave and vigilant,

"this self which wills what's good and genuine.
My mission now religion for those free
from groundless idle faith and thoughts of sin.

"So everyone can face reality
I preach my unbelief as common sense
And choose a crisp and clear-cut imagery

"that gives the average man such confidence.
To all my causes, anti-war or bomb,
I lend an academic eminence,

"sound-mindedness and self-assured aplomb.
Yet all I'm fond of stay outside a shell
of loneliness I never could flee from. . . ."

A life of love affairs, a carousel
of causes and such endless self-esteem;
this new hermetic self our deepest hell.

The sacred now becomes an absent dream
where all unspoken's analysed away
in logic's cool and down-to earth regime;

the rumour of our angels too passé
and so no longer worth our thinking of;
millennia of thought we can't relay

in free-fall vacuums of forgotten love.

(iv)

"I'm Heidegger and Messkirch's sexton's son,
the bumpkin seminarian they send
to Constance where, beholden to the one

"true church whose wisdom I at first defend
against a mania for all that's new,
I find a decadence that can't transcend

"itself, a slippery subjective view
as far from truth as reason's grasping hand;
both God and here-and-now play peek a boo.

"How we make truth I come to understand,
for human life eludes what logics snare;
I am *der Meister* from the fatherland

"who knows the queens of mood are angst and care
and dares to face no reason now nor rhyme,
There's only *Dasein*, only Being there.

"Abyss below, above the lost sublime,
the bridge we walk we make up as we go,
our Being's meaning just this passing time.

"All bonds of fellowship dissolve in flow,
authentic living's standing there alone;
our faith a flight, escapist empty show,

"ecstatic moments when you know you're thrown.
The naked it. The null and homeless you.
But, Hannah Arendt, no one else I've known

"could understand our fall the way you do,
my green-dressed muse of *Sein* und *Zeit*,
two years we had our secret rendezvous.

"*Der Führer* comes, the time is ripe and right
to turn our *Dasein* upside down; en masse
we'll leave the cave of shadows for the light.

"As Freiburg's rector some I now harass.
Since God is dead instead we birth a star
and yield to Being lest the moment pass.

"I'll be philosophy's *Reichskommissar*—
indeed, I even help a Jew or two—
and yet we must be true to who we are.

"My teacher Husserl who'd been born a Jew;
debarred from teaching didn't have to flee.
I sent him flowers but then, of course, withdrew.

"*Sieg Heil* to Being's grand epiphany,
our nation's existential Rubicon!
Don't Nazis understand philosophy?

"But Hölderin believed Napoleon.
Am I another man before his time?
In my Black Forest cabin I'll get on

"with Being, learning even now to climb
to ecstasy and 'goddings' thoughts incite,
my forest clearings for new words to chime

"like lovers in their coded *Einsamkeit*,
so *einfach, einfalt, einzig* that I start
my echoes in your own *Gewofenheit*.

"And yet two stakes were driven through my heart:
I failed as rector, left my childhood's church
to which I can't return though I depart. . . ."

A short brown man with Sheol angst will lurch
across our youth to let his mocking tone
undo but not repair. For all his search

the Nothing in his standing on his own
will overarch the ties of in between;
his Time and Being's broken bonds alone

don't know the theatre of the unforeseen
but always seem to want to disembroil
the self from loves and friends that intervene

in solipsistic dreams of blood and soil
which never trade in life's dramatic mess;
blank cheques and self-absorption's counterfoil,

our ego vault of all and nothingness.

(v)

Here in the frozen circle of the pit,
enclosed in ice Freud's grandson's muscle-lined
and inward-looking cold identikit

of Sartre now begins to speak its mind.
"From childhood on I always knew my aim,
the mark I'll make, the books I'll leave behind.

"My father dead, betrayed by those who claim
they love me. Mother marries *un bourgeois*;
her father needs in me his dying flame.

"Authority and power my lifelong dread—
and don't give me all that subconscious guff—
les salauds! I hate their *mauvaise foi*.

"A prodigy, my books become the stuff
of life. With words I know I'll ride roughshod,
disdain the bourgeois fools and call their bluff;

"within my world of thought I am my god,
yet know the nausea of will deterred
by things. I tread the path that Nietzsche trod.

"Blind chance makes all of human life absurd;
we are as we exist and what we choose.
Beauvoir and I have always both concurred

"that freedom is what we should never lose—
we live by everything thought clearly through,
all other loyalties we must refuse.

"I'm short and wall-eyed yet I always knew
  that I could talk my lovers into bed,
  though more to masturbate them than to screw.

"Beauvoir *ma femme de tête* and I both led
  our sideline lives as Europe's storms begin;
  resistance still resistance in the head.

"Camus and I so differently akin—
  I'm the ugly genius already known,
  he's handsome engagé and genuine,

"although he lacks my iron marrowbone
  and starts to think we change things by degrees.
  I learn to want the bastards overthrown.

"All change needs violence. You can't appease
  the bourgeoisie who always dominate.
  And if you lie with dogs you rise with fleas!

"For those in power will always say 'let's wait,'
  or 'let's be cool and calm and keep to fact,'
  debate's the tool of those who subjugate

"the working class. As artists we must act,
  destroy *les cons* who want the right to rule
  or talk of things objective or abstract.

"Beauvoir and I hold court at *La Coupole*;
  for *la famille* it's authenticity,
  our café life an existential school

"where we fuse Marx with my philosophy
  or argue through our wine how best to splice
  a communist control with anarchy,

"to plot posterity's new paradise.
  Is hell still other people in our way?
  I freeze again surrounded by this ice. . . ."

Such bright and wounded psyches on display;
  a war's detached mistrusting residue
  in overweening egos still holds sway.

And yet what loomed so large, so deep, so new,
what seemed a while the only way one thinks,
in hindsight soon begins to fade from view;

a skiff that rides its angry wave and jinks,
one small but self-important bagatelle,
a braggadocio of angst that sinks

to vanish in the nothingness of hell.

Canto 4
Deeper and Further

(i)

Before the satin dark kept closing in,
outsiders were preparing to break through
to where a hard-earned light might rebegin.

A high-coifed, thin-faced Dane has clue by clue
inveigled us until he dares to say:
"The truth which builds you up is truth for you.

"Johannes Climacus, whom I first portray,
is you and I before we climb the stair
from where we hold our own dismay at bay

"by wit, refinement or our savoir faire,
by moral sensibilities and art
but soon the mind can bring a dim despair.

"Our angst is never sudden like a dart,
but hovers vaguely in the head before
it slowly bores its way into the heart.

"Now let me tell you I am Kierkegaard,
who bears his father's sorrows in his bone;
his darkest secrets scar me to my core.

"A youthful fall with loneness I atone
as mine and jilt Regina, lifelong muse,
Ophelia this Hamlet loves alone.

"My father's narrow faith my dreams refuse.
  Though I reject his God I then relearn
  we're of the world and own no overviews;

"Our passion and all inner thoughts still yearn
  for existential truth where we belong;
  how can we speculate without concern?

"No faith unless the risk you may be wrong;
  a proofless truth this wagered surety
  you choose and come what may you plunge headlong

"just as you fall in love or trustingly
  can float above the fathoms of abyss,
  so confident in what it means to be.

"Yet getting there you walk the precipice
  of doubt, the bluff of all my noms de plume.
  Despite Georg Hegel's state you can't dismiss

"the daily here and now, our living room
  where unique selves imagine, think or dream
  up worlds of meaning which our hearts assume.

"I am the one who swims against the stream,
  perfection's loner, the psyche which explores
  beyond Judge Wilhelm's ethics Easter's gleam

"where Christ must enter walking through closed doors.
  I scorn would-be believers who still balk
  at scandals of a God whose death restores.

"Across my years my father's wrongs could stalk
  what in one cleansing moment seemed atoned;
  Thy sins forgiven. Now arise and walk!

"This introspective Hamlet now dethroned,
  as migrant geese can flap autumnal skies
  I take off with the joyous wings I've loaned.

"And still I hear the tamer grounded cries.
  A Brent goose loves its waddling counter-geese
  But, once enthralled by them, it never flies.

"A scapegoat for a love that will not cease,
  I'm Copenhagen's fool who stands apart,
  but *God's no God of tumult but of peace*."

We mend divides between the mind and heart
  to match existence with our ecstasy
  and move behind and yet beyond Descartes,

discovering in the pit's humility
  how objectivity we try to keep
  breaks down. The mind's no neutral referee.

Where Whitehead praises, Russell digs in deep.
  Must we relearn to choose the world we see?
  Hell's only exit passion's mindful leap;

we glimpse a light beyond dead certainty.

(ii)

"You gave me, Kierkegaard, a second sight;
  but loving Mozart, horses, peaks to climb,
  in me your glimpse becomes a dazzling light.

"Despite my father I embrace my time,
  the probed context, subjective faith within.
  Seven years in Safenwil as pastor I'm

"Red Comrade Barth who battles here to win
  his flock their wage. Believers à la carte,
  my once-progressive teachers all cave in

"and back the Kaiser's war. I had to start
  unveiling Schleiermacher's century.
  Are all great things contained within our heart?

"Then reading Romans by my apple tree
  I sense that something wild still lurks behind,
  a breath from Corinth blowing now through me.

"God is God above our human mind,
  beyond our selves and still beyond beyond;
  and free as light that can delight or blind,

"God self-disclosed to whom we can respond.
 Unasked-for gifts of grace. No compromise,
 no *Anknüpfungspunkt*, link or place to bond

"but in the story of Christ's crux and rise;
 like Anselm we discern with faith's desire
 God's scandal bared in his own chosen guise.

"Good Friday, Easter and the tongues of fire,
 A tangent touching on our circle's rim,
 the only point of contact we require.

"Cain and Saul each other's synonym
 though none escapes what grace can still redeem,
 foreshadowing what's taken up in Him.

"In politics I swim against the stream;
 dismissed by Nazis, back in Switzerland
 I fail to shake our cunning bland regime

"which loudens in its post-war reprimand.
 Three dozen years the only mode I know
 to hear the word and try to understand

"how God's own yes will overcome his no.
 Our task to witness. Often I gainsay
 too much but now more peaceful I can grow

"in happiness and so like Mozart play
 without my demons. Yet in every life
 those shadows we can never chase away;

"and Nelly Hoffmann, my long-suffering wife,
 who reared my five and always stuck by me;
 I bear the blame for years of triple strife.

"Yet Lollo spent her life and energy
 for me, remarking just when she began
 to fail *we had a good time, hadn't we?*

"My reconciliation doctrine's plan
 lets Jesus Christ be prophet, priest and king;
 the humbled and the raised, true God and man,

"so sin's a countermove too late to bring
   about our second fall from such earned grace;
   we can't go back behind our eastering.

"Both justified and blessed in medias res
   we have already touched the garment's hem,
   caress Him now in every face we face."

"A Barthian? I'm never one of them!
   I've no monopoly; just grateful I'm
   the ass which bore Him to Jerusalem."

Amazing how one story's truth can rime,
   as played-out life reveals its relevance;
   yet even in our shifting paradigm

once bitten by our reason's arrogance
   we fear a broken pride and can't quite dare
   the wholly other in our earthly dance.

As burrowers we love the breakthrough's glare
   but, dazed by that first shaft of purging light,
   our tunnelled vision waits for open air

where all-pervasive rays flood out the night.

(iii)

"Though Barth and I must thank you, Kierkegaard,
   condemning *Don Giovanni* went too far!
   Sometimes the beautiful can fly before

"the true and good. In Karl's own seminar
   where we first met, his work ploughed deep in me;
   so I'm the Catholic Barth, von Balthasar."

"You grasped me, Balthasar, and we agree
   on much; your pundit I become in turn,
   your Trojan horse in Rome's theology."

"As infants in our mother's smile we learn,
   for all the gap between our God and us,
   it is for love's analogy we yearn."

"But that analogy is dangerous;
   a witness, Balthasar, and nothing more,
   all such connection points are odious."

"All literature I study to explore
   the final things but then the cloudless blitz,
   God's lightning strikes; so like you, Kierkegaard,

"I leave that world. I joined the Jesuits
   where, bored by arid proofs and abstract thought,
   de Lubac shows patristics better fits

"a saintly life and, though I could have taught,
   as student chaplain I can steer young men
   and women, guiding now the grieved or fraught.

"These years my greatest convert, Adrienne
   von Speyr, mystic doctor, has begun
   to turn both friend and muse and so from then

"the sum of what we've written or have done
   belongs to both; John's Group and our new press.
   A single centre, we're two halves of one.

"Her visions' secretary when under stress
   to choose between my order and God's will,
   I know who I must serve and acquiesce.

"We make the rim the core and so fulfil
   God's promise in the ordinary heart.
   But Adrienne's confessor now she's ill,

"I watch her slowly dying as I start
   another book, a kneeling discipline
   inspired by years of your dogmatics, Barth!

"Before all beauty—should I say within—
   possessed by light that takes us by surprise,
   both saints and artists somehow are akin.

"*Die Herrlichkeit* in contemplation's eyes,
   a sudden flash, unbidden acts of grace,
   the glory of our God in human guise

"where understanding's nurtured in the face
    of Christ, who leaving God is then made sin
    in theodrama of the commonplace.

"No greater love, no love more genuine
    than Friday and yet all that Saturday
    of emptiness we now become one kin

"forgotten in death's endless dust and prey
    to the despair of silent Sheol where
    our God is dead and nothing praises day.

"As Christ shares hell we too in turn can share
    the eastering; unique inbreak and mend
    in timeless love to which we're also heir

"and all may seek forgiveness in the end.
    In Rahner's 'always' and 'already' done
    God's will and our desires too easily blend;

"if each anonymous good-living one
    unknowingly can let the kingdom come
    we blur the lines. The one true faith or none.

"Too facile. Much too bland a sugarplum.
    We must communicate the proper view;
    I fear some slipshod happy medium."

So easy to monopolise what's true,
    as if in leaving self's dark cul-de-sac
    we then divide the spectrum into two:

what lies ahead is bright, behind is black.
    In fuller light are boundaries precise?
    We balk at such nuances and pull back

to shy away from dazzling paradise.

(iv)

But now it's Levinas, a tight-knit ball
    of energy, and short compared with Barth
    or Balthasar, the tallest of them all.

"Like Heidegger, I'm sure that we must start
 afresh, though what for him is theory
 dictates my life, lays down a trace I chart,

"a tumour hidden in my memory.
 Let Nietzsche's red-tailed hawk become a dove
 in every stranger who approaches me.

"Another's face commands me from above
 and, called beyond reciprocal rapport,
 a love of wisdom now is wisdom's love.

"Good Dostoyevsky had prepared me for
 philosophy and Husserl's turning back
 to things as given, yet before the war

"I hit on Rosenzweig's reflecting track
 and ask with him what we as Jews can bring
 to mend both Grecian legacy and lack.

"I spend five years a war-camp underling;
 my student friend Maurice Blanchot now hides
 my wife and child with nuns, a cloistering

"which saves them, though our parents on both sides
 and my two brothers perish in that hell,
 a bleeding gap which nothingness elides.

"For years as head of school-life's carousel
 I teach Talmudic midrash and I pray,
 philosopher and teacher parallel.

"As Paris existentialists hold sway
 my Kovno wife (my parents' landlord's child)
 supports my night-time thought and teaching day.

"Although she felt that Shushani beguiled
 my mind, Monsieur would give me eyes to see
 the one and universal reconciled.

"In pure delight without utility,
 we think, we eat, we sleep and soak in sun,
 to love our life and seek security.

"Whatever cost, I think of number one
   though I deprive the other, take his place,
   until a face commands and I'm undone

"in sighs of passage that can know no place,
   God flickering in you my neighbour's glance.
   Like Moses, all I see is just a trace

"as out of the abyss of *jouissance*
   your word appeals beyond an overview
   to hear my reasons and to know my stance.

"Obsessed and hostage, I stand in for you
   who wake an infinite desire in me;
   the more I do, the more I need to do.

"I'm summoned to a hospitality,
   a debt of gentleness I must repay,
   my freedom this responsibility.

"For all my life I dread *totalité*.
   Believing's done in doing what is right
   so all I say I then again unsay."

Commanded by the other from a height,
   such self-effacing need to stand below
   atones our pride and still, though we're contrite,

we dream of heavens where in letting go
   that self which makes itself a whipping post
   allows a banquet's two-way overflow.

Less hostage, more a guest or lavish host
   whose care will turn the byway stranger friend
   at feasts beyond all duty's uttermost,

where obligation and delight can blend.

(v)

"We must interpret. Each philosopher
   has something of the truth, but none has all"—
   the slight and gracious figure of Ricoeur—

"For some the detour and the longer haul.
 Like Levinas, I too survived to see
 how many movements of our times would stall."

"And you, Ricoeur, have spent five years like me
 cooped up in camps; and orphaned young we are
 both heirs of war who dread all tyranny.

"Although we both believe, our bête noire
 is cryptic faith—our God must stand apart—
 philosophy remains just secular."

"And like you too I move between Descartes
 and Nietzsche with his ego's overthrow
 to mediate each polar counterpart.

"I see your face but not from there below,
 not *here I am* but rather *here I stand*
 responsible, though still I want to know

"who is this self that's hearing your command?
 I'm only I when you and I converse.
 My character's the same but much unplanned

"occurs, yet in the parts we can't rehearse
 I keep my word and you can count on me;
 our life's a narrative where we traverse

"a plot in time which is our history
 refigured in configuration's play,
 between our selfhood and identity.

"Of course the other is my protégé
 and yet in self-effacement self-esteem;
 I've promised trust I never will betray.

"Between an overreach and too extreme
 mistrust, we can attest to who we were
 and who we are; our self-becoming stream

"a spilling time we're flowing in, somewhere
 between the good life we keep aiming for
 and what we owe the next commanding stare.

"Our guiding ends and duties *en rapport*,
   I fold you in solicitude's embrace
   as neither willing slave nor conqueror

"but more disciple learning from your grace,
   as I receive a gift bestowed by friends
   in reciprocities of face-to-face

"and givings where my self-esteem extends;
   so loving who I am, I love you too.
   On such a sense of self our trust depends.

"In every work I struggle to undo
   polarities and give each tension scope,
   seeing what's best, carefully reading through.

"In polyseme, in metaphor and trope
   such interwoven meanings all are meant;
   Freud's symbols point to either guilt or hope.

"As so much is its opposite complement,
   the prophet and the sacred sign a to-
   and-fro between the word and sacrament.

"In summoned selves mandated to renew,
   good conscience strives to find a synergy
   where God and our free will can rendezvous.

"Beyond equation, generosity—
   a foolish gift the Christ-shaped heart can pour;
   a lovely risk become our destiny.

"Analysis or Hermes both explore
   an optative that underpins my thought;
   abundant joy that's always so much more."

We double back to tie the *is* and *ought*,
   relearning love's responsible embrace;
   departures quick, returns are long and fraught.

We glimpse the infinite. Our face-to-face
   a hint of Eden lost, not once but twice.
   In slow detours we open up a space

where we can dare desire a paradise.

Canto 5
Burning Bush

(i)

I hesitate. What business have I here
among the saints? But suddenly your face
rewelcomes me; just as when I'd appear

in your midmorning class our eyes embrace
and once enfolded in your smile I dare
the company of saints, whose days of grace

across all time invisibly repair
whatever peccadilloes wound our pride
and seal the cracks in brittle earthenware.

But tell me now, my earthly bride and guide,
who are these shining faces at the feast,
like sacred lanterns glowing from inside?

That many come from both the west and east
and shall sit down with Abraham. Is that
Jean Vanier in love with all the least,

that tall and gentle presence laughing at
whatever Dietrich Bonhoeffer just said?
They're bubbling in an ease of trust and chat.

I recognise his fair Germanic head,
the hair receding over glinting eyes
and Bonhoeffer's slight hint of midriff spread.

That woman next with eyes so dark and wise,
with pearls and glasses dangling just below
and forthright air that bends to compromise?

She's Hannah Arendt raising her Bordeaux
To toast eternal now, *une femme de tête*,
her face alive with age's afterglow

and wisdom reaping youth's imprudent debt.
And who's the moustached man she's turning to,
who sipping sweetened tea his angel wet,

explains to her what Muslims need to do
to hear compassion in the prophet's word,
how Islam from within must now renew?

It's Said Nursî the dream-filled Kurd
who reads through Allah's lens love's origin;
and there beside him John the twenty-third,

a saint who knew the greatest mortal sin
was lack of human warmth. So breaking bread
he blesses his companions and tucks in.

And what a table! Such a lovely spread!
Gruyère, Roquefort, Boursin and Camembert;
papayas, grapes and apples Cézanne red

against the table's folded linen glare.
*I tell of things the eye had never seen
nor ear had heard* that angels here prepare:

Rambutan, cherry, kumquat, tangerine,
La France or Japanese or Thai or Greek,
the endless more and more of each cuisine,

all herbs and local seasoning to tweak
the taste or untried variants instead
with newer tangs to savour, each unique

as sentences still waiting to be said,
abundance so beyond our need or lack,
a bubbling outflow from the fountainhead

in unheard lines, fresh angles of attack,
a riot in the heart the will can't earn . . .
Love bade me welcome yet my soul drew back.

O tell me saints what have I still to learn?
Is something in me still too proud to die?
Do tell me saints before I must return.

The turbaned Nursî stares me in the eye:
"My Western friend, there is no resting place
while in the cosmic glass you see your eye

328

"and not the image of the Owner's face.
Islam's a yielding to that counterclaim
that everything you learn is still a trace.

"In such surrender there's no sense of shame;
unlike the angels who must just obey
you're trusted to become each holy name."

Here Dietrich nods, "I'd meditate and pray
but still my inner discipline despaired
of others' dreads until my heart gave way

"to find in my surrender that I dared
God's own compassion and at last I knew
all wounds in our humanity are shared."

"*O si*," adds John, "a younger man, I too
disdained my brothel-going soldier friends;
with age I cried against those wars that slew

"such youth and snuffed their flame for others' ends.
My widening heart keeps learning how to match
the all-including arms His cross extends."

"But," Hannah sighs, "we thought we could detach
our being, leap our shadows, somehow sleuth
a human essence only God can catch.

"Desire for jumping shadows signed our youth
but now we see how we can ruin the earth;
we know we are God's guardians of the truth."

"Although we plot and hatch for all we're worth
what's new remains a miracle unearned,
a gift we don't expect, another birth,"

Jean Vanier joins in, "I think I yearned
to soothe a human wound of loneliness
which each of us alone has slowly learned

"to heal in yielding to a greater yes
that bends to wash the bruised and unloved feet,
to tend with water and the towel's caress,

"to live by folly winning in defeat.
  What if the weak become our first concern,
  what if such love decides our balance sheet?

"*And God so loved the world.* We each in turn
  knew wounds and gains we had to reconcile;
  how Hannah's father's early death would burn

"a girl's so eager wick too quickly, while
  Pope John, you too, although you understood,
  a twelve-year-old still in your childlike smile

"remembers how you left your home for good
  and, Dietrich, just at thirteen years or so,
  you lost your brother in green adulthood.

"The refugees our ship left at Bordeaux
  endure in me, a young marine cadet,
  at thirteen far away from home, although

"the dream that's *L'Arche* was years from me as yet.
  But what of Said Nursî? How was it
  to live so long in jail or under threat?"

"Bones," he smiles, "grow stronger when reknit
  and wounded healers all we mend and praise;
  our breakage is a first prerequisite.

"*Then eat of all the fruits and follow ways
  your Lord made smooth and from their bellies drinks
  of diverse hues to heal mankind.* A vase

"needs cracks, my friends. The Westerner who thinks
  a thought is watertight will lack the ease
  to let both light and moisture through the chinks."

The angels turn to serving herbal teas—
  chrysanthemum, hibiscus, ginger root,
  hydrangea, camomile. As palates squeeze

the tang and zing of blossom, plant or fruit,
  a mood of jokes and laughter now pervades
  the evening light that catches each minute

detail. A feast of countless forms cascades
the images each artist cries to know—
a moment snatched in all its hues and shades.

"In your compassion, Bríd, I think I grow
and understand how only love can heal;
I learn to feel what others undergo.

"But though I know my empathy is real
I never wore their shoes or bore their cross
Or ever put my shoulder to their wheel.

"Do all these words I write then double-cross
so false hopes raised fall lower than before,
what seemed a gain become a double loss?

"My warm-sleeved heart much colder at its core,
a life at one remove, a broken reed,
an oil-less virgin rattling heaven's door?"

"*Das kann ich aber gut verstehen*; indeed
both you and I have shared a temperament
and lived our youth's desires at breakneck speed.

"Of course both John and Dietrich have a bent
for music; John's Claudel and Charles Péguy
were guides, and during lonely months he spent

"in jail a newer Dietrich dared to be
a poet he'd suppressed whose words caress
the moods of his slow garden agony.

"I too have turned to poems under stress
and broken Auden asked to marry me;
I knew the poet Jarrell and T. S.

"Like you I fell for Rilke. *I would be
like her . . . and is there not a time in love
we're freed from our beloved one so we*

"*endure like trembling arrows aimed above
ourselves.* Dear Rilke striving to transcend,
but like Augustine far too little of

"this world of flesh and clay and in the end
  his angels never know redemptive grace.
  But listen to me carefully, my friend,

"eternal now hides in this time and place.
  Franz Kafka is all future, Proust the past;
  A poet's work must be the interface

"embracing all the wonders we've amassed
  with gratitude but also, in the light
  of what we've lost or thought we had surpassed,

"motifs of wisdom you with second sight
  will slowly rebegin to interweave.
  You won't look back to try to underwrite

"all loss or hanker for some make-believe,
  but in the glare of here and now to find
  a vision for our world you must conceive;

"as Dante once prepared the modern mind
  you too must show a depth and breadth of view
  that lets the future in our now unwind."

But Dietrich sings Franz Schubert's *Gute Ruh*;
  My straying child, you're home, let me entice
  your eyes to close, so *tu die Augen zu*,

until one phrase both liquid and precise
  contains all songs. Unless you too become
  like little children, there's no paradise.

I let sleep fall as once more I succumb;
  my yielding to eternal lands of nod
  a recreation in what's yet to come,

tomorrow brewing in the womb of God.

(ii)

"I'm A'isha the Prophet's best-loved wife;
  today here under heaven's complex dome
  I'll host your second glimpse of afterlife."

It's morning in this sun-fed honeycomb
of floors and Jacob's ladders slung between
the many mansions of my father's house,

and taking breakfast on a mezzanine
now Dietrich, Hannah, Nursî, Jean and John
relax and chat together overseen

by A'isha, who—after Abd had gone
had moved between her roles as rebel chief,
believer's mother, hadith passer-on—

here loves to watch the morning guests convene
and how this house contains so many rooms
no earthly eye could ever have foreseen,

how last night's conversation soon resumes,
though some may switch to other rooms nearby
to where some unexpected friendship blooms.

"It's strange that history's criss-cross should now tie
these five saints' lives together. Vanier
and John had met; then John's remains would lie

"in state when Hannah was on holiday
in Rome and as the crowds said their goodbye
she praised this man who could so simply say

"as lilies of the field and birds comply,
so everyday it's lovely to be born
and everyday a lovely day to die.

"She knew there wasn't any need to mourn.
In paradise there is no clock to beat
and friendships here once made are never torn

"by partings haunting every time we meet.
Pope John was Turkey's papal nuncio
but Nursî still exiled, they'd never meet."

Detailing history's strange undertow
it seems that A'isha begins to souse
my mind in heaven's sweeping overflow.

I feel the warmth and vastness of this house
across so many floors and shapes of space,
where through its windows streams of sunlight douse

these rooms with morning, lavishing a grace
of generosity, a givingness
which both can go beyond and still embrace

compassion, delight needing to address
before I even am addressed. There is
a sense of fullness in today's caress

as though my being grows to fathom this
our manifold and tiered reality
refusing any easy synthesis;

an open multistoreyed house where we
can move so simply now from floor to floor,
from porous room to room and, fancy-free,

can love the brand-new morning rays that pour
unstinting light all over us again;
this same and varied endless more and more.

"In childhood we could slip from plane to plane—
Don Bosco walked the streets of our Turin,
Our Lady full of grace lived down the lane,

"The good Samaritan our next of kin,
bound up the man who went to Jericho.
How could the likes of me be genuine

"and not cross over? Then, as pope, although
on Christmas day they tried to hem me in,
I blessed those children who'd had polio

"and hugged that prisoner bowed down by sin—
you couldn't come to me, I came to you—
To be, I told him, is to rebegin."

"Pope John, although throughout my childhood too
the world held up a mirror to His names,
and we all knew how every name rang true,

"yet godlikeness may stake its counterclaims
until reflections in that mirror seem
to have their discrete being and their aims

"and miss their role within the greater scheme,
like signs forgetting that they're pointing to
the generous Lord who shaped you, al-Kharīm."

But look how sunlight plays at peek a boo,
you see me now and now you don't as though
delighting in each shifting point of view

it still ascends its noonday indigo
and switching focus on our mezzanine
its spot now catches Dietrich in its glow.

"I know," said Nursî, "that you were keen
to find how nature runs itself and still
somehow believe a God can intervene.

"I too had grappled with the human will
and how in this our world that's come of age
we must exploit our mastery and skill

"and can for God's sake never disengage
our knowledge from the cause of all that's right
and fair, and in our housekeeping we gauge

"economies to boost the widow's mite
although we are all heirs before a God
who fathers us and who will underwrite

"whatever we must undertake. How odd
that being both a child and fully grown
is love beyond the carrot or the rod,

"a life that's tensioned in a middle zone
and switching roles, like A'isha, between
the moments when it seems we stand alone

"and moments when, our hand still held, we lean
back on our father's arm to bask in trust
as on this Jacob-laddered mezzanine."

"O yes," smiles Jean, "no wonder we're nonplussed—
  the world is more like heaven than we dare
  admit and yet the star is not its dust.

"O look at this midday so debonair
  at its delighted zenith and how we
  increase just marvelling at *notre Père*."

"Is this the fun for you it is for me
  when drawn-out breakfast turns to chatting fest?"
  A beaming Hannah loves this bonhomie.

"You see, I've thought both long and hard how best
  to grasp just how economies are made
  from labour, work and action. We invest

"in *Arbeit* all the sweat which has conveyed
  our DNA along the human line,
  while what we fabricate instead displayed

"how we could own what then became a sign
  that we belong, our home, our tools and art;
  but action is the way we redefine

"a polity, so we're allowed depart
  from our survival's daily breaking wheel;
  natality can be another start

"so every new arrival here can deal
  another way with life, reshape the earth.
  Our destinies of clay again reveal,

"no matter what our being may be worth,
  each generation can reset the scene;
  the core of human action must be birth

"and in what's random, in our shuffled genes,
  our *amor mundi*'s fleshy by-and-by,
  a God still loves to work the in-between."

I bring a vision now to amplify
  that first abundance and to overhaul
  the generous desires that underlie

a universe's being here at all.
I conjure up economies of gift
to counteract the meanness of our fall,

a sharing of resources to uplift
each heart that lets the poor and broken thrive.
Is giving then the secret of all thrift?

I love a lavishment of self that I've
discerned in each of you, my saints and stars,
a breadth of view, a mix of grace and drive

that soars and still can tend particulars
of everyday, the slow minutiae
within a long-range vision nothing mars.

Yet all of you once had your feet of clay
and surely you like me knew dark days when
a hollow voice within the mind held sway

until your soul rejected once again
the desert stones of vision turned to dough.
But you, my saints, had trust beyond my ken.

"Of course, there were the days of touch and go"—
It's Jean who laughs and turns to answer me—
"How could I live at *L'Arche* and never know

"such steel-grey moments of despondency?
But I rejoiced now even in the day
when nothing big or worthy seemed to be

"achieved and relished moods of come-what-may
which let the slow osmosis of all time
seep through the day's unplanned cantabile

"and made that habitat a paradigm
of how in healing others we are healed—
a catalyst, a beautiful enzyme

"thrown in to leaven now a world congealed
in grids of power and gain, a tiny rift
where wounded glory is again revealed.

"So little, you can say, so slight a shift
  and yet enough to let the grapevine spread
  a rumour of love's overfall as gift.

"I still can wonder where it all has led
  or how it will expand or change its tack.
  To look behind or look too far ahead

"can mean we lose the chance to be a sign
  of light, however small just here and now,
  a heaven's faint and earthly countershine;

"just as perhaps in ways you don't know how
  this poem may be a slow fuse to ignite
  the moments in our psyches which allow

"an amplitude, a deeper second sight
  that knowing weakness dares to love the weak,
  begin a new economy of light."

I think of how a morning's lemon streak
  became the flood of midday's warm cascade;
  so much begun from angles so oblique.

Some joy exceeds the to and fro of trade;
  a recklessness that takes a pen to mark
  all debts as cancelled and our bills prepaid.

A generous breath still fans a cosmic spark;
  that first largesse on which we still rely
  lets sunlight burgle every room of dark.

Our signs become the things signs signify.

(iii)

"Don't gaze at me because I'm dark, because
  the sun has gazed on me, for I am black
  and beautiful, a Shulamite who was

"the bride-to-be whose song held nothing back;
  and since there is a loner still in you
  that woman's love must always keep on track,

"I am the one now sent to guide you through
   another day of learning not to care,
   just cutting loose while keeping each note true,

"and letting rip a bebop laissez-faire
   of riffs as all *the saints go marching in*,
   so recklessly and utterly aware

"of how a chord's progressions underpin
   a saxophone's own sweated ad-libbed lines,
   which soar above a secret discipline

"in freedoms which a judgement countersigns—
   a politics of sound decisions made
   to trust a melody's covert designs."

O Shulamite, your song of songs relayed,
   in all its voices as you wake or dream,
   the passions which love's promise had prepaid;

and every time a bugle plays I seem
   to hear the cross-talk rhythms of your song
   in new elaborations of a theme

unfolded by no easy right or wrong—
   just single notes we know we have to choose,
   then play as if we'd known them all along.

But Dietrich has begun to hum "*O Blues
   please tell me what you're doing here so soon.*
   I saw how need could turn its rusty screws

"on Harlem, where each Sunday afternoon
   I learned to love the lost bush meeting cry
   that in a post-crash angst could shout and swoon

"in upbeat moods *I spread my wings and fly,
   O Lawd, sometimes I don't know where to roam,
   I'm praising Jesus, ain't got time to die.*

"I bought their songs on records to bring home;
   all jazz now banned we listened stealthily
   like first raw converts in their catacomb

339

"as Joshua and Moses led them free;
a fire by night, a cloud by day to what
will be, become *de year of Juberlee*;

"their lives so woven in the Spirit's plot.
We've borne our burdens in the heat of day
and still to sing *swing low, sweet chariot*

"in Harlem psalms that seeped into my clay.
I heard their voices in my agony . . .
but Hannah what were you about to say?"

"It's just to emphasise the what-will-be,
the openness of music's trusting mix
of well-planned chords and spontaneity.

"You see how Marx's take on politics
still rides the narrow gauge of history
along predicted lines we need to fix,

allowing nothing that we can't foresee,
the things successors change against the odds;
a band of angels coming after me."

"*Genau!* and so we perfect," Dietrich nods,
"our blissful moment holding freedom's key,
by giving it again to what is God's.

"But *look over yonder, what do I see*—
the hissing stylus sings its *hallelu*—
the Holy Ghost a coming over me

"and so *if you git dere before I do*—
I'm go'n'ter feast on milk and honey, yes—
tell all ma friends that I'm a comin' too.

"The faith that Luther wanted to express—
I tell my students. *There's a better day
a comin'.* Glory in the wilderness."

"Has this," asks Hannah, "always been the way?
Pariahs show the parvenus the light
they think they own by simply holding sway

"and I who've known exile and had to fight
  to make a life in my adopted land
  believe that politics can't be a flight

"to half-remembered pasts or to some grand
  utopia, an end for all our means
  with everything tied down and overplanned.

"Though even from my early German teens
  I thought I'd master truth, I slowly grew
  to love the shuffled chance and jazz of genes

"we can't control and so like Lessing knew
  I tell the truth I see yet still prefer
  to leave to God a grander overview.

"Utopians who weave their gossamer
  ideal never see the here and now;
  for such far sight the present is a blur,

"a mess a neater mind must disavow
  so they are blind to how things really are,
  to where all politics begin and how

"it's less about the far-fetched and bizarre
  and more our every day's old battered tune,
  the criss-cross notes that sometimes clash or jar

"in time that's filled with now; yet no cocoon,
  of course the present looks to what's to come
  and echoes still a past from which it's hewn.

"Although extremists beat their tight-skinned drum,
  I've learned to plump for ambiguity,
  a twilight which refuses to succumb

"to either-or but chooses to stay free,
  to keep two poles in tension so they both
  can bring their own to where they don't agree.

"Extremism is for some a kind of sloth,
  which, balking at the thought of afterthought,
  denies the risk of chaos in all growth."

"Like you I realise too well how fraught
   change is or just to try to understand
   where we must compromise or where we ought

"resist. If ever doubt got out of hand
   in Tegel, Harlem sounded in my ear:
   a great camp meeting in de promised land.

"*So splendidly consoled and sheltered here—*
   behütet und getröstet wunderbar—
   I couldn't be a prisoner of fear."

Now Jean, who hadn't talked today so far,
   chips in a stooping gentle caveat:
   "we make our judgements just as though we are

"the ones who choose and opt for this and that,
   but are we shaped to be an instrument
   blown through, as if our fluttered tongues just scat,

"our voices riff and hum and we consent?
   I know de Lawd has laid His hand on me—
   in retrospect it all seems heaven-sent."

"Yes, looking back our lives appear to be
   a line we improvise above and yet
   I know—as Jew and German refugee—

"within a polity we can't forget
   we act in concert, never one by one.
   You see as in our paradise quintet

"or any conversation just begun
   good politics is endless interplay,
   discourse where all is never said and done

"that finds a new negotiated way
   between my will and those who share my place—
   an interchange where both sides have their say."

For just a moment staring at her face
   I see a combo riffing on a tune,
   imagine Hannah playing double bass

as Ella-like she sings "How High the Moon";
on keyboards Dietrich, Jean on saxophone,
with John's wild trumpet's soar and Myles-like croon

and Nursĭ on percussion and trombone. . . .
Then suddenly I wake from reverie.
"How easy to imagine that we own

"our lives and gifts when we should only be
a moon reflecting one eternal light,
giving back to *Al-Wakīl*, the Trustee,

"the One, the First, the Last. As I recite
my rhythmic prayer in drunk sobriety
I thrill inside as heart-throbs too delight

"in naming one another lovingly;
it's where you are the darkest night would shine."
Had Nursĭ also seen my reverie?

I love how topics shift and realign,
the way the spirit moves us to allow
our conversations switch and intertwine,

but as my third day here is closing now
and I am learning slowly to let go,
I'm still a little anxious as to how

relaxing in the tune I'll ever know
what I will add or what I can achieve,
surrendering and going with the flow.

"At first so many saw me as naive
because I didn't doubt or second-guess
the plans that God was keeping up his sleeve.

"A child *la mia Mamma* could address
The Virgin Mary, lifting me to say
Ma ecco Angelino so she'd bless

"my life and make me her own protégé;
Madonna's shine my first epiphany.
Since then I learned how every day to pray

"until my prayer became its own reward;
 I carry now my Lord deep down in me
 and let myself be carried by the Lord.

"So trust love's giddy bird and set it free
 to improvise, allow it soar within,
 ascend with debonair humility

"as notes that scale Grapelli's violin;
 abandon now the tick-tock metronome
 and dare *rubato* earned by discipline.

"You know when I was made the pope of Rome
 before the conclave leaving from Milan,
 I'd bought my ticket for returning home.

"Once pope, I knew throughout my five-year span
 I'd blow a Pentecost across the globe;
 my master plan was not to have a plan

"but just to give to God the scope to probe
 our trust, in chancing once again a make
 or break, so we'd begin afresh like Job

"to love God only for his own love's sake."
 I'm too old now to fret about a name
 or reputation. What is here at stake

is how we after years of taking aim
can try to acquiesce in skills well honed
that follow every phrase's counterclaim

extempore, relending tunes once loaned
in riffs that ride a breeze's free-for-all,
where everything belongs and nothing's owned.

I trust each day's pneumatic overhaul
and glory in the Spirit's overplus.
I gonna be there when the trumpets call.

My Madam Jazz keeps breathing life in us.

(iv)

Desires are fathomed in her eyes' embrace;
she starts and laughs with such a happiness
that God appeared delighting in her face.

"Have I to tell you? Will I let you guess?"
She jokes, "The only clue I'll give is this:
my name contains the Latin word for bless."

Don't tell me that it's Dante's Beatrice!
Look how my God is spoiling me for choice,
who as a young man courted the abyss!

But I have learned to yield and so rejoice
in each of you. The Shulamite was right:
my God has spoken in a woman's voice.

First Bríd, then A'isha, the Shulamite
and now *la mia donna* Beatrice,
who face by face conduct me to the light.

How could I ever have expected this?
But wrapped up in this woman's mystery
I start my fourth day here foretasting bliss.

"You mortals down below can fail to see
how marvels coded in the universe
reflect the face of God's infinity.

"Too graceless, too constrained, you still immerse
yourselves in steps and miss out on the dance—
the scientists and poets don't converse

"or celebrate each quantum of advance,
discovering a heaven's cameo
in God, the gambler's mix of love and chance.

"As Peter once warned Dante years ago
you must not hide what I don't hide from you—
and tell them all when you return below

"you glimpsed how out of the eternal blue
a love let loose our universe, and sensed
the breath behind the aeons' derring-do,

"the cosmic trust that since our world commenced
 allowed the soup to cool and ages on,
 in spite of all the loaded odds against,

"the perfect matching up and liaison
 of push and pull that let our earth begin
 to grow beyond its dark oblivion."

"When young I too had felt to underpin
 our universe with nature's reasons why
 could somehow mean that science then would win

"hands down and oust my God so we'd rely
 on human will. No truck with that, I told
 my brother. How could we see eye to eye?

"I didn't know how physics would unfold—
 Karl Friedrich's world remained an unread page;
 I thought there was a line I had to hold.

"In Tegel I would reach another stage—
 though to the father God I'm still a son—
 I saw the world had come at last of age

"and through the sciences we'd now begun
 to know God less as need than overflow,
 our more than requisite abundant One.

"We search for God in all of what we know,
 a presence found in each discovery,
 in every problem solved God's counterglow."

"The marvels, Dietrich, we still need to see,
 the wonders which I showed to Dante grown
 more beautiful in their complexity.

"Let us delight in what we'd never known,
 in someone's principle and someone's law,
 and use their names for things we never own

"because they were the first of us who saw
 another angle to God's wondrous mind.
 How could we ever lose our sense of awe?"

"Indeed," says Hannah, "everything we find
   that's true will start again with *thaumazein*;
   in each fresh cache the beauty's realigned,

"the subtler for another new-found sign.
 A girl from tutor Adolf Posterman,
 I learned how Einstein's world would undermine

"the mind with which my century began
 and yet it seems to take so long before
 each -ism learns how life rejects their plan

"and comes up with the unexpected more
 as somehow every fragile human truth
 is keeping some surprises still in store."

"Although," says John, "my background seems uncouth—
 at least compared with Dietrich or with Jean—
 I always had, and even from my youth,

"an eagerness to study all I can,
 a restlessness which longs to understand
 and so, while yet a seminarian

"in Rome, I wished to read the greats and planned
 to be au fait with all that science might
 reveal to help us try to understand

"God's wonder, find new ways to reunite
 theology and science and allow
 us view both kinds of knowledge in the light

"of how our lives evolve as even now
 our mode of thought reflects an age's needs;
 our times a friend we dare not disavow.

"Just as my dear Baronius succeeds
 in weaving God into the secular,
 I sail between where frightened Scylla feeds

"on fears of growth, insists that we debar
 all change, avoid at once whatever's new,
 the obscurantists sticking as they are,

347

"and on the other side Charybdis too
  a whirling pool where all is relative,
  and everything and nothing both are true."

"In *L'Arche*," Jean nods, "at first we tried to live
  by trusting only in God's providence
  but looking back I think we did not give

"ourselves the time to see the common sense
  of turning to professionals' advice.
  We had to learn to have the confidence

"to balance science with our passion, splice
  our trust and know-how; skilled and spirit-filled,
  to taste the fruit yet not lose paradise.

"It's not that we were proud or too self-willed
  but more a fear that skill might undermine
  the ark of love we worked so hard to build.

"But Nursî, you're the one who'll best combine
  the sense of wonder with a prayerful awe
  and read in nature's works God's countersign."

"Madrasas seemed too willing to withdraw
  from all the wonders which modernity
  can still reveal and bit by bit I saw

"the need to study every ology,
  to find in every atom's charge and star
  another angle on God's synergy.

"For me no knowledge can be secular—
  in all our mathematics' formulae
  I read the All-Embracing's aide-memoire

"as here in heaven too I've watched the way
  the subatomic world's own mystery
  dissolves in chambered skips and ricochet

"and how the ballroom of our stars runs free,
  ballooning out its curves of time and space—
  O Lord, increase my marvelling at thee!

348

"Each day on knees and palms just as I place
my forehead on the ground in prayer I feel
a galaxy of particles that race

"and interact at speed where some reveal
themselves and disappear as happenings,
events still showing less than they conceal.

"And then I rise between two schemes of things
to stand below a whirl of quark-like stars
still spinning in their roundabouts and swings,

"a cosmos turning on its axle bars
that wheels in love's galactic dance routine.
There's nothing in this universe that jars

"with how I move in faith here in-between
two vastnesses that stretch beyond my ken,
keep praying to a God who breathes unseen,

"a wooer trusting to the mise en scène,
determined still to let the drama run
its course. For me it's somehow strange that when

"Copernicus revolved us round the sun
the West should lose their image of the light.
Already knowing hubris had begun

"to wear the clothes of God. We must delight
in each discovery and praise His names,
our only fear our own pride's oversight."

I know how science makes no counterclaims—
although a schoolboy I had chosen Greek—
once adult, just like John, one of the aims

I set myself has been at least to seek
to follow now as best a layman can
unfoldings of our skill and each technique

revealing more of how it all began
an outburst filling all space from the start.
I thrill at glimpses of God's open-plan,

A soup both table d'hôte and à la carte
as particles disperse or gravitate
and life becomes creation's counterpart

throughout the hyperspace genes navigate,
converging on their islands of success
as if attractors beckon us and wait—

our evolution earned by time and guess
in balances of trial's loss and gain.
And yet, my saints and stars, I must confess,

although I know the cost of freedom's rein—
the push and pull of nature realigned—
I still can't understand the birthing pain,

the breed that dies into another kind,
the grieving drone that serves his royal bee,
creation's need to leave so much behind.

Each wonder still a fresh epiphany
and yet I puzzle how to see such loss;
I stumble on life's darker mystery.

"But none of us escape that pitch and toss"—
It's Dietrich speaking slowly and with care—
"before the resurrection, first the cross."

No sparrow falls and no unnumbered hair.
So many trillion years since time began
and yes, the loving One who's still aware

of wrinkles on the face of Gallagh man.
But how can I envisage such a mind?
I think of how a microchip can scan

across a globe of networked signs to find
when confidently we begin to prod
our touchscreens teams of human brains designed.

Beside that mind in all we do we plod;
my stylus still a probing broken wand.
Imagine then the motherboard of God!

I only know one way I can respond.
Between the subatomic whirling maze
and galaxies that spiral out beyond,

surrendering now to wonder, I just praise.

(v)

This final day before I must depart,
my Mary show me how to face the light
that can both know and honour every heart.

From Bríd I learned to trust life's own delight,
for A'isha I roamed this mansion's rooms,
and jazzed with Solomon's dark Shulamite,

with Beatrice my praise could just assume
how marvel leads to marvel in our growth;
but you I greet with wonder in the womb's

still childish leap, my Jewish girl who, loath
at first to hear the word of joy and grief,
cried "here I am" and served by bearing both.

On this fifth day of light, my leitmotif
and guide, prepare me for the burning bush,
come shine in me the sun of self-belief.

"Although of course I flinched in my first blush,
perplexed by that announcing, still I knew
I was the one the angel's wing would brush.

"I did what any mother needs to do
and loved less in heroic things but more
by stealth and daily nurturings, the few

"alleviations, burdens which I bore,
the easings of a background tenderness
which leaves a confident magnetic core.

"Before the hyssop thirst that last address
I heard: O woman, *here behold your son!*
So let me be your fifth-day stewardess.

"Our heaven's not the same for everyone,
   though *life is sweet to all in different ways*,
   sometimes the sword foretold by Simeon

"can pierce the heart and hollow out a vase
   that's deeper and can take a larger joy
   and so delight for longer in God's gaze.

"I know your mother loved her elder boy.
   that all her sunlight filled you with self-trust
   which even years of doubt could not destroy.

"There were those years of dangerous self-disgust
   at hurts and scars of some perceived disgrace
   and yet false shame can be a kind of rust.

"Remember heaven is a playful place;
   as Dante with Cunizza tried to show,
   we need a self-forgiveness to efface

"what God more easily than we lets go.
   Piaf and Caitlín here both lavish songs,
   keep singing out their hearts of *artichaut*.

"In paradise full-heartedness belongs
   as much and more as toeing of the line;
   eternity won't clock up minor wrongs.

"Our clay is seldom whole or anodyne;
   I'm both the Morning Star and mother who
   could nudge the thoughtfulness of Cana's wine.

"A love that loves no matter what you do
   will always keep the choicest wine till last . . .
   But saints are waiting here to talk to you."

"It's strange," says Vanier, "how Freud has cast
   so long a shadow over motherhood;
   my life has been a kind of counterblast.

"Strong sunlight opens out the tightest bud
   and those who never knew a first caress
   unclench by being loved and understood.

"We all must bear the wound of loneliness;
    although in love we often glimpse a trace,
    a gash still yearns for God and nothing less

"can answer our desire or take its place—
    and even though such glimpses can prepare
    us all to stand before the dazzling face,

"attracted even while we're unaware
    by light that floods the satin darkness out,
    our wound remains a lifelong love affair."

"No Thomas with his itchy-fingered doubt"—
    now Dietrich turning towards Jean replies—
    "a boy I knew what wounds were all about,

"my brother's death had made me realise
    how deep the lesion of desire must run;
    I touched the wound and heard my mother's cries.

"Like Mary, whom the sword of Simeon
    would pierce, my vase once hollowed out for more,
    now all the deeper I enjoy the One."

"My mother's fourth of seven and before
    I'm ten I leave my home in Nurs behind,
    madrasa to madrasa, then the war

"and on through all the years I was confined
    I know I carried her first warmth in me,
    A self-belief which nothing undermined."

"Like you, Nursî, and you too, Jean, agree—
    a priest I too had left before my teens—
    a voice imprinted deep in memory

"escorted us, a prompt behind the scenes,
    a lullaby's internalised refrain
    recurring unawares like long-lost genes."

"That grief," now Nursî adds, "lets us attain—
    God's deepest joy belongs to Islam too;
    our Mary cries out in her childbirth pain."

"I too," nods Hannah, "chime with all of you;
  my namesake's song like Luke's Magnificat
  claims joy repays our suffering's IOU.

"But no more cautious talk or caveat—
  yes, vessels deepen with each sacrifice—
  the day is passing and I'm certain that

"our poet guest has heard enough advice.
  We should remember that before tonight
  he's due to glimpse the core of paradise."

I thank my saints but now a dazzling light
  begins to draw me to itself and woo
  me in the way a lover can invite

you closer still without compelling you;
  at once your oldest and your latest flame
  renewing thrills of your first rendezvous,

a date with your one love and lifelong aim,
  a sweet compulsion burning from within
  that makes you want to drop your lover's name.

To miss this mark is still the only sin.
  But following a gleam I'm now drawn home,
  a love returning to its origin.

Is this the pull of wholeness, a shalom
  that both attracts and gives a prepaid peace?
  I'm walking an arcade of trees, a dome

of branches thickly leaved and of a piece
  as though I'm moving in parentheses
  where there is both excitement and release

from any inattention or unease
  which could distract me from the arch's eye,
  where flooding light and rumours of a breeze

round off a blazing horizontal sky
  which beckons me onwards and I respond.
  And yet for all this tunnel vision I

am certain still that this is not some fond
farewell and that I've never been so close
to all I love as, moving now beyond

the time and place of two-dimensioned prose,
I hunger for the eye that beckons me
along a funnelled path between two rows

of slightly tilted boles where every tree
is interwoven with its counterpart,
convexing such a leafy canopy

where opposites can meet and then depart
in curves of paradox which shape the light;
I can't yet understand but know by heart

that nothing but desire can underwrite
my passage through this vaulted light-led zone,
that in this arch's eye all things unite.

I'm solo here but still not on my own;
becoming more myself in resonance
with those I love, I'm never all alone.

Already in this arch as I advance
my loneness wound is healing in the eye
whose rays now lead me to a skylit dance,

a dizzy whirl, a giddy dervish high
that pulses onwards to an ecstasy
once savoured for its wistful passing by;

but dance no longer needs a brevity
to add an edge to what might quickly pall.
It peaks beyond my wildest fantasy,

then as it climaxes and seems to fall—
the moment when a pleasure might abscond—
it hasn't neared its apogee at all

but peaks again and so beyond beyond,
surprising me with infinite excess,
that nothing I have known can correspond

to such abundant joy or could express
a sweetness like the moment lovers bond
in dewy aftermath without tristesse,

so glistening and delighted in their fond
embrace, just thrilling at each tipping kiss.
As willows glance the surface of a pond,

my vase remembers every touch of bliss,
each love knot in our pleasures' daisy chain.
Although no memory compares with this,

each nervelet and synapse inside my brain
finds images among its bric-à-brac
to help an ageing vessel to contain

such joy. Just as some jumper stepping back
before a leap recalls an old success,
I bring to mind from my own beaten track

delights I've known, the follies of *jeunesse*,
the throb of what's achieved or things explored,
each rush when head and heart could coalesce;

the high those times the body too had soared
and years of training paid off dividends,
the ball I intercepted and so scored;

but most of all together with my friends
around a table when we drank and ate,
those evenings when time's rigid arrow bends.

But now such pleasures all accumulate
in tributaries that can amplify
a whole creation flowing here in spate.

Be with me so, my saints and stars, as I
approach this glory hole of light which shone
all day and now fires up the evening sky

like Moses' burning bush that draws me on
along this rouging corridor to where
the last loose branches in their pink chiffon

of leaves half-roof the gap to form a pair
and every bole and limb begins to dance;
the universe's light-fantastic prayer

now lauds a wooer taking still a chance
on just this cosmic ballet's elegance
where nothing is decided in advance,

where hadrons jiggle in their resonance
while galaxies bebop and flowers blaze;
in cedars and wild animals I glance

a daily choreography of praise.
O suitor never holding us in thrall
but trusting to the ragtime of our ways

as in our brokenness we only fall
to rise where all who've come have come by choice;
let's dance across creation's dancing hall.

In shadows of your wing will I rejoice.
Sound now the bird of jazz's trumpet call!
"O Micheal, Micheal!" cries a lover's voice.

Yes, here I am, my Madam All in All.